Select Winning Stocks Using Financial Statements

Select Winning Stocks Using Financial Statements

RICHARD LOTH

DEARBORN™
A **Kaplan Professional** Company

Editorial Director: Cynthia Zigmund
Managing Editor: Jack Kiburz
Project Editor: Trey Thoelcke
Interior Design: Lucy Jenkins
Cover Design: Jody Billert
Typesetting: Professional Resources & Communications, Inc.

Published by Dearborn
A Kaplan Professional Company

Printed in the United States of America

99 00 01 10 9 8 7 6 5 4 3 2 1

Library of Congress Cataloging-in-Publication Data

Loth, Richard B.
  Select winning stocks using financial statements / Richard Loth.
      p. cm.
  Includes bibliographical references and index.
  ISBN 0–7931–3152–9 (pbk.)
    1. Stocks—United States. 2. Investments—United States.
  3. Financial statements—United States.   I Title.
  HG4910.L67 1999
  332.63'22—dc21   98–53431
                                                            CIP

Dedication

To individual investors—may they continue to learn
and prosper in their investing activities.

Contents

List of Exhibits

Preface

KNOWING HOW TO WORK WITH THE NUMBERS

Some 20 years ago I came across a wonderful book, which, unfortunately, is no longer in print, entitled *How to Keep Score in Business*. The author, Robert Follet, was a businessman, not an accountant. He wrote the book to share his experience with young managers in running his own and other companies. His principal point was that in business you keep score with dollars, and the scorecard is a financial statement. He recognized that "a lot of people don't understand keeping score in business. They get mixed up about profits, assets, cash flow, and return on investment." The same thing could be said today about a large portion of the investing public when it comes to considering the investment information value of financial statements. It is the purpose of this book to do for investors what Follet did in his book for business managers—to provide an easy-to-understand framework for analyzing a company's financials to determine its investment qualities.

Respected investment authorities and authors like Peter Lynch (*Learn to Earn*) and John Train (*The Craft of Investing*) counsel individuals, if they are serious about investing, to become conversant with basic accounting. What they really mean by accounting is financial accounting, which is, essentially, the interpretation and analysis of financial statements. This book is designed to do that—to teach number-crunching skills to beginning investors and to improve the evaluative skills and understanding of those investors who already have some degree of financial statement know-how. Knowing how to work with the numbers in a company's financials—that is, its financial statements—will make you a smarter investor and consequently a better investor. You will spend less time on a company's stock price and more time inside its financials learning how the numbers reflect its operational strengths and weaknesses and its financial condition. You will learn the value of buying into good companies, which should translate into buying good stocks. This book will not make you a crack investment analyst—that takes more sophisticated material than that presented here, as well as professional coursework—but this book will help you master the fundamentals of financial statement analysis, which is the basis of effective investment research. For those of you who feel mathematically challenged, you'll see that basic math skills—addition, subtraction, division, and multiplication—are all you need to analyze a company's financials. Don't let the numbers scare you!

In view of the abundance of books on investing produced in recent years, do we really need a book on financial statements as they relate to the investment process? As I see it, the answer is a definite yes for three rather obvious reasons. First, a number of books on investing, all of which contain sections on financial statements, have been on the business best-seller lists for weeks on end over the past few years. If we just focus on the content of their chapters dealing with financial statements, none of these works would come close to receiving a passing grade. To protect the guilty, the books and their authors will go unmentioned here, but their errors of omission and commission are numerous and egregious. That means that thousands of readers of these very popular books are walking around misinformed, and/or confused, and probably both—not a healthy condition for the investing public.

Second, often good books on investing, like those mentioned above by Lynch and Train, are highly recommended for their general content, especially for the beginning or less experienced investor, but their treatment of financial statements is limited in scope. Train, for example, dedicates only 3 pages in the *Craft of Investing* out of the book's total 206 pages to a company's financials. Lynch, in his *Learn to Earn,* does slightly better with 10 pages out of 260 on financial statements. Lynch's approach, while interesting, focuses almost exclusively on how a balance sheet is created as opposed to providing a comprehensive view of financial statement analysis. It's also surprising to find that an illustration of a cash flow statement reflects a format for the obsolete Sources and Application of Funds, which has not been used since the late 1980s, even though the book carries a 1995 publishing date! It would appear that even the good books on investing could use some improvement when they deal with the subject matter of financial statements.

Third, during the 1990s until the writing of this book, investors have experienced a highly favorable stock market, one in which stock and mutual fund values have experienced extraordinary rates of appreciation when compared to the historical record. It's unlikely that such an environment in which it has been fairly easy to succeed as an investor will be permanent. When, not if, the market comes back to earth from the stratosphere, intelligent stock-picking skills, including financial statement analysis, will once again be appreciated, and necessary, as tools for identifying quality investment opportunities. In addition, it appears likely that sometime in the near future investors in managed mutual funds are going to recognize the limits (relative underperformance and the impact of expenses) of this popular investment vehicle. For those millions of individuals who invest strictly in managed mutual funds, it would be prudent to explore some diversification into direct stock investing, which would require sharpening their basic investing skills.

For sharpening investing skills, this book offers several unique features. The traditional approach to understanding financial statements has been one size fits all. Differences in financial statement components and presentations among companies in different industries or lines of business are both numerous and obvious. These differences in financial statements are explained here, instead of trying to fit all companies into the conventional manufacturing company mold. In some cases (e.g., banks and utilities) the differences are so great that they are treated separately in chapters of their own. Analytical worksheets, which can be copied and used by readers, for the evaluation of a company's financial statements are provided along with instructions for their use. Unfortunately, corporate financials evidence a variety of terminology that is often confusing, particularly for the less experienced investor. I have made it a point to translate this jargon into plain English. This helps investors to better understand the computation of financial indicators that are used in financial statement analysis. I also have made extensive comparisons of actual companies to illustrate how investment evaluators can differ depending on the type of company involved.

I have written this book to help individual investors use financial statement information to evaluate the investment qualities of a wide variety of companies. For those inclined to be do-it-yourself investors, the investment evaluators will provide a reliable framework for identifying quality companies. Like any other confusing or unknown terrain, financial statements are easier to navigate with a helpful guide. The book should be of particular value to the millions of Americans who, as part of their 401(k) plans and/or as ESOP participants, own shares of their company's stock and need to objectively evaluate their investment. For those investors who use investment information services to evaluate companies, the book should improve your understanding of the data provided—also true for investors who work with investment professionals. You'll be prepared to know what questions to ask about a company's financial position and performance and to participate intelligently in investment discussions with your adviser.

Last, I think it is appropriate to mention here that *Select Winning Stocks Using Financial Statements* has relevance for those not directly involved in the investing process. Skills needed for understanding and using financial statements can be highly beneficial to an audience beyond individual investors. I believe that students of financial accounting, small business owners/operators, entry-level credit managers, investor relations and investment professionals and nonfinancial managers could all benefit from the book's unique approach to financial statement know-how. Knowing how to work the numbers can work for everyone!

Acknowledgments

I received the help of a number of persons in writing this book. I would like to acknowledge their contributions and express my gratitude for the efforts they made on my behalf.

First in line is my wife, Nancy. Without her support I could not have undertaken these writing endeavors. I value her critical editorial eye on the written text and her commonsense questioning of the content. Also, without Tanya Miller's assistance, I would still be struggling with the many charts and tables.

I thank Jan Fedrizzi and other staff members of the Avon and Eagle, Colorado, public libraries for the opportunity to conduct our monthly seminars on investing basics for local community members. These encounters have kept me in close contact with the educational needs of the investing public and provide perspective on the best ways to respond. This book contains answers, I hope, to a lot of the questions coming out of these sessions.

Two friends of many years helped refresh my memory—Bill Murphy on several corporate finance items and Marc Gilmore on banking material. Marni Pont O'Doughtery of Keefe, Bruyette & Woods, New York, came through with some timely statistical bank data that was much appreciated. Without the interest and encouragement of Cynthia Zigmund, Editorial Director, Dearborn Financial Publishing, this book would not have been written.

Last, I need to make an unusual acknowledgment. When suffering moments of writer's block, I turn to a great friend and constant companion. Her joyful countenance of eternal devotion to her master makes everything seem just fine, and the words flow. Thanks, Daisy, the "bestest" basset hound in the whole world. I look forward to *our* next project!

INTRODUCTION

What Investors Need to Know about Financial Statements

During the 1990s, millions of Americans discovered the stock market, and investing has become what some observers have called the new national pastime. Stocks have surpassed the value of real estate as the most significant component of household balance sheets. Nearly half of all American households are now invested in the stock market. Equity mutual funds have been the vehicle of choice for the vast majority of these relatively new individual investors. Many individuals, however, have also chosen to invest directly in stocks through company employee stock plans, as well as independently. Investment clubs have proliferated, and the number of companies offering direct stock purchase plans is expected to grow from approximately 425 to over 1,500 in the next few years.

The growth in the size of the investing public has been accompanied by a corresponding growth in investment advisory and information services, publications, and media coverage directed at individual investors. Unfortunately, not all of this material is of good quality. The intelligent investor must be selective, seeking out and identifying the most reliable and relevant data. There's no question that a company's financial statements are a primary source of reliable and relevant investment data. Whether investors analyze a financial statement themselves or depend on services such as Value Line and Standard & Poor's, they must have at least a basic knowledge of a company's financials to effectively judge its investment qualities. *Select Winning Stocks Using Financial Statements* is specifically designed to provide the skills to help investors become effective number crunchers and, as a consequence, to develop appropriate financial statement analysis skills. As an investor with these skills, you'll be able to determine the investment qualities of companies and improve your stock selection capability.

A key tool of stock analysts, particularly those employing fundamental analysis techniques, is the interpretation of financial statements. Fundamental analysis is one of the two schools (the other is technical analysis) that are used to appraise a company's investment prospects. Michael C. Thomsett, an author of several works on business and investment topics, has recently written the excellent *Mastering Fundamental Analysis* (Dearborn Financial Publishing, 1998), which he says "is written for investors, not for financial experts." I would like to say the same about *Select Winning Stocks Using Financial Statements*. If you feel intimated by the thought of performing financial statement analysis and think it's only for the experts, Mr. Thomsett makes this cogent observation:

> That there *is* no secret is the biggest secret of Wall Street—and of any specialized industry. Very little in the financial world is so complex that you cannot grasp it. The fundamentals are—as their name implies—fundamental, basic, uncomplicated. The only factor complicating financial information is jargon, overly complex statistical analysis, and complex formulas that don't convey information any better than straight talk.

Putting into practice some of Thomsett's straight talk, this book addresses what investors need to know about a company's financials. Prudent investing dictates that we seek out quality companies with strong balance sheets, solid earnings, and positive cash flow. This is a nice-sounding phrase, but what does it mean in practice? For much of the investing public, these conceptual terms require practical definition. Before we plunge into the trees—financial statement components—to look for explanations, let's look at the forest—the general characteristics of financial statements. In the following pages I explain 12 critical items investors need to know—my Decisive Dozen àla Dave Letterman.

1: WHAT FINANCIALS TO USE

The financial statements that are used for analytical purposes, are the balance sheet, the income statement, and the cash flow statement. In popular investment literature, the cash flow statement is often overlooked, even though it's a source of key investment information. The statements of shareholders' equity and retained earnings contain nice-to-know, but not critical, information, and are not used by analysts.

Chapters 1 through 9 provide investors with a comprehensive understanding of the information the balance sheet, income statement, and cash flow statement contain and how it can be used for investment evaluation. Each statement is examined as a whole, and then its individual components are examined. The financial statements of Procter & Gamble are presented as typical examples. Variances from these forms and differences in statement components, as well as account captions, are illustrated with examples from other companies' financials. From this review, a framework of investment evaluators are identified and computed to reveal a company's liquidity/efficiency, asset productivity, leverage, profitability, key growth rates, and cash generation.

A sample of 20 companies in various types of business illustrate the results of applying my investment evaluators to the companies' financial condition and performance. I refer to the companies in the sample throughout as the G20. The companies are not homogeneous, and I don't intend to make direct comparisons. My purpose is to use the financials of well-known companies, which are widely held by the investing public and represent a diversity of industries, to illustrate a variety of financial statements and their form of presentation. In Chapter 10, I present an actual case study of Modine Manufacturing Company for a five-year comparative financial statement and investment evaluator analysis, which employs specially designed worksheets.

2: KNOWING WHAT'S BEHIND THE NUMBERS

The numbers in a company's financials reflect real world events. These numbers and the financial ratios/indicators that are derived from them for investment analysis are easier to understand if you can visualize the underlying reality of this essentially quantitative information. A comprehensive understanding of what a company does helps to make the numbers come to life.

Financial statement analysis, per se, is an exercise in quantitative analysis. To be meaningful, a company's numbers need to be analyzed within the context of the products and services it produces, its customers, and the markets it serves. For this analysis, you could follow no better example than that of the widely acclaimed investor Warren Buffett. As Robert Hagstrom, Jr., explains in his book *The Warren Buffett Way*:

> The most distinguishing trait of Buffett's investment philosophy is the clear understanding that, by owning shares of stock, he owns businesses, not pieces of paper. The idea of buying a stock without understanding the company's operating functions ... is unconscionable, says Buffett. This mentality is reflected in the attitude of a business owner as opposed to a stock owner. In the summation of *The Intelligent Investor*, Benjamin Graham wrote, 'Investing is most intelligent when it is most businesslike.' These words are, Buffett says, 'the nine most important words ever written about investing.'

3: THE DIVERSITY OF FINANCIAL REPORTING

The diverse nature of companies and types of business activity result in a diversity of financial reporting. This phenomenon is reflected principally in the configuration and composition of company balance sheets and income statements. Don't expect these financial statements to fit into a single mold. Many of the popular books on investing take a one-size-fits-all approach to interpreting financial statements. The less experienced investor is going to get lost when he or she encounters a presentation outside the mainstream company, which is used as the "typical" example. As I mentioned in number 1 above, uniformity is not the norm for most corporate financial reporting. Understanding the variances in financial statement presentations makes it easier to understand a company's financials and to know how to correctly interpret its numbers.

A number of types of business use unconventional financial reporting formats. Banking, utilities, insurance, security brokerage, and real estate are some of the more prominent industries that fall into this category. I have chosen to take a special look at banks and electric utilities as widely held companies. It is necessary to review their financials in a completely different way, so much so that I have devoted a separate section to them—Chapters 11 and 12 for banks, and Chapter 13 for electric utilities.

4: THE CHALLENGE OF FINANCIAL JARGON

Financial reporting terminology is a problem. To illustrate, I often ask my seminar attendees to explain the difference between net earnings, net income, and net profits. The response to this question, even from some of the more experienced investors, is rarely clear or straightforward. Just for the record, the terms are synonymous.

Financial jargon unnecessarily complicates understanding relatively simple evaluative techniques. There's little hope that this situation will change in the foreseeable future. Therefore, investors have no other recourse than to develop a working knowledge of this language. Apart from the specialized nature of this jargon, there is little standardization in its application. The variety of nomenclature used by companies to describe their statement accounts is confusing, especially for the beginner. The balance sheet and income statement are more susceptible to nomenclature variety than is the cash flow statement, but readers are advised to consult the glossary in this book frequently.

5: ACCOUNTING IS AN ART, NOT A SCIENCE

There are generally accepted accounting principles (GAAP) and rules for the preparation of a company's financial statements. Nevertheless, the presentation of a company's financial position, as portrayed in its financial statements, is influenced in many instances by management estimates and judgments. Financial accounting is not an exact science. In the best of circumstances, management is scrupulously honest and candid, while the outside auditors are demanding, strict, and uncompromising. Even in this best-case scenario, the opportunity exists for selective interpretations of financial accounting principles by management. Some companies abuse this latitude although I suspect most don't. Whatever the case, the imprecision inherent in the accounting process means that the prudent student of financial statements should adopt what Leopold Bernstein, a recognized authority on financial analysis, calls "an inquiring and skeptical approach" to financial statements. In a *Business Credit* article (February 1992), he advises that "analytical safety resides mostly in an attitude of skeptical and informed alertness toward all accounting presentations." In this regard, I suggest you read (in Appendix A) excerpted remarks from a speech by Arthur Levitt, chairman of the Securities and Exchange Commission, on certain present-day financial reporting problems.

Investors should also be aware that companies are permitted to use two sets of books for their accounting records. They can apply different accounting policies to the financials used for their tax returns and to the financials prepared for pubic disclosure. The expression *tax reporting purposes* refers to the former and the expression *financial statement purposes* to the latter. For example, using accelerated depreciation provides a faster write-off on the tax return and thus lowers a company's taxable income. For creditors and investors, however, the company wants to show maximum profit performance and therefore uses straight-line depreciation, which, comparatively, helps to boost income by stretching out the expense over a longer period. The timing differences between the two depreciation methods is what creates deferred taxes as either a liability or an asset in the balance sheet.

6: TWO KEY FINANCIAL ACCOUNTING CONVENTIONS

Accountants use a large body of accounting concepts and assumptions in preparing financial statements. The sum total of all these accounting conventions established over the years is formidable. For financial statement users, a basic understanding of at least two of these conventions—historical cost and the accrual basis for financial accounting—is particularly important. Assets are valued at their purchase price (historical cost), which may be significantly different than their market value. Also, depreciation applied to certain fixed assets may have reduced their accounting value to zero, but they continue to be productive and of significant value to a company.

Under accrual accounting, revenues are recorded when goods are shipped or services rendered and expenses recorded when incurred to produce these revenues (the matching concept). Generally, this flow does not necessarily coincide with the actual receipt and disbursement of cash. Hence, the importance of knowing the difference between profits and cash flow. A company can be highly profitable, but if it runs out of cash, it is out of business!

Investors should also be acquainted with three organizations that establish and monitor the accounting "rules of the game." The Securities and Exchange Commission (SEC) has the ultimate authority over publicly held companies. However, as a practical matter, it has delegated its rule-making responsibility primarily to the Financial Accounting Standards Board (FASB), which in turn works closely with the American Institute of Certified Public Accountants (AICPA). Both the FASB and the AICPA are private business organizations. From time to time, FASB issues Statements of Financial Accounting Standards (SFAS) that affect the form and substance of financial statement accounting. When reviewing a company's financials and their related notes, investors should be aware that changes occasioned by the application of an FASB standard can affect a company's financial condition and performance.

7: NONFINANCIAL STATEMENT INFORMATION

Financial statement information, while obviously important to the investment research process, has its limitations. Nonfinancial statement information, such as the state of the economy, industry and competitive considerations, market forces, the effect of technological change, and the quality of management and the workforce are not directly reflected in a company's financials. A good example is the current debate about the need for change at General Motors. In a *Business Week* article (July 27, 1998), "GM: It's Time to Face the Future," by Kathleen Kerwin, a comparative "GM vs. Ford" table was included that revealed the following excerpted data, which would not be found in either of the companies' respective financials:

	GM	FORD
Labor hours per vehicle	46.5	34.7
Unit output/worker	27.3 units	45.6 units
Number of senior managers and	72	46
change since 1992	Up 47%	Down 37%
Senior management productivity:		
Revenue per officer and change	$2.12 billion	$2.67 billion
since 1992	Down 22%	Up 91%
Market share per model	0.56%	0.93%
Units sold per dealership	552	761

Reprinted from the July 27 issue of *Business Week* by special permission; ©1998 by McGraw-Hill Companies.

You don't have to be an analytical genius to recognize that these data imply that GM faces a significant challenge as a car maker when compared with Ford, a close competitor. Information of this nature is becoming increasingly available to the average individual investor through the financial press and other media, investment research reports, and specialized investment information services, both in print and through the Internet. Investors need to recognize that financial statement insights are but one piece, albeit an important one, of the larger investment information puzzle. Smart investors use a company's financials in combination with nonfinancial data to make informed investment decisions. In other words, economic and industry conditions, favorable and unfavorable, dictate against viewing any company's financial statements in isolation.

8: FINANCIAL RATIOS AND INDICATORS

The absolute numbers in a company's financial statements are of little value for investment analysis. Therefore, the numbers are transformed into ratios and indicators to reveal relationships that provide evaluative insights into a company's financial performance and condition. Dozens of ratios are used by credit and investment analysts to examine companies. I have chosen 23 basic ratios from this universe and refer to them as key investment evaluators, all of which are relatively easy to calculate and understand. They fall into six broad categories that measure a company's financial performance and position: liquidity/efficiency, asset performance, leverage, profitability, key growth rates, and cash flow generation. In subsequent chapters I explain how they are calculated and what they mean to the investor, but a few general characteristics of ratios must be clarified.

First, ratios and indicators must be looked at over an extended period to find trends, which are the meaningful feature of ratios. Second, beware of so-called good ratios because companies differ in size, financial condition, stage of development, and line of business. Applying a single standard to all of them is a mistake. Rather, I would suggest looking for consistency or improving quality in a company's historical ratios. Third, compare these ratios to one or two competitors, but be aware that differing accounting policies among companies can make comparisons a bit tricky. I'm somewhat skeptical about industry comparisons. Ideally, it would be extremely helpful to compare a company's investment evaluators with those of other companies in its industry sector. In today's complex business environment, however, a company is often a hybrid, operating in several lines of business. Industry categorizations often bring together very disparate businesses, which puts in question the comparability of individual component companies. Because comparability is an essential analytical technique, the simple solution here is to compare apples with apples, (i.e., companies that are direct competitors). Last, while there is general agreement on how most ratios are calculated, differences do occur, especially with the important debt ratios in the leverage category. If you are using prepackaged ratios—those calculated and supplied by a company (in its annual report) or an investment information service—be sure you know what numbers are being used in the calculation. Charles Gibson, author of one of the best textbooks on using financial accounting information, *Financial Statement Analysis,* makes this observation about financial ratios:

> At present, no regulatory agency such as the SEC or the FASB accepts responsibility for determining either the content of financial ratios or the format of presentation for annual reports, except for the ratio earnings per share. Many practical and theoretical issues relate to the computation of financial ratios. As long as each firm can exercise its opinion as to the practical and theoretical issues, there will be a great divergence of opinion on how a particular ratio should be computed.

9: NOTES TO THE FINANCIALS

It's difficult for financial statement numbers by themselves to provide the disclosure required by regulatory authorities. Also, professional analysts universally agree that a thorough understanding of the notes to financial statements is essential to properly evaluate a company's financial condition and performance. These notes, often incorrectly referred to as footnotes, are not easy reading. In Chapter 11, I try to make this task somewhat easier for investors by demonstrating how to focus on critical points of information to be found in the notes.

10: AUDITED FINANCIAL STATEMENTS

Prudent investors should only consider investing in companies with audited financial statements, which is the case for all publicly traded companies. Before digging into a company's financials, the first thing to do is read the accompanying auditors' report. It is important to understand what an auditors' report does and does not represent. In Chapter 9, I guide you through these considerations.

11: CONSOLIDATED STATEMENTS

Often, especially with larger, more complex companies, the word *consolidated* appears in the titles of financial statements—as in Consolidated Balance Sheet. Consolidation of a parent company and its majority-owned (more than 50 percent ownership) subsidiaries means that the combined activities of a number of separate legal entities are expressed as one economic unit. The presumption is that the consolidated financial statements are more meaningful than separate statements for different entities.

Beginning in the late 1980s, companies were required to consolidate majority-owned subsidiaries regardless of any dissimilarities in their respective operations. While observers generally applauded the move, it was nonetheless controversial. James E. Ayers, Dana Corporation's (an affected company) treasurer in those days, expressed the opinion of many financial professionals by saying, "Mixing assets from finance subs and manufacturing companies is like mixing apples and oranges . . . you get fruit salad, not financial statements." No one questioned the rule's motive—to require companies with sizable finance subsidiaries to fully disclose the debt associated with these operations, but the coherent presentation and analysis of distinctly different businesses isn't easy. Most companies with large finance subsidiaries have adopted Dana's pioneering decision to present two sets of figures in their financial statement presentations—one for the core business and another for the finance business. For example, companies in the G20 sample, such as General Electric and Ford, include their finance companies in their consolidated financial statements. To get an accurate view of companies with consolidated but disparate businesses, the investor needs

EXHIBIT I.1 • Ford Motor Company and Subsidiaries—Consolidated Statement of Income

Ford Motor Company and Subsidiaries

CONSOLIDATED STATEMENT OF INCOME
For the Years Ended December 31, 1997, 1996 and 1995
(in millions, except amounts per share)

	1997	1996	1995
AUTOMOTIVE			
Sales (Note 1)	$122,935	$118,023	$110,496
Costs and expenses (Notes 1 and 15):			
Costs of sales	108,907	108,882	101,171
Selling, administrative and other expenses	7,082	6,625	6,044
Total costs and expenses	115,989	115,507	107,215
Operating income	6,946	2,516	3,281
Interest income	1,116	841	800
Interest expense	788	695	622
Net interest income	328	146	178
Equity in net loss of affiliated companies (Note 1)	(88)	(6)	(154)
Net expense from transactions with			
Financial Services (Note 1)	(104)	(85)	(139)
Income before income taxes - Automotive	7,082	2,571	3,166
FINANCIAL SERVICES			
Revenues (Note 1)	30,692	28,968	26,641
Costs and expenses (Note 1):			
Interest expense	9,712	9,704	9,424
Depreciation	7,645	6,875	6,500
Operating and other expenses	6,621	6,217	5,499
Provision for credit and insurance losses	3,230	2,564	1,818
Asset write-downs and dispositions (Note 15)	-	121	-
Total costs and expenses	27,208	25,481	23,241
Net revenue from transactions with Automotive (Note 1)	104	85	139
Gain on sale of Common Stock of a subsidiary (Note 15)	269	650	-
Income before income taxes - Financial Services	3,857	4,222	3,539
TOTAL COMPANY			
Income before income taxes	10,939	6,793	6,705
Provision for income taxes (Note 6)	3,741	2,166	2,379
Income before minority interests	7,198	4,627	4,326
Minority interests in net income of subsidiaries	278	181	187
Net income	$ 6,920	$ 4,446	$ 4,139
Income attributable to Common and Class B Stock			
after preferred stock dividends (Note 1)	$ 6,866	$ 4,381	$ 3,839
Average number of shares of Common and Class B			
Stock outstanding (Note 1)	1,195	1,179	1,071
AMOUNTS PER SHARE OF COMMON AND			
CLASS B STOCK (Note 1)			
Basic income	$ 5.75	$ 3.73	$ 3.58
Diluted income	$ 5.62	$ 3.64	$ 3.33
Cash dividends	$ 1.645	$ 1.47	$ 1.23

The accompanying notes are part of the financial statements.

to segregate or unbundle the consolidated financial information and look at the parts. Most such companies, realizing the complexity of their operations, have adapted their financial statement formats to conform to reality (see Exhibit I.1). Otherwise, the interpretation of their financial statements and the calculation of standard ratios and indicators of financial condition and performance would suffer considerable distortion and lack meaning.

Just as majority ownership obligates a parent company to consolidate an investment, it follows that the lack of majority ownership, 50 percent or less, permits the nonconsolidation of a subsidiary, even though such a subsidiary could be a significant business under the effective control of a de facto parent. In most instances, the subsidiary carries substantial debt that is not reflected in the de facto parent company's financials, making the parent company's balance sheet look financially healthier. In the late 1980s, Jefferson Smurfit, a large paper/paperboard manufacturer, financed its acquisition of Container Corporation, for example, by loading it with the acquisition debt. Cynics refer to this as the *50 percent solution* to what would otherwise be a much higher level of indebtedness for the de facto parent. Over the years, the accounting authorities and the Securities and Exchange Commission have tightened up the definition of control, whatever the ownership percentage, so this form of hiding debt is no longer a major problem for investor analysis, at least for publicly held companies.

12: FINANCIAL STATEMENT TRIVIA

Financial statement trivia would probably be the best way to describe the three elements that I lump into this item. While not of transcendental importance, they are worth mentioning, particularly for readers inexperienced in the workings of a company's financials.

First, the SEC requires publicly held companies to include three years of audited income, cash flow, and shareholders' equity statements, but only two years for the balance sheet, in their annual reporting presentations. Unfortunately, most companies, in lemminglike fashion, follow this practice. This practice is unfortunate because comparing only two years of any financial information is relatively meaningless—the focus is just too narrow. Also, and more important, the need to calculate averages of certain balance sheet items to compare them with income statement items (e.g., return on equity = net income ÷ average shareholders' equity) would be greatly facilitated by having three-year balance sheet data readily available. Otherwise, if you're trying to do multiyear financial statement analysis, you have to obtain and handle a number of annual reports or 10-Ks just to get the balance sheet data you need. Companies that spend an additional fraction of a penny to print a third column of figures in their balance sheet presentation are to be praised.

Second, the larger the company, the larger the numbers in its financial statements. It is helpful when numbers are rounded off to thousands or millions, which are more readable. Most companies, unfortunately, present their annual figures in reverse chronological order—the most recent year in the first column with one year ago (for the balance sheet) and two years ago (for the income, cash flow, and equity statements) following in adjacent columns. Unless you are proficient in

Hebrew or Arabic, which are written from right to left, your eye must move unnaturally from right to left. This style of presenting figures is not helpful and may be part of a larger conspiracy to confuse the general public (have you noticed that the numbers on a calculator keypad are in the reverse order of those on your Touch-Tone telephone?). Once again, praise to those companies (e.g., Microsoft) that present their numbers chronologically from left to right, just the way the eye moves naturally. This format really does make it easier to track the trend of numbers, calculate averages, and make interannual comparisons.

One last comment on numbers. A number of financial ratios and indicators, including some that I present in this book as investment evaluators, are calculated from numbers in both the balance sheet and the income statement. In these instances, it is more accurate, and is the practice of analysts, to use an average number for the balance sheet amount. This is often done for you in company and investment information service reports; other times it is not. Averaging simply involves taking appropriate year-end figures (e.g., shareholders' equity), adding them together, and dividing the total by two. This is a rough but useful approximation of a balance sheet amount for the whole year, which is what the comparative income statement number (e.g., net income) represents, as opposed to just using the amount for the last day of the year in the balance sheet. When we next talk about financial statement dates, you'll see that income, cash flow, and equity statement figures represent flow numbers, and the balance sheet figures represent point-in-time numbers.

Third, as I have just alluded to, some things investors should know about financial statement dates, particularly as these indicate the periods covered in a company's financials. A photographic metaphor is often used to explain the difference between a balance sheet and an income statement (the same would be true for the cash flow and the equity statement); the former is akin to a snapshot and the latter a movie. The balance sheet represents a company's financial position at its fiscal year-end (i.e., the last day of its accounting period). In contrast, the other statements reflect a company's operations for the whole fiscal year—365 days. A company's fiscal year is its business year, which does not necessarily correspond to a calendar year. Companies generally select a period that ends when their business activities have reached the lowest points in their annual cycles, a period referred to as a natural business year. For example, you'll note that some G20 component companies like retailers Albertson's and Wal-Mart, use January 31 as the end of their fiscal year.

Some companies choose a year-end by designating a point in time (e.g., the first Friday in September), which can produce fiscal years different in size from one year to another. For a company with a relatively large sales volume, the difference in sales and earnings between a 52-week and a 53-week fiscal year can be significant. You must be aware of the number of weeks in a company's fiscal year when comparing the company's year-to-year results as well as its results vis-à-vis other companies. You won't often find companies whose fiscal year weeks vary from one year to another, but consider the comparative challenges involved in this company's (name withheld for obvious reasons) fiscal year, as described in a note to its financials:

Fiscal Year: The Company's fiscal year is the 52 or 53 weeks ending the last Saturday in May. The 52-week years are comprised of 13 four-week accounting periods separated into two 12-week quarters ending during August and November, a 16-week quarter ending March, and a 12-week quarter ending during May. A 53-week year results in a five-week accounting period and a 13-week quarter at the beginning of the fiscal year.

Say what? Thankfully, the vast majority of company fiscal years are conventional 52-week affairs, most of which have year-ends of December 31 and June 30, but a large number of companies also spread out their year-ends rather evenly over the other months of the year as well.

This brings us to the end of my Decisive Dozen. Other general comments could probably be made on corporate financials, but these are the critical points for investors to understand. In the preceding pages you've been given the big picture on financial statements. Now it's time to get inside a company's financials to determine its value as a business and as an investment opportunity.

CHAPTER 1

Understanding the Balance Sheet and Its Components

A company's balance sheet is comprised of assets, liabilities, and equity. Assets represent things of value that a company owns and has in its possession or is due to it, which can be measured objectively. Liabilities are what a company owes to others, including creditors, suppliers of goods and services, tax authorities, and so on; liabilities are obligations that must be paid under certain conditions and time frames, excepting any fixed obligation to investors. A company's equity (i.e., what's left after liabilities are subtracted from assets) is what is owed (actually a misnomer) to shareholders as owners of the business. They accept the uncertainty that comes with ownership risk in exchange for what they hope will be, over the years, an increase in the company's equity value and a satisfactory return on their investment in the form of dividends and/or appreciation of the stock's price.

Standard accounting conventions generally present the balance sheet in one of two formats: horizontal (the account form) or vertical (the report form); most companies favor the report form. Another format, the financial position form, is found very infrequently in the United States but is commonly used by international companies, particularly European ones. See Exhibit 1.1 for examples of the three formats and their general account structure. Most companies refer to their financial statement as a balance sheet, but a small number of companies use alternative names such as a statement of financial position or a statement of financial condition.

Although specific captions that define the various sections of a balance sheet are not always used, the individual accounts fit into these major classifications:

- Current assets (short-term)—items convertible into cash within one year
- Noncurrent assets (long-term)—items of a more permanent nature
- Current liabilities (short-term)—obligations due within a year
- Noncurrent liabilities (long-term)—obligations payable beyond one year
- Equity—shareholders' investment

EXHIBIT 1.1 • Balance Sheet Formats and General Account Structure

REPORT FORM

Current Assets	$262,006
Fixed Assets	59,929
Other Assets	2,240
Total Assets	$324,175
Current Liabilities	$76,763
Long-term Liabilities	54,126
Shareholders' Equity	193,286
Total Liabilities/ Equity	$324,175

ACCOUNT FORM

Current Assets	$262,006	Current Liabilities	$76,763
Fixed Assets	59,929	Long-term Liabilities	54,126
Other Assets	2,240	Shareholders' Equity	193,286
Total Assets	$324,175	Total Liabilities/ Equity	$324,175

FINANCIAL POSITION FORM

Current Assets	$262,006
Less: Current Liabilities	-76,763
Working Capital	185,243
Plus: Noncurrent Assets	62,169
Total Assets Less Current Liabilities	247,412
Less: Long-term Liabilities	54,126
Net Assets	$193,286

Generally, assets are listed in the descending order of their liquidity (i.e., how quickly and easily they can be converted to cash). Similarly, liabilities are listed in the order of their priority for payment. One last minor point: in financial accounting, the terms *current* and *noncurrent* are synonymous with the terms *short-term* and *long-term*, respectively, and are used interchangeably.

As mentioned before, the balance sheet is a photograph at a specific point in time of a company's financial position as reflected in the fundamental accounting equation: Assets = Liabilities + Equity.

You don't have to be a sophisticated financial analyst to understand what the equation very clearly indicates: As the assets of a company grow, its liabilities and/or equity also must grow for its financial position to stay in balance. What is so important about this rather obvious relationship? A company grows by increasing its sales, either directly or through the acquisition of other businesses. In both cases, growth more than likely results in higher levels of accounts receivable and inventory, and it requires a greater investment in property, plant, and equipment (fixed assets) to support the growth or expansion. As a generalization, these accounts—receivables, inventories, and fixed assets—typically reflect the big numbers in most companies' asset position in their balance sheets. These statement components are discussed in more detail later, but for now it's important to realize that growth generally dictates a larger asset base, which in turn requires a larger debt liability/equity base. Within this phenomenon lie important clues to a company's investment qualities.

How assets are supported, or financed, by a corresponding growth in liabilities—most important, debt liabilities—and equity reveals a lot about a company's financial health, particularly in the case of growth-oriented companies. According to a basic rule of finance, short-term (current) and long-term (noncurrent) assets should be financed by sources of funds with the same characteristics as those on the liability/equity side of the balance sheet equation. A reasonable mix of short-term and long-term debt liabilities and proportionately appropriate levels of long-term debt and equity are the signs of a financially healthy company, but no absolute right mix or proportion applies equally to every company. Different industries, as well as companies' various stages of development, influence the proportion. However, taking a conservative stance, it is essential for investors to look at balance sheets with a critical eye when appraising how assets are supported. Various investment evaluators, discussed in the following chapters, will help you analyze this important aspect of a company's financials—how assets are supported.

As recommended in the second item of my Decisive Dozen, you should know something about the company whose 1998 financials I'm using as our mainstream example. Procter & Gamble (P&G) is a large, well-known worldwide manufacturer and marketer of household/consumer products. Its more than 300 brands include, among others, such names as Tide, Pampers, Pringles, Crest, Pantene, Bounty, Ivory, and Crisco. Messrs. William Procter (a candlemaker) and James Gamble (a soapmaker) joined forces to found the company in 1837. Today, the company is still Cincinnati based with sales exceeding $37 billion and a workforce of some 110,000 employees. P&G is a Fortune 500 company and one of the components of the Dow Jones Industrial Average. In my opinion, Procter & Gamble does a good job of presenting in its financial statements as seen in its 1998 annual report. It's now time to get into the details of a balance sheet to learn what the financial statement numbers tell us about a company's business and its financial position. Refer to Exhibit 1.2 as you read the following commentary.

ASSET ACCOUNTS

Current Assets

Cash and cash equivalents. This is the most commonly used terminology to describe an asset account that includes a company's most liquid assets. Procter & Gamble's cash and cash equivalents amount to $1.5 billion for 1998. With the exception of retailers and food service businesses, most companies, generally speaking, provide payment terms to their customers, and their cash accounts are fed by the collection of their accounts receivables, which have in turn been generated by sales with payment terms.

Cash refers to cash on hand (petty cash), negotiable checks received but not yet deposited, and balances in a company's operating checking accounts. If no cash equivalents are held, the account will appear just as cash. Cash equivalents, as the term implies, are the result of a company's desire to earn interest on available cash in excess of current operating needs. The company elects to invest excess funds on a short-term or temporary basis—sometimes this very terminology is used to identify cash equivalents. Accounting rules define cash equivalents as high-grade securities readily convertible to cash with an insignificant risk of any change in value and with maturities of less than three months. Such items would include, among others, such financial instruments as U.S. government Treasury bills, bank certificates of deposit, bankers acceptances, and commercial paper. In other words, cash equivalents are as good as having cash. Sometimes funds are earmarked for a specific purpose (e.g., an obligatory prior deposit for a major purchase) and are then identified as restricted cash, are deducted from the cash account, and are generally classified as noncurrent assets. So-called compensating balances, which can be a condition of a bank loan agreement, are not considered restricted funds. While not terribly significant, investors should be aware that corporate treasurers sometimes go to great efforts to build up cash balances at their company's year-end closing to enhance the company's liquid asset position. Such window dressing, if it occurs at all, is virtually impossible to detect from the numbers in a company's balance sheet.

It's nice to see a large cash position in any company's balance sheet, but investors need to understand that a large cash position originates from events recorded in the cash flow statement, which we discuss in Chapters 5 and 6. It is a company's strong cash flow that produces its liquidity, and it is the statement of cash flow that provides clues as to how this liquidity is achieved. In the balance sheet we simply see the year-end result of a company's increase or decrease in cash for the period reviewed.

EXHIBIT 1.2 • Procter & Gamble 1998 Balance Sheet

CONSOLIDATED BALANCE SHEETS   The Procter & Gamble Company and Subsidiaries

	June 30	
Amounts in Millions Except Per Share Amounts	1998	1997
ASSETS		
Current Assets		
Cash and cash equivalents	$ 1,549	$ 2,350
Investment securities	857	760
Accounts receivable	2,781	2,738
Inventories		
Materials and supplies	1,225	1,131
Work in process	343	228
Finished goods	1,716	1,728
Deferred income taxes	595	661
Prepaid expenses and other current assets	1,511	1,190
Total Current Assets	10,577	10,786
Property, Plant and Equipment		
Buildings	3,660	3,409
Machinery and equipment	15,953	14,646
Land	539	570
	20,152	18,625
Accumulated depreciation	(7,972)	(7,249)
Total Property, Plant and Equipment	12,180	11,376
Goodwill and Other Intangible Assets		
Goodwill	7,023	3,915
Trademarks and other intangible assets	1,157	1,085
	8,180	5,000
Accumulated amortization	(1,169)	(1,051)
Total Goodwill and Other Intangible Assets	7,011	3,949
Other Non-Current Assets	1,198	1,433
Total Assets	$30,966	$27,544

See accompanying Notes to Consolidated Financial Statements.

EXHIBIT 1.2 • Procter & Gamble 1998 Balance Sheet, continued

The Procter & Gamble Company and Subsidiaries

Amounts in Millions Except Per Share Amounts	June 30 1998	1997
LIABILITIES AND SHAREHOLDERS' EQUITY		
Current Liabilities		
Accounts payable	$ 2,051	$ 2,203
Accrued and other liabilities	3,942	3,802
Taxes payable	976	944
Debt due within one year	2,281	849
Total Current Liabilities	9,250	7,798
Long-Term Debt	5,765	4,143
Deferred Income Taxes	428	559
Other Non-Current Liabilities	3,287	2,998
Total Liabilities	18,730	15,498
Shareholders' Equity		
Convertible Class A preferred stock,		
stated value $1 per share		
(600 shares authorized)	1,821	1,859
Non-Voting Class B preferred stock,		
stated value $1 per share (200 shares		
authorized; none issued)	–	–
Common stock, stated value $1 per share		
(5,000 shares authorized; shares outstanding:		
1998–1,337.4 and 1997–1,350.8)	1,337	1,351
Additional paid-in capital	907	559
Reserve for employee stock ownership plan debt retirement	(1,616)	(1,634)
Accumulated other comprehensive income	(1,357)	(819)
Retained earnings	11,144	10,730
Total Shareholders' Equity	12,236	12,046
Total Liabilities and Shareholders' Equity	$30,966	$27,544

Investment securities. Other account captions include marketable securities, short-term investments, securities for sale, or other securities. In 1998 P&G records $857 million for this current asset, which is, most likely, comprised of the same or similar instruments as those recorded in cash equivalents. The only difference is that these short-term invested funds have maturities beyond 90 days, possibly out to one year. Because of their maturities, accounting rules require them to be classified apart from cash equivalent, even though it is still management's intention to sell these securities over the short term. If management intended to hold these securities on a semipermanent basis, they would be classified as a noncurrent asset. Investment securities are valued at cost, which approximates their market value. If there is a material variance between the book, or recorded, value of the securities and their market value (i.e., the carrying value does not approximate market value), the variance will be disclosed in a note to the financial statements.

Accounts receivable. Receivables, generally trade receivables (i.e., amounts due within the following year from customers for the goods and/or services they have purchased) are reflected in this account. However, sometimes small amounts of nontrade receivables (e.g., an insurance settlement, tax refund, or asset sale) are also included in accounts receivable. A note receivable is simply a receivable that has been documented by a written, formal instrument and usually relates to some nontrade transaction. Businesses whose sales, for the most part, are paid for on a cash basis—for instance, retailers and restaurants—will have relatively small receivable positions compared to their sales volume. In general, however, the use of trade credit—that is, extending reasonable payment terms to customers—is common commercial practice and one that generates accounts receivable.

Procter & Gamble's terminology for accounts receivable is the most common, followed by receivables, trade accounts receivable, and accounts and notes receivable. Whether indicated or not in the balance sheet, the receivable amount is a net amount (in order to conform to generally accepted accounting principles). Prudent management dictates the establishment of an allowance for estimated (as opposed to actual) uncollectible or doubtful accounts, which reduces the gross amount of accounts receivable. For a company that extends payment terms on its sales, customers who don't pay are, unfortunately, a part of doing business. If the allowance is not shown in the balance sheet, it is generally disclosed in a note to its financial statements.

It is not always apparent, but analysts like to make a distinction between trade and nontrade accounts receivable. The former are a part of a company's normal operations and are considered liquid assets, one step away from being converted to cash. Generally, nontrade receivables are not accorded the same status. If an account receivable, or a portion of it, is not going to be collected within a year, the appropriate amount will be classified as a noncurrent asset. Sometimes receivables are sold to a lender to accelerate the flow of cash to a company. If sold without recourse, title actually changes and these receivables are no longer assets of the company. This practice is known as factoring and is common in some industries. It is just another form of financing when receivables are sold with recourse, and the receivable amount and financing amount should be added back into the company's current assets and liabilities positions in the balance sheet.

Retailers and restaurants generally have little or no receivables because their sales are paid for, for the most part, at the point of sale. However, in contrast to retail businesses, heavy equipment manufacturers, like Caterpillar, are in just the opposite situation. Because of the large dollar amounts involved in the sale of heavy equipment, the majority of financed transactions average in the $100,000 to $125,000 range, Caterpillar, for example, offers various financing plans designed to increase the opportunity for sales. Caterpillar Financial Services Corporation, whose financials are part of Caterpillar Inc.'s consolidated financial statements, handles customer financing. Exhibit 1.3 shows how Caterpillar discloses this component of its business in its balance sheet. Note that Caterpillar's finance receivables, both short-term and long-term, are substantial ($6.6 billion) and are supported principally by equally large debt facilities ($6.1 billion). Obviously, with companies like Caterpillar, Ford, and General Electric, which own and operate large finance subsidiaries, the analyst must evaluate these businesses by looking at the parts as well as the whole. Including finance receivables in a company's mainstream trade receivables would totally distort its financial position.

P&G had net accounts receivable of $2.8 billion in 1998, representing thousands of customers—retail stores ranging from small mom-and-pop shops to giants like Wal-Mart. Any concentration of receivables with a customer or group of customers in this type of customer base is unlikely. A wide diversification of customers is a risk-mitigating factor for this aspect of P&G's business. However, one only needs to recall Chrysler's near bankruptcy in the late 1970s to appreciate the importance of the quality of a company's accounts receivable, their timely collection, and their conversion to cash. It's quite likely that the managers of numerous automotive parts suppliers with substantial sales to Chrysler, and therefore a large receivable exposure, were wondering if they were ever going to get paid.

Investors need to pay attention to the quality of a company's accounts receivable, which are a key current asset and generally an important component of a company's total asset base. One practical measurement of receivable quality is in the calculation of a company's days sales outstanding (e.g., its receivables turnover), which is discussed as an investment evaluator in Chapter 2.

QUICK ASSETS

You won't find this caption in P&G's or any other company's balance sheet, but quick assets are the relatively liquid current assets just discussed—cash and cash equivalents, marketable securities, and accounts receivable. Procter & Gamble's quick assets computation for 1998 would look like this (figures rounded off in millions):

Cash and cash equivalents	$1.5
Investment securities	$ .9
Accounts receivable	$2.8
Total quick assets	$5.2

EXHIBIT 1.3 • Caterpillar Inc. Balance Sheet

STATEMENT 3
Financial Position at December 31
(Dollars in millions)

Caterpillar Inc.

	Consolidated			Machinery and Engines[1]			Financial Products		
	1997	1996	1995	1997	1996	1995	1997	1996	1995
Assets									
Current assets:									
Cash and short-term investments	$ 292	$ 487	$ 638	$ 241	$ 445	$ 580	$ 51	$ 42	$ 58
Receivables — trade and other	3,331	2,956	2,531	3,346	2,960	2,910	285	175	132
Receivables — finance (Note 6)	2,660	2,266	1,754	—	—	—	2,660	2,266	1,754
Deferred income taxes and prepaid expenses (Note 7)	928	852	803	935	876	834	9	15	13
Inventories (Notes 1C and 5)	2,603	2,222	1,921	2,603	2,222	1,921	—	—	—
Total current assets	9,814	8,783	7,647	7,125	6,503	6,245	3,005	2,498	1,957
Property, plant, and equipment — net (Notes 1D and 8)	4,058	3,767	3,644	3,483	3,242	3,199	575	525	445
Long-term receivables — trade and other	134	128	126	134	128	126	—	—	—
Long-term receivables — finance (Note 6)	3,881	3,380	3,066	—	—	—	3,881	3,380	3,066
Investments in unconsolidated affiliated companies (Note 9)	751	701	476	751	701	476	—	—	—
Investments in Financial Products' subsidiaries	—	—	—	882	759	658	—	—	—
Deferred income taxes (Note 7)	1,040	1,093	1,127	1,075	1,132	1,171	5	3	—
Intangible assets (Note 1D)	228	233	170	228	233	170	—	—	—
Other assets (Note 17)	850	643	574	510	368	330	340	275	244
Total assets	**$ 20,756**	**$18,728**	**$16,830**	**$14,188**	**$13,066**	**$12,375**	**$7,806**	**$ 6,681**	**$ 5,712**
Liabilities									
Current liabilities:									
Short-term borrowings (Note 11)	$ 484	$ 1,192	$ 1,174	$ 53	$ 36	$ 14	$ 431	$ 1,156	$ 1,160
Accounts payable and accrued expenses	3,358	2,858	2,579	3,020	2,556	2,358	654	520	776
Accrued wages, salaries, and employee benefits	1,128	1,010	875	1,120	1,005	873	8	5	2
Dividends payable	92	76	68	92	76	68	—	—	—
Deferred and current income taxes payable (Note 7)	175	142	91	46	70	40	129	72	51
Long-term debt due within one year (Note 12)	1,142	1,180	1,262	54	122	156	1,088	1,058	1,106
Total current liabilities	6,379	6,458	6,049	4,385	3,865	3,509	2,310	2,811	3,095
Long-term debt due after one year (Note 12)	6,942	5,087	3,964	2,367	2,018	2,049	4,575	3,069	1,915
Liability for postemployment benefits (Note 3)	2,698	3,019	3,393	2,698	3,019	3,393	—	—	—
Deferred income taxes and other liabilities (Note 7)	58	48	36	59	48	36	39	42	44
Total liabilities	**16,077**	**14,612**	**13,442**	**9,509**	**8,950**	**8,987**	**6,924**	**5,922**	**5,054**
Contingencies (Notes 17 and 18)									
Stockholders' equity (Statement 2)									
Common stock of $1.00 par value (Note 13):									
Authorized shares: 450,000,000									
Issued shares (1997, 1996, and 1995 — 407,447,312)									
at paid-in amount	1,071	881	901	1,071	881	901	403	353	333
Profit employed in the business	5,026	3,904	2,840	5,026	3,904	2,840	506	404	320
Foreign currency translation adjustment (Note 1E)	95	162	215	95	162	215	(27)	2	5
Treasury stock (1997 — 39,436,972 shares; 1996 — 26,745,092 shares; and 1995 — 19,417,076 shares) at cost	(1,513)	(831)	(568)	(1,513)	(831)	(568)	—	—	—
Total stockholders' equity	**4,679**	**4,116**	**3,388**	**4,679**	**4,116**	**3,388**	**882**	**759**	**658**
Total liabilities and stockholders' equity	**$ 20,756**	**$18,728**	**$16,830**	**$14,188**	**$13,066**	**$12,375**	**$7,806**	**$ 6,681**	**$ 5,712**

Supplemental consolidating data

[1] Represents Caterpillar Inc. and its subsidiaries except for Financial Products, which is accounted for on the equity basis.

The supplemental consolidating data is presented for the purpose of additional analysis and to provide required supplemental disclosure of information about the Financial Products' subsidiaries. See Note 1A on Page A-7 for a definition of the groupings in these statements. Transactions between Machinery and Engines and Financial Products have been eliminated to arrive at the consolidated data.

Analysts refer to quick assets as cash or assets close to being converted to cash. Essentially, this concept excludes inventory from current assets because it is susceptible to problems that could hinder its quick conversion to cash. A high degree of liquidity allows a company to lower or even eliminate the need to borrow funds and thus save on interest expense. Liquid companies can also take advantage of discounts on cash purchases from suppliers. In general, being liquid enhances a company's investment qualities. In Chapter 2, I discuss the calculation and application of the quick assets ratio, a frequently used indicator of corporate liquidity.

A number of books on investing instruct readers to calculate quick assets by simply subtracting inventories from the total amount of current assets. Although almost correct, the approach is wrong and in some cases could result in a materially misstated amount. Using P&G's 1998 numbers as an example, this approach would overstate quick assets by $2.1 billion ($7.3 billion versus $5.2 billion) or plus 40 percent! My advice is to add up current assets that we know to be liquid (e.g., cash and cash equivalents, marketable securities, and accounts receivable) and consider the total to be quick assets. Backing into a figure by just subtracting inventory from current assets can, by the inclusion of nonliquid current assets, overstate the amount of a company's quick assets.

Let's return to our review of Procter & Gamble's remaining current assets.

Inventories. As a manufacturer, P&G has total inventories ($3.3 billion in 1998) consisting of raw materials, work in process, and finished goods. Unlike P&G's balance sheet presentation, most companies provide a breakdown of inventory in a note to the financial statements, stating just the total amount under an inventories account in the balance sheet. The inventory of wholesalers and retailers, while generally a large asset, consists of finished goods only; and service companies have little or no inventory at all. Inventory usually represents a sizable asset for companies that have to carry it. The valuation and management of this asset, which is discussed later on, are key concerns for the investor.

First, however, we need to address how to classify materials, supplies, and spare parts, which, while not all that important, is worth clarifying here. Materials, supplies, and parts are consumable items that a company uses in its operational activities (i.e., they're not for sale to customers). Conservative analysts would normally not consider these items as inventory, but the amounts involved are generally not that material and aren't of major analytical concern. Nevertheless, some companies, like those in the transportation industry, will state an inventory amount in their balance sheet. For example, AMR Corporation, parent of American Airlines, has an account entry in its balance sheet for inventories, which are clearly described in a note to its financials as "spare parts, materials, and supplies relating to flight equipment." So AMR's inventories are really fuel, tires, engine parts, and so on for its airplanes, all consumable in its operations. Yet many investment information services express the amount as if it were conventional, salable inventory. The problem for investors, albeit a relatively small one, is to avoid making the same mistake when analyzing a company's current position.

Of much greater analytical importance is inventory valuation, which can be a complicated subject, but I'll try to keep it simple. The standard accounting convention is to value inventory at the lower of cost or market (LCM), which is an example of the principle of conservatism practiced by the accounting profession. The market value (current price) of an inventory item is fairly easy to determine. But what about historical cost? Most companies handle thousands of inventory items that are bought and used over time. What has been used? What's still in inventory? Generally, companies use one or more of the following four methods for costing inventory: first-in, first-out (FIFO); last-in, first-out (LIFO); average; and specific identification (not practical for most businesses). P&G's note on its accounting policies states that inventory cost is "primarily determined by either the average cost or the first-in, first-out method." Further along in the note is an indication that the last-in, first-out method is also applied to some inventories. So Procter & Gamble uses three different types of inventory valuation—not an uncommon practice for many companies.

EXHIBIT 1.4 • Understanding the Effects of FIFO and LIFO *Some misplaced numbers here*

The cost of sales, a key number in the income statement, is discussed in Chapter 3, but because the inventory cost valuation is directly related to the calculation of this figure, it's helpful to look now at how FIFO and LIFO, the two most used valuation methods, impact the cost of sales and the recorded amount for inventories in the balance sheet. We'll understand this impact better by using a simplistic example—the Jones family jellybean jar.

First, some assumptions: One week is equal to a company's fiscal year; Saturday is the same as a company's fiscal year-end; and jellybeans represent a company's inventories.

We begin Sunday with a full jar of jellybeans—60 of them. Mom paid $2.40 (4¢ each) for these jellybeans. On Tuesday, daughter Jane buys 40 jellybeans for $2.00 (5¢ each) at a school sale. On Thursday, Dad buys a package of 30 jellybeans for $2.40 (8¢ each) from the candy store. While these purchases (40 + 30 = 70) have been added to the jellybean jar, the family has been eating jellybeans, randomly selecting them from the jar. On Saturday, Mom gets the accounting bug, puts on her green eyeshade, and pulls out her calculator to determine the cost of the remaining jellybeans in the jar.

Mom's count shows 35 jellybeans remaining, but because they've been mixed together and consumed randomly, which ones are the ones that remain? Are they the ones attributable to Mom, Jane, or Dad? And how does Mom cost them? Under the first-in, first-out (FIFO) method of inventory cost evaluation, the ending inventory count would be 35 jellybeans having a cost of $2.65. FIFO assumes that items are consumed on the basis of what comes in first to inventory and goes out of inventory first. Therefore, of the 95 jellybeans eaten (60 + 40 + 30 = 95), 60 were Mom's and 35 were Jane's. Thus, the remaining inventory includes 5 jellybeans from Jane's purchase and all the jellybeans (30) from Dad's purchase and is worth $2.65. Continuing on, here is how the cost of sales is calculated under FIFO:

EXHIBIT 1.4 • Understanding the Effects of FIFO and LIFO, continued

Beginning inventory (Mom's 60 jellybeans @ 4¢ each)	$2.40
Plus purchases:	
Jane's 40 jellybeans @ 5¢ each	+2.00
Dad's 30 jellybeans @ 8¢	+2.40
	$6.80
Less ending inventory:	
35 jellybeans (5 @ 5¢ and 30 @ 8¢ each)	−$2.65
Equals cost of sales	$4.15

What the example shows is that, generally, with prices tending to rise over time, the ending inventory under FIFO reflects a higher value than the older inventory. This phenomenon is what produces a comparatively (to LIFO) lower cost of sales, higher earnings, and, consequently, more taxes paid.

Now let's take a look at how LIFO works using, once again, the Jones family jellybean example. The facts of the case are identical. We pick up the story at the point where Mom is trying to determine the cost of the remaining 35 jellybeans in the jar.

Under the last-in, first-out (LIFO) method of inventory cost evaluation, the ending inventory of 35 jellybeans would have a cost of $5.40. LIFO assumes that the latest items added to inventory, which should be the most expensive because of rising prices, are the ones sold first. Therefore, of the 95 jellybeans eaten, 30 were Dad's, 40 were Jane's, and 25 were Mom's. In effect, all the ending inventory of 35 jellybeans is attributable to Mom's initial purchase and is worth $1.40. Here is how the cost of sales is calculated under LIFO:

Beginning inventory (Mom's 60 jellybeans @ 4¢ each)	$2.40
Plus purchases:	
Jane's 40 jellybeans @ 5$ each	+2.00
Dad's 30 jellybeans @ 8¢ each	+2.40
	$ 6.80
Less ending inventory:	
35 jellybeans @ 4¢ each	−$1.40
Equals cost of sales	$5.40

In this example, we see that with prices tending to rise over time, the ending inventory under LIFO reflects a lower value than the newer inventory. This phenomenon is what produces a comparatively (to FIFO) higher cost of sales, lower earnings, and, consequently, less taxes paid.

Using these simplistic examples, wherein all the facts are the same, a FIFO company would have inventories in its balance sheet amounting to $2.65, whereas the LIFO company

EXHIBIT 1.4 • Understanding the Effects of FIFO and LIFO, continued

would only record an amount of $1.40. The cost of sales, a major expense in the income statement, of the FIFO and LIFO companies would be $4.15 and $5.40 respectively. The impact on the respective reported earnings is obvious. Financial analysts tend to like the understated or conservative impact on a company's financial position and earnings that are generated by the LIFO valuations.

The related note on inventories of a company that has LIFO inventory will indicate its current cost or FIFO value. The difference between the two values is referred to as an adjustment of inventories to LIFO or as the LIFO reserve. In effect, this difference represents the amount by which the balance sheet inventory figure is understated when compared to current cost. Trade creditors and bankers, who traditionally extend credit against current assets, like to see this cushion. Also, the phrase LIFO inventory reduction or liquidation describes what happens when LIFO inventory levels reduce down (goods are sold in greater quantities than purchased) to the cost layers of previous years. The concept is complicated, but when low-cost inventory is sold at current prices—nice if a bit artificial—earnings get a boost and the sale is explained in a note to the financials.

What does all this mean to investors? Simplifying things greatly, I suggest that they keep three points in mind. One, be aware that if a company changes its inventory cost valuation method(s), it will be mentioned in the notes to the company's financials along with explanations about the effect on its balance sheet and income statement. Two, there is no good or bad inventory cost valuation method, and the issue is not a major determinant of a company's investment value. However, the inventory cost valuation employed does have a significant impact on the calculation of the cost of sales. And the cost of sales is a major expense against revenues. As shown in Exhibit 1.4, the LIFO method is considered a more conservative statement of earnings and therefore as providing a higher quality of earnings. Also, LIFO tends to understate the true value of inventory, which translates into a more conservative balance sheet. Three, as a consequence of the previous point and depending on the degree of impact, a direct comparison of the financial condition and profitability performance of companies with differing inventory cost valuation methods is problematical. At the very least, investors should understand that such comparisons have a certain apples and oranges quality about them.

The impact on the balance sheet and the income statement of the FIFO, LIFO, and average methods of inventory cost valuation can be summarized as follows:

	Balance Sheet	**Income Statement**
FIFO	Most realistic (higher) current value of inventory	Lower cost of sales; higher profits; more taxes paid
LIFO	Inventory amount understated, thereby understating assets and relevant ratios	Most realistic in inflationary environment; higher cost of sales; less taxes paid.
AVERAGE	A compromise position between LIFO and FIFO for both financial statements	

Last, for investors the issue of inventory management is fairly straightforward and easy to understand. Turnover is the key concept in measuring the effectiveness of a company's inventory management. The faster inventory moves, the greater its liquidity and quality. In the following chapter you will learn how to calculate and use an important investment evaluator of inventory turnover.

Even though rapid inventory turnover is obviously desirable, a company has to maintain enough inventory on hand to serve customer needs for prompt delivery. Also, turnover measurements, as with all ratios, vary among companies and industries—there is no one absolute standard.

Deferred income taxes, prepaid expenses, and other current assets. These accounts that round out Procter & Gamble's current assets are quite common. Contrary to P&G's balance sheet, these accounts, in most instances, don't involve large monetary amounts (i.e., they are generally not material) and therefore are of little analytical significance. Deferred income taxes ($595 million in 1998) are caused by the timing differences occasioned by tax and financial statement reporting; by appearing as an asset, they indicate a credit due. Prepaid expenses, or prepaids, represent advance payments for services and/or supplies. As such, prepaids will not be converted to cash but rather will conserve the outlay of cash. Examples of prepaid expenses would include, among others, insurance premiums, advertising services, subscriptions, and memberships. Other current assets are generally insignificant items that don't fit anywhere else! In 1998, P&G's prepaid expenses and other current assets amounted to $1.5 billion.

Current assets are totaled and a caption is generally provided to show the total, but sometimes not. The next component of the balance sheet's assets is comprised of accounts representing noncurrent (long-term) assets, although a caption to this effect is seldom provided. Anything in the asset section of the balance sheet appearing after current assets is a noncurrent asset.

Noncurrent Assets

This section of the balance sheet generally includes long-term investments, property, plant, and equipment (so-called fixed assets), intangible assets, and other (noncurrent) assets. There is no universally accepted order of presentation, and the intangibles are often included in other assets and the detail of this account disclosed in a note to the financials.

Long-term investments. Procter & Gamble does not carry any long-term marketable securities or receivables, or any minority equity positions in affiliated companies. If all or some of these types of assets were held, they would be accounted for here in the balance sheet with an account caption conveying the nature of the holding.

Property, plant, and equipment (PP&E). For most companies, this is another big number in the balance sheet, indicating assets of a permanent nature required to operate a business and varying according to the type of business. Items generally included in PP&E are land, buildings, plant facilities, machinery, equipment, furniture, fixtures, construction in progress, capital lease equipment, and leasehold improvements. The reader should note that the term *fixed assets* is the financial professional's shorthand for property, plant, and equipment, although investment books and articles sometimes refer to a company's total noncurrent assets as its fixed assets. Don't let this confuse you, and stick with the professionals on usage. As can be seen in Exhibit 1.5, fixed assets is a handy term given the variety of language and form of presentation of PP&E in company balance sheets.

Fixed assets, except for land and leasehold improvements, are subject to depreciation. Land, for obvious reasons, is not depreciated and leasehold improvements (e.g., renovations or remodelings of properties) are subject to *amortization,* the term applied to a capitalized expense of this nature. Depreciation, amortization, and depletion all represent the same financial accounting concept that recognizes the gradual reduction in value of an asset on a systematic basis over a given period of time. Depreciation is used with fixed assets, amortization with capitalized expenses and acquired goodwill, and depletion with natural resources like oil, minerals, and timberland. All represent a logical decline in value as the items in question are used or used up. As we discuss in Chapter 5 on cash flow, it's important to remember that depreciation, amortization, and depletion are noncash charges—no cash leaves the company—that are recorded as expenses in the income statement.

In terms of financial statement format, Procter & Gamble has elected to put its complete PP&E account in its balance sheet. Its presentation includes a breakdown by land, buildings, and machinery and equipment less the total amount of accumulated depreciation for a 1998 net total for PP&E of $12.2 billion. Companies often provide these details in a note to their financials and simply state the net property, plant, and equipment figure in the balance sheet. Refer again to Exhibit 1.5 for examples of the variety of corporate practices for expressing PP&E data in balance sheets.

Investors should understand a number of points related to a company's fixed assets. First, many companies use operating leases for buildings, machinery, and equipment, but these items are not recorded as assets—that is, they're not in the balance sheet of the company because they don't convey ownership. Capital leases do convey ownership and thus are recorded as assets in a company's PP&E account in the balance sheet. Transportation companies like airlines and trucking, and retailers and restaurants make heavy use of operating leases to meet their equipment and space (premises) needs; and noncancelable operating leases have debtlike qualities—we'll look at the implications of this aspect of operating leases in our discussion of long-term debt as part of a company's noncurrent liabilities.

Second, several aspects of depreciation are important to investors. Companies don't randomly establish depreciation schedules; rather, the IRS provides depreciation guidelines for the different types of fixed assets, which have a variety of estimated useful lives, from as little as a few years to decades. Many of these assets, nevertheless, experience extended use beyond their useful lives without requiring replacement; and yet they have been fully depreciated and their value no longer appears on the company's balance sheet. Depreciation also affects the income statement as a yearly expense with the accumulation of these amounts appearing in the balance sheet or notes as a reduction to gross fixed assets. As mentioned above, depreciation is a noncash charge to income and generally represents a significant component of a company's operating cash flow. Last, the two principal methods of depreciation, straight-line and accelerated, are most often applied to a company's financial statement reporting and tax reporting, respectively (refer to the Introduction). However, no matter what depreciation method a company uses, the total depreciation is always the same (i.e., eventually the amount of depreciation expense is the same).

Third, a company often can be the beneficiary of hidden value in its fixed assets. For example, because assets are booked at historical cost, the market value of a piece of land, a strategically located manufacturing facility, or store location, and the like could be significantly higher than the carrying value in the company's balance sheet. This is particularly true of urban properties that are located near high-growth areas.

Fourth, some businesses are more capital intensive than others. Companies requiring large investments in fixed assets—for example, energy, natural resource companies, and heavy equipment manufacturers—must be able to generate strong internal cash flow as well as have the capability to raise appropriate levels of debt and equity capital to fund their higher levels of fixed investment.

Last, a leasehold represents a right to the use of a property under a lease. The property is not owned by the lessee company and therefore is not part of its asset base. Leasehold improvements represent expenditures, which have been capitalized, for renovations and remodelings of such property. Obviously, improvements to someone else's property, involving mostly retailers and restaurants, don't represent a strong asset value for the lessee, but operating leases and leasehold improvements are a fact of life for certain businesses. Investors need to be aware that conservative analysis would most likely view leasehold improvements as an intangible asset (see the following section) just as it does other deferred charges of this nature.

EXHIBIT 1.5 • Property, Plant, and Equipment Captions and Presentations

This sampling of G20 companies serves to illustrate the diversity of language and form of presentation of fixed assets evidenced in corporate balance sheets:

- **AMR Corporation** uses two captions – *Equipment and Property* and *Equipment and Property Under Capital Leases* – with details and accumulated depreciated disclosed in the balance sheet. The totals for each category have to be added to get the Company's total fixed assets.
- **Boeing** uses a "one-liner" approach – *Property, plant and equipment, net* and the amount. Details are found in the note to its financials.
- **Ford** with its "dual personality" balance sheet, which separates its automotive and financial services operations, provides a single account entitled *Net Property (Note 5)* and the amount. Details are in a note.
- **Coca-Cola** has a straightforward *Property, Plant and Equipment* in its balance sheet with details, accumulated depreciation, and a net amount for its PP&E without any identifying caption.
- **IBM** uses the *Plant, rental machines and other property* captions for gross and net (accumulated depreciation shown) PP&E in its balance sheet. One should note that his form of presentation mixes the fixed assets IBM uses to support its activities and the equipment it owns and rents to customers. A breakdown of the two different kinds of assets is provided in a note.
- **Microsoft** provides a bare-bones balance sheet caption – *Property, plant, and equipment.* The word "net" is not mentioned, but it is understood that the fixed asset amount in any balance sheet is stated as net of accumulated depreciation. Details are provided in a note to the financials.
- **GE,** like IBM, includes both conventional fixed assets and the equipment leased by its financial services subsidiary, GE Capital Corporation, it its *Property, plant and equipment (including equipment leased to others) – net (note 15)* in its balance sheet. A breakdown and details are provided in the referenced note.
- **Merck** uses the balance sheet caption *Property, Plant and Equipment (at cost)* to express gross fix assets, followed by a breakdown and accumulated depreciation, for a net PP&E figure with no identifying caption.
- **Exxon** has a line entry in its balance sheet for *Property, plant and equipment, at cost, less accumulated depreciation and depletion* and the corresponding amount. Details are provided in a note to its financials.
- **Disney** "personalizes" its PP&E presentation in its balance sheet with a literal description of its detail of fixed assets (e.g., *theme parks, resorts, attractions*) along with accumulated depreciation, and a net fixed assets amount with no identifying caption.

EXHIBIT 1.5 • Property, Plant, and Equipment Captions and Presentations, continued

- **3M** uses the conventional one-line balance sheet caption of *Property, plant and equipment – net* with the corresponding amount. Details are in a note.
- **Gannett** uses the introductory caption *Property, plant and equipment* and provides details in the balance sheet along with accumulated depreciation. The net PP&E amount is identified as *Net property, plant and equipment.*
- **Cyprus Amax,** economizing on language, provides a brief *Properties – At Cost, Net* caption in its balance sheet. The note in the financials covers the details.
- **McDonald's** uses gross *Property and equipment* , *Accumulated depreciation* and *Net property and equipment* captions to present its fixed asset position in the balance sheet – further details are in a note.
- **Albertson's** balance sheet has a one-line entry for *Land, Buildings and Equipment, net,* with the PP&E details included in a note.
- **Wal-Mart** presents a two-part picture of its fixed asset position in the balance sheet. First, there are captions for *Property, Plant and Equipment, at Cost,* followed by details and accumulated depreciation, and ending with *Net property, plant and equipment.* Second, captions for *Property Under Capital Lease* and *Net property under capital leases* provide details and accumulated amortization on capital lease equipment. There is no sum for the two categories of fixed assets.
- **Manpower** uses a *Property and Equipment* caption to introduce its fixed asset disclosure in its balance sheet, which is then followed by details, accumulated depreciation, and a net amount, captioned *Net property and equipment.*
- **Intel** prefaces its balance sheet presentation of fixed assets with the caption, *Property, plant and equipment.* Details and accumulated depreciation are provided that result in a line item for *Property, plant and equipment, net.*
- **Ameritech** uses *Property, plant and equipment* in its balance sheet, wherein it distinguishes between PP&E in service and under construction, the latter being a general characteristic of a telecommunications company's operations. A note to the financials provides details.

Albertson's, the large food supermarket chain, discloses (not all companies do) the amount of leasehold improvements in a note on its property, plant, and equipment account (see Exhibit 1.6). As of its 1998 balance sheet, this $372 million represented a relatively small (7 percent) amount of total gross assets ($5.2 billion) but over 15 percent of shareholders' equity of $2.4 billion.

Intangible assets. Numerous nonphysical assets are considered intangible assets, which can essentially be categorized into three different types: intellectual property, deferred charges,

EXHIBIT 1.6 • Albertson's—Note on PP&E with Leasehold Improvements

Land, Buildings and Equipment

Land, buildings and equipment consist of the following (in thousands):

	January 29, 1998	January 30, 1997	February 1, 1996
Land	$ 795,246	$ 700,208	$ 611,588
Buildings	2,055,276	1,799,976	1,525,769
Fixtures and equipment	1,779,469	1,607,454	1,427,047
Leasehold improvements	372,428	328,249	315,658
Capitalized leases	203,217	186,768	183,316
	5,205,636	4,622,655	4,063,378
Less accumulated depreciation and amortization	1,822,263	1,568,015	1,365,896
	$ 3,383,373	$ 3,054,640	$ 2,697,482

and purchased goodwill. There is little uniformity in balance sheet presentations for intangibles or the use of descriptive language for the account captions. Intangibles are often included as other assets and only disclosed in a note to the financials.

Investment analysts generally recognize that intangible assets have value; the problem lies in making a reasonable determination of the intangibles' monetary value, which is recorded in a company's balance sheet. Conservative financial statement analysis like that done by bank lenders and credit-ranking agencies often reduces a company's assets, and consequently equity, by the amount of a company's intangibles based on the premise that this type of asset has little or no liquidation or collateral value. This reduction produces tangible net worth—that is, Assets – Intangibles = Liabilities + Tangible net worth (Equity – Intangibles). I'd not suggest that investors automatically dismiss intangible assets, but as you'll see in the following, a material amount of intangibles in a company's balance sheet needs to be considered carefully from both a negative and positive standpoint.

Intellectual property intangibles are probably the easiest to understand because such items as patents, copyrights, trademarks, and brand names obviously have value. From an accounting standpoint, companies are allowed to record their value based only on the cost involved in developing an item or on an item's price if purchased from another party. What value would you place on the Coca-Cola formula? Or its brand name? Obviously, the market value of Coca-Cola's formula and brand name, which is not reflected in a balance sheet, is worth billions of dollars to The Coca-Cola Company. On the other hand, today's billion-dollar patent in the high-end technology field may be eclipsed by a superior invention next year and be relatively worthless.

Deferred charges represent an expense that has been capitalized—instead of being a cost in the income statement, the item becomes an asset in the balance sheet. Sounds like magic, but this practice conforms to accounting conventions that permit a company to record a cost as an asset (it's capitalized), which is subject to amortization. The rationale for capitalizing these costs rests on their long-term benefit to the company; for example, interest on loans during the construction phase of a plant, fees paid to investment bankers for the arrangement of debt and equity issues, and start-up or development costs of a new product or line of business. Remember leasehold improvements? They are a deferred charge recorded in a company's property, plant, and equipment account.

Companies like to capitalize costs whenever possible. If expensed, such charges are deducted from income and reduce profits immediately as opposed to being amortized over several years. Generally, deferred charges, which tend to overstate balance sheet assets, are not material, and the investor need not be overly concerned about this particular asset value unless the amount is significant. With the exception of some narrowly defined instances for computer software and natural resource companies, research and development costs are not allowed to be capitalized, leading some analysts to feel that many technology-driven companies' asset positions are substantially undervalued.

The layperson thinks of goodwill in different terms than the accountant. Although a company's reputation is important, reputation is not an intangible asset we're talking about. A more descriptive term would be *purchased goodwill*, which represents to the acquiring company the cost of the investment in excess of the equity (book value) of the acquired company. In plain English: Company ABC pays $100 for Company XYZ, and the latter has only $90 worth of recorded equity (Assets – Liabilities = Equity). This means that Company ABC will have to record $10 as goodwill (purchased goodwill) in its balance sheet and have this amount amortized over a period not to exceed 40 years. In theory, future cash flows, profits, business synergies, and so on justify the overpayment, but today's acquired beauty sometimes turns into tomorrow's beast. Investors should be aware that some investment professionals become uncomfortable with a relatively large amount of purchased goodwill in a company's balance sheet. Leopold Bernstein, a recognized expert on financial statement analysis writing in *Business Credit* (October 1994), expressed this concern in these words:

> The nondescript asset "goodwill" can range greatly in both meaning and value. The accounting process that led to its recording provides little, if any, clues to its economic worth. It can represent solid value such as the purchase of widely accepted brand names which required many years of costly development and promotion. It can, at the other extreme, represent overpayments for assets due to unrealistic expectations, undisciplined zeal, or lack of sound judgment and proper analysis. There are, of course, a whole range of possibilities in between.

Only time will tell if the acquisition price paid by an acquiring company was really fair value. The return to the acquiring company will be realized only if it is able to turn the acquisition into productive earnings.

Procter & Gamble has a rather complete balance sheet presentation for its intangible assets (net), which include goodwill—approximately $7 billion for goodwill, trademarks, and other intangible assets. This information is generally found in a note to the financial statements. In the case of purchased goodwill, an especially jargon-prone term in financial reporting, other expressions used to describe this item include the following:

- Cost in excess of fair value of net assets acquired
- Cost in excess of net assets of acquired businesses
- Excess of acquisition cost over fair value of assets acquired
- Excess of cost of acquired companies over equity
- Excess of cost over fair value of net assets acquired
- Excess of investments over net assets acquired
- Excess of purchase cost over fair value of net assets of acquired companies, net of amortization

Other noncurrent assets. Procter & Gamble uses this account caption in its balance sheet ($1.2 billion in 1998), which is typical of the presentation used by many companies as a catchall account for such miscellaneous items as prepaid pension costs, sundry assets, and minor investments. Normally, the dollar amount of other noncurrent assets is not material, but if it is, investors should look for details of this account in a note to the financials.

Total assets. This is the sum of current and noncurrent assets—everything a company owns. For P&G, total assets amounted to almost $31 billion in 1998.

LIABILITY ACCOUNTS

A company's liabilities represent money owed to others. The word *debt* is often used to mean liabilities, which I think is confusing, so I make a distinction between operational liabilities and debt liabilities, with the latter being true debt. Operationally, a company incurs a number of obligations such as accounts payable, accrued expenses, taxes payable, and pensions, which certainly represent obligatory future payments but are not debt obligations. Debt infers a formal, contractual relationship requiring the payment of interest and principal at fixed maturities, particularly if the company expects to continue to tap lenders for funds to finance its activities. All liabilities are equal (i.e., all are obligations that must be honored), but some are more equal than others. Debt is one of those liabilities that is more equal, and investors should be aware of a company's debt liabilities and how these affect a company's financial position and performance.

Current Liabilities

Notes payable. This account records short-term borrowed funds. The caption originated with the practice of lenders using a written promissory note to document a debt. Over the years, other forms of financing have evolved (e.g., commercial paper), but the traditional caption has remained in use by many companies. Whatever the account caption used, these short-term borrowings from financial institutions and /or outstandings for commercial paper are what's used to finance current assets such as accounts receivable and inventories. Current debt liabilities should be self-liquidating; a company, for example, may take out a loan to help buy raw material inventory that, when processed, sold, and the money collected, is repaid. Procter & Gamble uses a single account, debt due within one year, (almost $2.3 billion in 1998) to capture both short-term borrowings ($1,995 million) and the current portion payable of long-term debt ($286 million), which is discussed below. The latter is often shown in a balance sheet as a separate account entry; in the case of P&G, a breakdown of this nature is provided in a note.

Current portion of long-term debt. P&G includes this account, which simply records the current maturities of long-term debt, in a note to its financials for long-term debt. However, it is more common to see this information in the balance sheet, generally paired with short-term borrowings (notes payable). Unlike other current liabilities, which depend on the conversion of current assets for repayment, the current maturities of long-term debt are paid from a company's cash flow. This is one of the reasons for considering the current portion of long-term debt as part of long-term debt.

Accounts payable. Generally, this account, also referred to as trade credit, represents amounts owed by a company to suppliers (trade creditors) for the purchase of goods and services under varying terms of payment. Obviously, it is to a company's advantage to obtain as much of this interest free money as possible. Companies with a strong financial position and good reputation are usually able to obtain favorable terms of payment (the more time the better), which has a positive effect on its cash flow. Procter & Gamble certainly falls into this category and carried a hefty $2,051 million in 1998 as accounts payable. Investors can make a rough calculation to determine a company's days payable with this simple formula, which uses P&G's 1997–98 numbers (in millions of dollars):

Average accounts payable : 2,051 + 2,203 = 4,254 ÷ 2 = 2,127
[The concept of cost of sales is discussed in Chapter 3—Statement of Income]

Cost of sales per day: 21,064 ÷ 365 days = 57.7

Average accounts payable ÷ cost of sales per day = days payable: 2,127 ÷ 57.7 = 37 days payable

This calculation tells us that on average in 1998, P&G had approximately 37 days to pay its suppliers. The behavior of this indicator, expanding or contracting over time, provides a clue to how effective a company is at maximizing its trade credit, which is, among others, an important source of cash.

Accrued expenses. At a company's year-end statement date, a number of operational obligations are outstanding and recorded as accruals, accrued expenses, or accrued liabilities. Items recorded in this account, which are sometimes broken out separately, could include, for example, salaries and wages, employee benefits, dividends payable, interest due, rent, legal/accounting services, sales commissions, deferred income, and, in some cases, taxes, although this last item often has a line entry of its own. Procter & Gamble uses the caption accrued and other liabilities ($3,942 million in 1998).

Income taxes payable. If you are a investor, you want to see something recorded in this account, or otherwise it means that the company hasn't generated enough income to incur a tax liability: not good! Procter & Gamble had taxes payable of $976 million for 1998.

Current liabilities are totaled and a caption is usually provided to show the total, but not always. Next in the balance sheet's liabilities are accounts representing noncurrent (long-term) liabilities, although a caption is seldom provided. Everything below current liabilities is a noncurrent liability.

Noncurrent Liabilities

Long-term debt. Long-term debt represents borrowed funds with payments due beyond one year; usually the payment period covers several years. As mentioned above, payments due on long-term debt due within one year are recorded in current liabilities. The larger the company, the larger the spectrum and complexity of its borrowing arrangements. As presented in the balance sheet, these typically include long-term notes payable; commercial paper and bank loans; bonds; debentures; mortgages; revolving credit agreements; and capital leases. The note to a company's financial statements on long-term debt generally provides a lot of detail regarding the tenor, interest rates, and conditions related to these obligations. Generally, long-term debt is an important component of a company's total *capitalization* (the sum of long-term debt and equity), which represents the permanent capital used by a company to support its investment in fixed assets, equity investments, and permanent working capital. Procter & Gamble has a relatively uncomplicated long-term debt situation, recording $5.8 billion in its 1998 balance sheet. However, there is much more to the debt story, and investors should become conversant with what radio commentator Paul Harvey calls "the rest of the story."

First, the word *debt,* a seemingly uncomplicated financial term, means different things to different people. I commented earlier on the distinction between operational and debt liabilities, a distinction not always made in investment literature. For many, as I've said, a company's debt is synonymous with its total liabilities; for example, as you will see in the next chapter, a much used financial ratio compares total liabilities to total assets and is called the debt ratio—the debt in this case being total liabilities. Second, for others a company's debt refers to just the amount of its recorded long-term debt and doesn't even include the current portion payable in current liabilities. Third, some financial analysts would consider this last definition of long-term debt too narrow. They would include the current portion payable and add in a portion of operating leases and redeemable preferred stock (discussed below). Last, conservative financial analysts would not only incorporate all the items in this third point but would go even further. They would also include operational long-term liabilities, such as deferred income taxes, pension obligations, other postretirement employee benefits, and warranties as part of a company's long-term debt.

So then, just what is long-term debt? I have an answer that investors can use, but it's better to wait until the next chapter. Suffice it to say here that there is little definitional uniformity in corporate financial communications, the financial media, and investment information services. The critical consideration for investors in using debt information is to know the precise definition of the term being used. What accounts are included? The same would be true for the calculation of the various financial debt ratios—what are the components? Unless the source of the information clearly indicates what it considers debt, it would be unwise to take the related narrative and ratios at face value.

Two debt-related items that investors need to know about don't pertain, or are not material, to Procter & Gamble's financial position—operating leases and redeemable preferred stock. Operating leases are considered *off-balance sheet* items (i.e., there is no amount recorded, as either asset or liability, in a company's balance sheet for these items) and the information about operating leases is found in a note to a company's financials. An operating lease is a contract whereby the lessor maintains formal ownership of the property or equipment under lease and grants its use to the lessee in return for rental payments, which figure as an expense in the income statement. Because operating leases generally represent multiyear, noncancelable, irrevocable obligations, they have all the qualities of debt and are considered so by most financial analysts. Therefore, a company's long-term debt is usually adjusted to include two-thirds of the total minimum operating lease payments as long-term debt principal—the other one-third is considered interest expense. Some analysts will include the total amount as debt, making no distinction between principal and interest.

Redeemable preferred stock, which has more characteristics of debt than of equity, cannot be shown in the equity section of the balance sheet under existing accounting conventions. It must be shown, when it exists, in the no-man's-land between the liability section and the equity section of the balance sheet. In reality, because these securities have a mandatory redemption requirement similar to the repayment of debt, financial analysts consider them long-term debt.

Other noncurrent liabilities. Several items could be included in this type of account. As in the case of Procter & Gamble (almost $3.3 billion in 1998), many companies aggregate other noncurrent liabilities in a single-line entry in the balance sheet. In other companies, they'll be separated out and will generally include the following items: deferred income taxes, pension obligations, other postretirement employee benefits (OPEB), and warranty liabilities. As mentioned in the discussion of long-term debt, conservative analysts consider these long-term operational liabilities as part of a company's debt liabilities. I think that from the investor's point of view, this view is not altogether correct. No doubt these are true obligations of a company that would have to be met if the company ceased doing business (e.g., on a liquidation basis), but from an investment point of view, a company is looked at as a going concern and these obligations, to one degree or another, are going to be part of its liability position forever. No fixed repayment schedule or interest charges are attached to these obligations. For a company, one could make the case that these operational liabilities can be considered a form of interest-free permanent capital. When calculating a company's leverage ratios in Chapter 2, I don't include a company's long-term operational liabilities as debt.

Total liabilities. The sum of current and noncurrent liabilities gives us the total liability figure. Many companies omit this caption and corresponding monetary amount in their balance sheet, which is unfortunate because it's a useful number for calculating a number of financial ratios, and it's nice to have the math done for you. P&G's total liabilities in 1998 amounted to approximately $18.7 billion.

Two special items, which sometimes appear in the no-man's-land between the liability and the equity section of the balance sheet, warrant explanation—minority interest and commitments/contingencies.

Minority interest is seen only in the balance sheets of companies with investments in consolidated subsidiaries that are not wholly owned by the companies. The process of consolidation, as noted in the introduction, considers the parent company to have absorbed 100 percent of the net asset value (equity) of the investee company (subsidiary). However, if the majority investor owns only 80 percent of the subsidiary, the minority investor's interest must be recognized, which financial accounting does by recording a minority interest on the liability side of the majority investor's balance sheet. If this were not done, the equity of the majority investor company would be overstated. Minority interest is not a true liability because there's no mandatory payment of interest, dividends, or principal. Although opinion differs on this issue, investors are safe in considering this a balancing item. The amount is usually not material, so any argument over its precise classification is academic.

Sometimes companies include a notation for commitments and contingencies in the no-man's-land that looks like an account caption, but no corresponding amount appears. Regardless of whether or not the item is mentioned in the balance sheet, there is usually a note to the financial statements covering commitments and contingencies. These are potential liabilities and/or obligations that are not quantifiable in accounting terms but could have an impact on the financial position of the company in the future. The circumstances and explanations of these commitments and contingencies can be unusually complex (lengthy) or routine (short). (I go into more detail on this topic in Chapter 8 where notes to the financial statements are reviewed.)

EQUITY ACCOUNTS

Shareholders' or stockholders' equity, common shareholders' equity, shareholders' investment, book value, net worth, net assets, and, simply, equity, all mean the same thing; they identify ownership interest in a company—what's owed to investors after liabilities are subtracted from assets. The word *owed* is perhaps a misnomer because, unlike creditors, equity investors can't expect any fixed return on the money they have put into the company. They expect to get a return on their investment through the price appreciation of the company's stock and/or dividends paid, but no fixed obligation exists as it does with the money owed to creditors.

At the risk of oversimplification, I think what investors need to know about a company's equity position is found in one number—total shareholders' equity. Equity is one of those items characterized by the rule of thumb that more of a good thing is better. A strong equity position provides a company with a margin of safety in difficult times and allows it to take advantage of acquisition and expansion opportunities with relative ease. In the case of Procter & Gamble, the amount of shareholders' equity was $12.2 billion for 1998. All the other account entries and their respective numbers are nice to know, but it's the total equity number that is critical. What follows, therefore, is just a brief descriptive narrative of the components of the equity section; and readers can consult the glossary for formal definitions of the various equity components.

The equity section starts with a listing of a company's capital stock—preferred and common. The former isn't used very much but does appear on occasion in a company's balance sheet. P&G is one of those cases; it has approximately $1.8 billion of preferred stock in its equity position. Notations generally indicate the number of shares authorized and actually issued (outstanding) for the stock that is recorded in shareholders' equity. Additional paid-in capital and retained or reinvested earnings are the other positive contributions to a company's equity position. In 1998 Procter & Gamble registered roughly $1.3 billion, $0.9 billion, and $11.1 billion for its common stock, additional paid-in capital, and retained earnings, respectively. The large amount of retained earnings, the profit that has been left in the company after paying out dividends, is explained by P&G's very long operating history—over 160 years!

A number of adjustments (increases and decreases) to equity that are required by accounting conventions often appear. The most prominent of these include treasury stock, foreign currency translation, unearned compensation, unrealized gain (loss), and ESOP loans/guarantees. Users of financial statements should note that, effective December 15, 1998, all financial statements will reflect a change in the balance sheet presentation for the first three items. Financial Accounting Standards Board's SFAS No. 130—Reporting Comprehensive Income—means that reductions with a link to income/expense items will be accumulated in a separate account in the equity section described as accumulated other comprehensive income, discussed in more depth in Chapter 3. Procter & Gamble's midyear 1998 balance sheet presentation anticipated this change by using the caption suggested by FASB.

Total liabilities and shareholders' equity. The sum of total liabilities and equity are added together and balanced against total assets. Procter & Gamble's total 1998 "footings"—assets and liabilities/equity—equal approximately $31 billion for each side of the balance sheet. Although assets and equity are obviously measurements of company size, it's a company's sales/revenue figure that is most often used for this purpose by financial professionals.

Now that you have an understanding of the general anatomy of a balance sheet, let's see how you can use key parts of this anatomy to build financial ratios and indicators to evaluate the balance sheet. Becoming conversant with these measurements allows individual investors to apply the same criteria to judge balance sheet strength as that used by investment professionals.

CHAPTER 2

Key Investment Evaluators for Balance Sheets

For investors, the strength of a company's balance sheet is measured by three broad categories of investment evaluators: liquidity/efficiency, asset performance, and leverage. In the following pages, you'll learn how to calculate and interpret a series of financial ratios and indicators that allow you to apply these key investment evaluators to a company's balance sheet. I'll continue to use the numbers from Procter & Gamble's 1998 balance sheet in Exhibit 1.2, which is now familiar to you, for this purpose. The exhibits in this chapter are intended to expose you to a variety of results of different measurements as they are applied to a diverse group of companies and industries.

LIQUIDITY/EFFICIENCY INVESTMENT EVALUATORS

First, as we discovered in the discussion of current assets in the previous chapter, the faster a company can convert its working assets, principally accounts receivable and inventories, into cash, the more liquidity it enjoys. A company is said to be liquid when it carries a high proportion of its assets as liquid assets. Investors should also be alert to spotting liquidity enhancers in a company's financial information. For example, for a company that has noncurrent investment securities, there is typically a secondary market for the relatively quick conversion of all or a high portion of these items to cash. Also, unused committed lines of credit, usually mentioned in a note to the financials on debt or in the management discussion and analysis (MD&A) section of a company's annual report, can provide quick access to cash.

At a macro level, a company's liquidity is determined, to a large degree, by the type of product or service it provides and its customer base. As you will see, it's easier for a retailer that is simply turning over merchandise for cash to be liquid than it is for a manufacturer of industrial products. The latter has to maintain inventories of raw materials and work in process and generally provide terms of payment with its sales. The manufacturer's cash conversion cycle, which we discuss later, is, because of the nature of its business, much longer than that of the retailer.

At the micro or company level, whatever the nature of a company's business, a key management function is to make sure that the receivable and inventory positions are managed efficiently. That means ensuring an adequate level of good customer service—for example, appropriate payment terms and product availability—while at the same time making sure that working assets don't tie up undue amounts of cash. This is a balancing act for managers, but an important one. Important because with high liquidity, a company is able to take advantage of price discounts on its cash purchases, easily meet its short-term obligations, benefit from a good credit rating, and take advantage of market opportunities. The old adage that "cash is king" is as important for investors evaluating a company's investment qualities as it is for the managers running the business. A liquidity squeeze is worse than a profit squeeze. Management expert Peter Drucker has observed that "in a profit crunch a company typically sells off or cuts its least profitable and most obsolete businesses or products. In a liquidity crunch, it typically sells its most profitable or most promising units since these bring in the cash soonest."

Before discussing the ratios and indicators you should use to measure a company's liquidity, I feel compelled to correct some conventional wisdom on two of the most popular, albeit misleading, liquidity indicators: the current ratio and its close relative, working capital. Contrary to their apparent value as analytical tools, they don't convey the evaluative information about a company's liquidity that an investor needs to know. Alternative analytical tools are more insightful, just as easy to understand, and readily computed from financial statement data with which you are already familiar. Before discussing these alternatives, it behooves investors, nevertheless, to fully understand the limitations of the current ratio and working capital concepts because they are so widely used and commented on in investment literature.

The current ratio measures the amount of current assets that are available to pay current liabilities. It is easily calculated by dividing current assets by current liabilities and is expressed as a times factor (x). For example, Procter & Gamble's 1998 current ratio is 1.14 to 1, or simply expressed as just 1.14. The most often expressed assumption is that the higher the current ratio the better. For years, scores of books and articles on investing have preached that the general rule of thumb is the current ratio should be 2 to 1 or higher. While not that critical to our discussion here on liquidity, Exhibit 2.1, I hope, puts that myth to rest. What is important for investors to know is that the current ratio, as an indicator of liquidity, is flawed because it's based on a company's liquidation of current assets to meet its current obligations. In reality, this is not likely to occur. Because investors have to look at a company as a going concern, it's the flow of funds or the time it takes to convert a company's working assets into cash that is the key to its liquidity. You'll see how this concept works when, in the pages below, we discuss a company's operating cycle, which is the most effective way to measure liquidity.

Working capital, as a real-life element in the operation of a business, is absolutely essential. Working capital, as a number—the difference between current assets and current liabilities—has little or no relevance to an assessment of a company's liquidity. Nevertheless, this number is duly

EXHIBIT 2.1 • Current Ratios for Companies in the Dow Jones Industrial Average*

COMPANY	CURRENT ASSETS	CURRENT LIABILITIES	CURRENT RATIO (x)
AT&T	16,179	16,942	0.95
Allied Signal	5,573	4,436	1.26
Alcoa	4,417	2,453	1.80
Boeing	19,263	14,152	1.36
Catepillar	9,814	6,379	1.54
Chevron	7,006	6,946	1.01
Coca-Cola	5,969	7,379	0.81
Disney	11,283	6,572	1.72
DuPont	11,874	14,070	0.85
Eastman Kodak	5,475	5,177	1.06
Exxon	21,192	19,654	1.08
General Electric	212,755	120,668	1.76
General Motors	101,449	66,837	1.51
Goodyear	4,164	3,251	1.28
Hewlett-Packard	20,947	11,219	1.87
IBM	40,418	33,507	1.21
International Paper	5,945	4,880	1.22
Johnson&Johnson	10,563	5,283	2.00
McDonald's	1,142	2,985	0.38
Merck	8,213	5,569	1.47
3M	6,168	3,983	1.55
Phillip Morris	17,440	15,071	1.16
Procter & Gamble	10,786	7,798	1.38
Sears	30,682	15,790	1.94
Union Carbide	1,866	1,504	1.24
United Technologies	9,248	7,311	1.26
Wal-Mart	17,993	10,957	1.64

Notes:

* Less financial service companies: American Express, J.P. Morgan, and Travelers.

recorded in many corporate financial communications such as the annual report and investment information services. If it has any value, as a number that is, it would need to be compared to a company's sales or assets to have meaning. As a stand-alone number, working capital sheds very little light on a company's liquidity position. Investors need to understand that working capital and cash flow are not synonymous.

A simplistic, but accurate, comparison of two companies' current position will illustrate the weaknesses in relying on the current ratio and/or a working capital number as liquidity indicators:

	Company ABC	Company XYZ
Current assets	$600	$300
Current liabilities	−300	−300
Working capital	$300	0
Current ratio	2:1	1:1

Company ABC looks like an easy winner in a contest of current positions and liquidity. It has an ample margin of current assets over current liabilities, a seemingly good current ratio and working capital of $300. Company XYZ has no current asset-liability margin and zero working capital. However, to illustrate my point, what if (1) both companies' current liabilities have an average payment period of 30 days; (2) Company ABC needs six months to collect on its accounts receivable, and its inventory turns over just once a year (12 months); and (3) Company XYZ is paid cash by its customers, and its inventory has a 20-day turnover. In this contrived example, Company ABC is very illiquid and would not be able to operate under the conditions described. Its bills are coming due faster than its generation of cash—you can't pay bills with working capital; you pay bills with cash! Company XYZ's apparent tight current position is, in effect, much more liquid because of its quicker asset conversion.

The quick assets ratio, which gets less attention than the current ratio, focuses on the coverage of total current liabilities by a company's quick assets (see Chapter 1). The ratio is also referred to as the acid test ratio, or the quick ratio. A company's quick assets—cash and cash equivalents, invested funds, and accounts receivable—are assumed to have a fairly dependable and relatively fast conversion to cash. Inventories and other current assets, although still in the liquid asset category, are perceived to be subject to longer cash conversion periods and potential value reductions, especially in emergency liquidation situations. As measured by this indicator, the higher this ratio is, the greater a company's liquidity. While of more value, in my opinion, than the current ratio, I would still urge investors to view the quick assets ratio only as a helpful, but not a critical, tool to measure liquidity. I repeat, a company's operating cycle is the primary evaluator of its ability to meet its short-term obligations.

THE OPERATING CYCLE

What is the operating cycle? All companies, apart from the financial services sector, have one—it's an approximation of the time it takes to convert accounts receivable and inventories, which are the two key components of current assets and generally major corporate asset values, into cash. This time span is usually measured by using the turnover ratios for receivables and inventory. The concept of turnover can be expressed as a number of times per year or as a number of days. It appears that financial professionals tend to use days with receivables and times per year with inventories to indicate turnover rates. I suggest investors use days for both indicators, which, when added together, provide a coherent time measurement of a company's operating cycle.

A turnover rate of four times a year, for example, if expressed as times per year, would be written as 4x, which is the same as approximately 91 days. Or, vice versa, 91 days approximate a turnover rate of 4x (per year). You can easily convert a times-per-year indication into days by simply dividing 365 (days in a year) by the times per year (e.g., $365 \div 4 = 91.25$).

A fast turnover rate of accounts receivable and inventories is what creates real liquidity and is a positive indication of the quality and efficient management of these important assets. As noted at the beginning of this chapter, a company's product line and customer base impose certain fixed conditions on a given company's accounts receivable and inventory turnover. Companies in the retail sector, which have to carry little or no accounts receivable, have to be concerned with inventory turnover only. This sector's customers, with either dollars in hand or a credit card, are paying for relatively fast-moving merchandise with cash or its equivalent. In contrast, a manufacturer of industrial products has to source and store raw materials, take time to fabricate the product, and, most likely, provide payment terms on its direct sales to customers as well as its sales through distributors. Favorable terms of payment offered to buyers can be a powerful marketing tool. For some companies, it would be counterproductive to overly restrict its extension of credit to reduce receivable collection time, which would have the effect, undoubtedly, of restricting sales.

Whatever a company's market conditions, the shorter the collection period for accounts receivable and the faster the turnover of inventories, the less cash is needed to carry these current assets. That's a very positive indicator of investment value. A company needs to borrow less, stays more flexible, and incurs less interest expense. Common sense tells us that having more cash available for acquisitions and business expansion is better than having it tied up in operating assets. What investors need to look for is the efficient management of these key assets and evidence of high quality working capital—a fast turnover of accounts receivable and inventories. This is one of those elements of a company's financial position where quality beats quantity! Factors such as the efficiency of collection efforts, industry conditions, competitive pressures, raw material sourcing, production time, and the nature of the product will all impact on a company's operating cycle. How effectively a company's managers deal with these factors will produce positive or negative trends, increasing or decreasing the number of days, respectively, in its cash conversion cycle—the best indicator of a company's liquidity.

Days Sales Outstanding (DSO)

Days sales outstanding, as the term implies, is the financial professional's description of the indicator used to measure the turnover of a company's accounts receivable. The numbers to calculate this component of the operating cycle are readily found in a company's balance sheet and its income statement. Using Procter & Gamble to illustrate, refer to its 1998 balance sheet and income statement figures (expressed in millions) in Exhibit 1.2 in the previous chapter and Exhibit 3.1 in the next chapter:

Step 1: Divide net sales by 365 to get sales per day.

$$\frac{\$37{,}154}{365} = \$101.8 \text{ sales per day}$$

Step 2: Calculate the average of accounts receivable for 1998.
$2,738 (1997) + $2,781 (1998) = $5,519 ÷ 2 = $2,760 average accounts receivable

Step 3: Divide average accounts receivable for 1998 by sales per day for DSO.
$2,760 ÷ $101.8 = 27.1 days sales outstanding

P&G collected its accounts receivable in 1998 at a fast pace, less than a month's time or, expressed as a turnover rate, more than 13 times a year.

One additional point about the DSO calculation needs clarifying. The accounts receivable number in the balance sheet is net of an allowance for uncollectible accounts. Technically, the allowance should be added back in to give us a gross number for accounts receivable, which would give us a more correct number to work with in the computation of days sales outstanding. However, because the allowance is usually a relatively small number, its impact would not be material on what is, admittedly, a rough approximation. For ease of calculation, therefore, investors are safe in using the net accounts receivable numbers in the balance sheet.

DAYS INVENTORY ON HAND

Because a company's operating cycle is calculated as a time period, we'll use days of inventory on hand as the concept to determine how fast inventory turns. Just as we did with the DSO, the numbers we need are found in Procter & Gamble's 1998 balance sheet (inventories) and income statement (for cost of sales P&G uses an equivalent term, cost of products sold). The computation of days inventory on hand is very similar to that for days sales outstanding except that instead of using the net sales figure, we use the cost of sales figure. Sales and accounts receivable numbers both include profit and are compatible. Inventory and cost of sales are recorded at cost before the inclusion of profit and therefore are compatible for the inventory turnover calculation (P&G's 1998 financials/amounts expressed in millions):

Step 1: Divide cost of sales by 365 to get cost of sales per day.

$$\frac{\$21,064}{365} = \$57.7 \text{ cost of sales per day}$$

Step 2: Calculate the average of inventories for 1998.

$3,087 (1997) + $3,284 (1998) = $6,470 ÷ 2 = $3,186 average inventories

Step 3: Divide average inventories 1998 by cost of sales per day.

$3,186 ÷ $57.7 = 55.2 days inventory on hand

In 1998, P&G turned over its inventory every 55 days, a period of less than two months, or more than six times a year. Just as we saw that overly aggressive receivable collection efforts could adversely affect sales, too tight an inventory period could make timely customer deliveries problematical. Here again, in the real world, management needs to perform another intelligent balancing act or sales could suffer.

Procter & Gamble's operating cycle improved in 1998 (82 days) over 1997 (84 days) by 2 days. Refer to Exhibit 2.2 to see that the company had 28 days for receivables and 56 days for inventory in 1997 versus 27 days and 55 days, respectively, in 1998. That might not seem like much of a difference, but think of it in real terms, the amount of cash it actually represents to the company: (1) one day's worth of sales ($102 million) for each turn of DSO during the year (approximately 12 times during the year) and (2) one day's worth of cost of sales days ($58 million) for each inventory turn (approximately 6 times during the year). By rough calculation the sum of these two days freed up over $1.5 billion worth of cash during 1998!

Investors will benefit from reviewing the performance of the G20 companies in Exhibit 2.2 to develop real-life insights into the operating cycle as an investment evaluator. First, it is worth repeating that ratios need to be looked at over time, preferably at least three to five years. Financial analysts like to look at ten years. Also, intercompany comparisons are only meaningful if they are done within the same or similar lines of business and industry sectors.

The first thing you'll notice in the G20 sampling is the diversity of liquidity positions, another reason it's a mistake to treat all balance sheets the same. One size does not fit all!

Microsoft is definitely a winner in the liquidity sweepstakes. Here is a company selling over $11 billion worth of computer software, and it doesn't have to carry any inventory. In addition, its market strength is such that its collection time on accounts receivable is very low, all of which results in an operating cycle of a couple of weeks—a very enviable position. Service companies such as AMR Corporation (American Airlines), Manpower (temporary employee staffing), and Ameritech (telecommunications) don't carry salable inventories. But in the case of the latter two companies, their businesses require offering payment terms to their customers and thus carrying relatively high amounts of receivables. In contrast, AMR gets paid rather quickly from the sale of its passenger tickets, so it's likely that most of its receivables relate to its commercial customers for freight services. Ford's very low DSO is deceptive. How can it sell a relatively high-ticket item like a motor vehicle and get paid in nine days? The secret for Ford, as well as for its automobile manufacturing competitors, lies in the use of a finance subsidiary—that's where you find a signif-

EXHIBIT 2.2 • Sampling of Industry and Company Liquidity/Efficiency Indicators

INDUSTRY	COMPANY	FISCAL YEAR	CURRENT RATIO (x)	QUICK ASSET RATIO (x)	DAYS SALES OUTSTANDING (days)	+	INVENTORY TURNOVER (days)	=	OPERATING CYCLE (days)
Airlines	AMR Corporation	12/31/97	0.9	0.7	27		(a)		27
Aerospace	Boeing	12/31/97	1.4	0.6	24		82		106
Automotive	Ford	12/31/97	1.1	0.6	9(b)		20(b)		29(b)
Beverage	Coca-Cola	12/31/97	0.8	0.5	32		58		90
Computer	IBM	12/31/97	1.2	0.7	109		42		151
Computer Software	Microsoft	06/30/97	2.9	2.8	14		0		14
Conglomerate	GE	12/31/97	0.9(c)	0.7(c)	67(b)		48(b)		115(b)
Energy	Exxon	12/31/97	1.1	0.8	29		29		58
Leisure Time	Disney	09/30/97	1.2(c)	0.4(c)	57		19		76
Manufacturing	3M	12/31/97	1.6	1.0	60		99		159
Media	Gannett	12/31/97	1.2	0.9	47		13		60
Mining	Cyprus Amax	12/31/97	1.4	0.5	23		68		91
Personal Care	Procter & Gamble	06/30/97	1.4	0.8	28		56		84
Pharmaceutical	Merck	12/31/97	1.5	0.9	43		66		109
Restaurant	McDonald's	12/31/97	0.4	0.3	16		9		25
Retailing—Food	Albertson's	01/31/98	1.3	0.2	3		42		45
Retailing—General	Wal-Mart	01/31/98	1.3	0.2	3		65		68
Service	ManPower	12/31/97	1.7	1.6	65		0		65
Technology	Intel	12/31/97	2.6	2.2	52		55		107
Telecomunications	Ameritech	12/31/97	0.6	0.4	70		(a)		70

Notes:

(a) Inventories are spare parts, supplies, and materials, which are not used for this calculation.

(b) Ford's and GE's financing subsidiary activities are not included in the calculations of these ratios.

(c) Balance sheet does not express current assets/liabilities, therefore, estimates were made.

icant amount of money due from its dealer-customers. In fact, companies' financials that consolidate commercial/industrial and financial activities, such as is the case with Ford, General Electric, and, to a lesser degree, Boeing in the G20 sample, don't lend themselves to a meaningful operating cycle analysis. As noted before, it's the trade, not the finance, accounts receivable whose turnover is effectively measured by the days sales outstanding calculation.

Another true liquidity winner, from the perspective of both receivables and inventory turnover, is McDonald's. Look at the numbers: 16 days and 9 days, respectively, for a total operating cycle of only 25 days. In this case, fast food equates to fast cash. It's easy to make these numbers come alive by visualizing those Big Macs, Cokes, and fries virtually flying across the counter. Retailers like Albertson's (food supermarkets) and Wal-Mart (food and consumer goods) enjoy the same type of cash sales as McDonald's, but they obviously have to carry large merchandise inventories not typical of the restaurant business. Mainstream manufacturers like Intel, 3M, and Merck all have triple-digit operating cycles, which is typical for a business that needs to transform raw materials into finished products and then sell them through industrial/commercial channels of distribution. IBM's days sales outstanding figure is high, not because of poor receivable quality, but rather because it carries a large amount of computer equipment leasing receivables, which is a long-established IBM business practice.

The operating cycle and its components are the best indicators of a company's true liquidity. In addition, the performance of days sales outstanding and days sales in inventory are good indicators of management's ability to efficiently manage such important assets as accounts receivable and inventories. The popular current ratio does not provide the same insights and to a large degree is deceptive. To prove this point, check out the current ratio for McDonald's in Exhibit 2.1. At 0.38 to 1, the conventional wisdom associated with the current ratio would consider that the company's current position as highly illiquid. On the other hand, using operating cycle analysis, we find a veritable cash machine that is very liquid.

ASSET PERFORMANCE

For most companies, fixed assets—property, plant, and equipment—represent the single largest component of their total assets. For example, Procter & Gamble's fixed assets represent 39 percent of its 1998 total assets, but other examples from our G20 company sampling (1997 financials) in Exhibit 2.3 indicate the diversity of fixed asset positions (fixed assets as a percentage of total assets) evidenced by companies in other types of business. As we learned in the discussion of PP&E in the previous chapter, these assets, which are of a fairly permanent nature, are required for the normal conduct of a company's business. Obviously, a company's investment in fixed assets is dependent, to a large degree, on its line of business. Thus, investors are reminded to make this distinction when considering the fixed asset turnover and return on assets ratios discussed below.

The large amount of fixed investment required by natural resource companies is reflected in Exxon's and Cyprus Amax's fixed asset positions of 69 percent and 77 percent, respectively. Also, the large amount of real estate required by retailers such as Albertson's (65 percent) and Wal-Mart (47 percent) requires a substantial investment in fixed assets. A company like McDonald's is in a similar situation to retailers—they all need lots of real estate—and has 82 percent of its total assets in property and equipment. On the other end of the spectrum, service companies and computer software producers like Manpower (7 percent) and Microsoft (13 percent), respectively, only need a relatively modest amount of fixed asset investment to run their business successfully. Mainstream manufacturers generally have around 30 to 40 percent of their total assets dedicated to property, plant, and equipment. The point for investors is that the larger the fixed asset requirements of a company, the more long-term capital, both debt and equity, are required to support this type of asset. A company with large fixed asset requirements needs to work hard at managing its debt intelligently and needs to have the ability to raise equity through retained earnings as well as through placements in the capital markets.

The Fixed Asset Turnover Ratio

Because fixed assets generally represent a big number in a company's balance sheet, the fixed asset turnover ratio is designed to reflect the efficiency of this significant asset investment by comparing it with the company's annual sales figure. It is a rough measure of the productivity of a company's fixed assets with respect to generating sales. Some financial analysts will use this same measurement with total assets.

Using Procter & Gamble's 1998 financials, we find the property, plant, and equipment numbers we need to calculate this ratio in the noncurrent section of the balance sheet, and the sales figure, which P&G expresses as net sales, in the income statement (amounts expressed in millions):

Step 1: Calculate the average fixed assets for 1998.
$11,376 (1997) + $12,180 (1998) = $23,556 ÷ 2 = $11,778 average fixed assets

Step 2: Divide sales by average fixed assets.
$$\frac{\$37,154}{\$11,778} = 3.15 \text{ fixed asset turnover (times per year)}$$

Procter & Gamble turned over its fixed assets in 1998 at a rate of approximately 3.2x. This indicator looked at over time, and compared with the performance of competitors, gives the investor some idea of how effectively P&G's management is using this large and important company asset. The higher the turnover rate the better.

Return on Assets (ROA)

The return-on-assets ratio is generally considered to be a profitability ratio—it shows how much the company is earning on its total assets. I have chosen to locate it here as an indication of asset performance. It is expressed as a percentage return by comparing net income (P&G expresses this as net earnings) to average total assets. A high percentage return implies well-

EXHIBIT 2.3 • Sampling of Industry and Company Asset Performance Indicators

INDUSTRY	COMPANY	FISCAL YEAR	FIXED ASSET TURNOVER (X)	RETURN ON ASSETS (%)
Airlines	AMR Corporation	12/31/97	1.4	4.8
Aerospace	Boeing	12/31/97	5.5	(a)
Automotive	Ford	12/31/97	0.6	2.6
Beverage	Coca-Cola	12/31/97	5.2	24.9
Computer	IBM	12/31/97	4.4	7.5
Computer Software	Microsoft	06/30/97	8.1	28.1
Conglomerate	GE	12/31/97	2.9	2.8
Energy	Exxon	12/31/97	2.0	8.8
Leisure Time	Disney	09/30/97	2.7	5.3
Manufacturing	3M	12/31/97	3.1	15.9
Media	Gannett	12/31/97	2.3	10.8
Mining	Cyprus Amax	12/31/97	0.5	1.0
Personal Care	Procter & Gamble	06/30/97	3.2	12.4
Pharmaceutical	Merck	12/31/97	3.8	18.4
Restaurant	McDonald's	12/31/97	0.8	9.2
Retailing—Food	Albertson's	01/31/98	4.6	10.4
Retailing—General	Wal-Mart	01/31/98	5.4	8.3
Service	ManPower	12/31/97	56.3	8.6
Technology	Intel	12/31/97	2.6	26.6
Telecomunications	Ameritech	12/31/97	1.2	9.4

Notes:
(a) Negative net income.

managed assets, but remember that the percentage return on assets of companies requiring heavy fixed investments will be limited.

Procter & Gamble's 1998 balance sheet (in millions) records total assets of $27,544 and $30,966 for 1997 and 1998, respectively. Net income (net earnings) for 1998 is $3,7880 (millions) and is considered the bottom line in the income statement. The ROA ratio would be calculated in the following manner:

Step 1: Calculate the average total assets for 1998.
$27,544 (1997) + $30,966 (1998) = $60,221 ÷ 2 = $29,255 average total assets

Step 2: Divide 1998 net income by average total assets for ROA.
$3,780 ÷ $29,255 = .1292 or 12.9 percent return on assets.

As is the case with the fixed asset turnover ratio, the return-on-assets ratio is best employed as a comparative analysis of a company's own historical performance and/or with companies in a similar line of business with similar balance sheet structures (i.e., parallel levels of asset investment).

A look at the fixed asset turnover ratios for the companies in the G20 sample in Exhibit 2.3 reflects the effect of size. Companies such as Exxon, Cyprus Amax, McDonald's, AMR, and Ameritech, which, because of the high amount of fixed asset investment their lines of business require, all evidence relatively low levels of turnover. At the other extreme, a service company like Manpower, which doesn't require much fixed investment, generates an extraordinary level of turnover.

Although size certainly has an effect on the return-on-assets ratio, the use of net income as the numerator in the calculation for ROA increases the variability of this indicator when compared with the turnover ratio, which uses sales as the numerator. Levels of sales and profits do not always run on a parallel course. And as you'll see in the next chapter, profit margins vary among companies. For example, Coca-Cola, a high-margin business, and Wal-Mart, a low margin business, while having a similar fixed asset turnover ratio, have a very dissimilar return-on-assets ratio—24.9 percent and 8.3 percent, respectively.

GE's return on assets highlights a point I made in the introduction about the importance of knowing what a company does and how it operates to better understand the numbers and ratios related to its financial statements. GE had a good year profitwise in 1997. So even with a very large asset base, how come its return on assets, which is one of the lowest in our G20 sampling, was a paltry 2.8 percent? This is a good example of the need to understand what is behind the numbers in order to make informed decisions. GE is perceived to be a giant commercial/industrial conglomerate, which, among other activities, includes a financing subsidiary, General Electric Capital Services (GECS). Few people in the general investing public realize that because of GECS, GE can also be considered one of the world's major financial institutions. As of year-end 1997, GECS had total assets of over $255 billion, which amounted to approximately 84 percent of parent GE's total assets. If we think of GE as more of a bank than a commercial/industrial company (and as you will see in Chapter 14 on bank investment evaluators), GE's return on assets of 2.8 percent would be the envy of bankers worldwide. There's a lesson here for beginning number crunchers—think before you crunch!

LEVERAGE

Leverage, also called financial leverage, is the expression used by financial professionals to refer to a company's use of debt as opposed to equity to support its assets, that is, the proportion of debt and equity in the balance sheet equation of Assets = Liabilities + Equity. For investors, the proper evaluation of a company's debt position is a key consideration in determining its investment qualities. In financial terms, debt is a good example of the proverbial two-edged sword. The prudent use of debt can increase the resources available to a company for expansion and ultimately benefit its shareholders. It is also true that the imprudent use of debt can burden a company's operations with high interest expenses and hinder or limit its ability to take advantage of market opportunities. There is no right amount of leverage. Conservative investors look for safety in companies with no debt or low debt. However, because of a company's line of business, its perceived strength and reputation in financial markets, and its history of good debt management, investors may be quite comfortable with higher levels of debt.

Before discussing the ratios used to measure a company's leverage, we need to clear up debt terminology. In Chapter 1 we established that in this book the term *liabilities* implies two kinds of obligations—operational liabilities and debt liabilities. Therefore, I don't equate the term *debt,* when used by itself, with total liabilities, as investment literature often does. For our purposes, a company's debt is defined as including the following items: short-term borrowings (notes payable), the current portion of long-term debt, long-term debt, two-thirds of the principal amount of operating leases, and redeemable preferred stock. Debt is also referred to as a company's indebtedness. Conventional wisdom holds less indebtedness to be greater solvency. Solvency is to a company's debt/equity position what liquidity is to its asset position—the more of either the better. Later I change some of the terminology associated with commonly used leverage ratios to make them easier to understand conceptually and therefore easier to apply to a company's financials.

While the previously mentioned leverage ratios are standard, what companies, financial analysts, and investment information services use as components to calculate these ratios is far from standard. To illustrate this point, which, because of a lack of uniform computation, is an important one for investors to appreciate, I divide debt classification into three general approaches. In addition, I assign a like numerical amount as a score to each category component to show how total debt figures can vary:

- A liberal interpretation tends to minimize the amount of debt—includes only long-term debt as recorded in the balance sheet under noncurrent liabilities. Total debt: 100.
- A moderate interpretation includes current borrowings and adjusted long-term debt (long-term debt as recorded in the balance sheet + the current portion of long-term debt + two-thirds of operating leases + redeemable preferred stock). Total debt: 500.
- A conservative interpretation includes all items in a moderate interpretation of debt and such noncurrent operational liabilities as deferred taxes, pension liabilities, and other postretirement employee benefits. Total debt: 800.

So what is debt? My recommendation for investors is to take the middle ground. While recognizing some validity to the conservative approach, realistically noncurrent operational liabilities represent obligations that will be with the company forever, at least if the company is considered a going concern. Also, unlike debt, there are no fixed payments or interest expenses attached to noncurrent operational liabilities. Bank lenders, or at least those who stick to the conservative approach, tend to look at the liquidation value of assets in their interpretation of a company's financial position. It's more meaningful for investors to view a company's financials as though the company is a going concern and therefore to use the moderate definition of debt in their leverage calculations.

One last term that warrants explanation is *funded debt,* a term not used much in financial reporting, but often considered in the analysis of a company's debt position. Technically, funded debt refers to that portion of a company's long-term debt comprising bonds and other similar long-term, fixed maturity types of borrowings. No matter how problematical a company's financial condition, the holders of these obligations cannot demand payment as long as the company pays the interest on its funded debt. In contrast, bank debt is usually subject to acceleration clauses and/or covenants (see Chapter 8) that allow the lender to call its loan (i.e., demand its immediate payment) under prescribed circumstances. From the investor's perspective, the greater the percentage of funded debt in total debt, the better. As Peter Lynch observed in his bestseller *One Up on Wall Street,* "Funded debt gives companies time to wiggle out of trouble."

Last, credit rating, discussed in Chapter 7, is another nonfinancial statement item that is a valuable source of investment information for investors. Credit ratings are formal risk evaluations by credit-rating agencies—Moody's, Standard & Poor's, Duff & Phelps, and Fitch—of a company's ability to repay principal and interest on its debt obligations, principally bonds and commercial paper (funded debt). Obviously, investors should be glad to see high-quality rankings on the debt of companies they are considering as investment opportunities and be wary of the reverse.

LEVERAGE INDICATORS

Because the so-called debt ratio measures the amount of total liabilities that are used to support a company's total assets, it seems logical to refer to this ratio as the liability/asset ratio. The debt-equity ratio is the other popular debt measurement that I have renamed, calling it the liability/equity ratio, another literal description of a comparative relationship important to investors.

Liability/Asset Ratio (aka Debt Ratio)

The liability/asset ratio indicates the percentage of assets that are supported by liabilities as opposed to the owners' equity. The lower the percentage, the less dependent the company is on financial leverage (i.e., funds borrowed from and/or owed to others). Using Procter & Gamble as our example, we can obtain the total liability and asset numbers from its 1998 balance sheet (figures in millions):

Step 1: Divide total liabilities by total assets.
$18,730 ÷ $30,966 = .6049 or 60.49% liability/asset ratio.

P&G, as is commensurate with its size and reputation as a blue-chip company, is using a fair amount of leverage. The company took on more debt to finance some major acquisitions in its 1998 fiscal year, which, as a consequence, resulted in a higher-than-normal liability/asset ratio.

Liability/Equity Ratio (aka Debt-Equity Ratio)

The liability/equity ratio compares total liabilities to total shareholders' equity—a measurement of how much suppliers, lenders, and sundry creditors have committed to the company versus what the shareholders have committed. The lower the percentage, the greater the company's financial safety and operating freedom. P&G's 1998 total liabilities and total equity numbers are taken from its balance sheet to calculate its liability/equity ratio (figures in millions):

Step 1:   Divide total liabilities by total shareholders' equity.
$18,730 ÷ $12,236 = 1.53 liability/equity ratio.

This ratio is generally expressed on a times basis (x), which in this instance would be expressed as Procter & Gamble's liability/equity ratio: 1.5 to 1 or 1.5:1, meaning that its liabilities are approximately 1.5 times its equity. Obviously, company size and reputation influence an interpretation of this ratio. A blue-chip company such as P&G, which is carrying a fair amount of debt—and probably more debt than normal because of major acquisitions undertaken during its 1998 fiscal year—is able to handle more leverage than a company of lesser standing.

A conservative variation of this ratio, which is seldom seen in corporate or investment information services presentations, involves the reduction of intangible assets from a company's equity position to obtain its tangible net worth. If this is ascertained with P&G's 1998 financial position, approximately $7 billion in total goodwill and other intangible assets would be subtracted from its total shareholders' equity of $12.2 billion, leaving a tangible net worth of $5.2 billion. Using this very tough measurement, P&G's liability/equity ratio would weaken to a more leveraged 3.6 times (liabilities compared to equity).

Capitalization Ratio

A company's *capitalization* (not to be confused with market capitalization—see the glossary), sometimes also called capital structure, is the term used to describe the makeup of a company's permanent or long-term capital, both debt and equity. The capitalization ratio measures the debt component of a company's capitalization—total long-term debt divided by the sum of total long-term debt and total equity. A healthy equity cushion is always more desirable than a high percentage of debt. In our calculation of this ratio, only the current portion of long-term debt and recorded long-term debt (as stated in the balance sheet) are used to compute the debt amount. Unfortunately, practice varies, especially with regard to the presence or absence of current long-term debt in the debt component. This is again one of those situations in which investors need to know how the ratio is calculated before using it in their evaluative deliberations.

EXHIBIT 2.4 • Sampling of Industry and Company Leverage Indicators

INDUSTRY	COMPANY	FISCAL YEAR	LIABILITY/ ASSET RATIO (a)	LIABILITY/ EQUITY RATIO (times)	CAPITALIZATION RATIO (a)	ADJUSTED CAPITALIZATION RATIO (a)(b)
Airlines	AMR Corporation	12/31/97	0.70	2.4x	0.42	0.73
Aerospace	Boeing	12/31/97	0.66	1.9x	0.34	(c)
Automotive	Ford	12/31/97	0.89	8.1x	0.76	(c)
Beverage	Coca-Cola	12/31/97	0.57	1.3x	0.14	(c)
Computer	IBM	12/31/97	0.76	3.1x	0.46	0.52
Computer Software	Microsoft	6/30/97	0.25	.34x	(d)	0.01
Conglomerate	GE	12/31/97	0.88	7.7x	0.65	(c)
Pharmaceutical	Merck	12/31/97	0.47	.95x	0.12	(c)
Energy	Exxon	12/31/97	0.52	1.2x	0.15	0.17
Leisure Time	Disney	9/30/97	0.54	1.2x	0.39	0.42
Manufacturing	3M	12/31/97	0.55	1.2x	0.17	0.18
Media	Gannett	12/31/97	0.49	.98x	0.34	0.35
Mining	Cyprus Amax	12/31/97	0.64	1.8x	0.51	0.53(e)
Personal Care	Procter & Gamble	6/30/97	0.56	1.3x	0.27	(c)
Pharmaceutical	Merck	12/31/97	0.47	.95x	0.12	(c)
Restaurant	McDonald's	12/31/97	0.52	1.1x	0.37	0.52
Retailing—Food	Albertson's	1/31/98	0.54	1.2x	0.34	0.44
Retailing—General	Wal-Mart	1/31/98	0.55	1.4x	0.37	0.43
Service	ManPower	12/31/97	0.70	2.3x	0.24	0.34
Technology	Intel	12/31/97	0.33	.5x	0.03	0.03
Telecomunications	Ameritech	12/31/97	0.67	2.1x	0.38	0.39

Notes:

(a) Percentage expressed as a decimal, (i.e.,100% = 1.00).

(b) Long term debt includes 2/3 of the principal of noncancelable operating leases and, if any, the amount of redemable preferred stock.

(c) Not Applicable, (i.e., no operating leases or redeemable preferred stock).

(d) No long-term debt.

(e) Also includes mineral royalities.

Procter & Gamble's 1998 capitalization ratio would be calculated in the following manner (amounts in millions):

Step 1:   Add the current portion of long-term debt, which for P&G is found in a note, to the amount for long-term debt recorded in the balance sheet in noncurrent liabilities. $286 + $5,765 = $6,051 total long-term debt.

Step 2:   Add total long-term debt to total equity to obtain the capitalization figure. $6,051 + $12,236 = $18,287 capitalization.

Step 3:   Divide total long-term debt figure by capitalization. $6,051 ÷ $18,287 = .33 or 33% capitalization ratio.

Adjusted Capitalization Ratio

If a company uses noncancelable operating leases (off-balance sheet) and/or carries redeemable preferred stock in its balance sheet, these items, as discussed previously, are considered long-term debt and should be added into the equation. Procter & Gamble does not have either of these in its 1998 financials. Refer to Exhibit 2.4 for examples of how adjusting long-term debt items affects certain companies with operating leases and/or redeemable preferred stock.

The companies in the G20 sample in Exhibit 2.4 reflect a wide range of leverage indicators as evidenced by the results of the liability/asset, liability/equity, and capitalization ratios. Intel's and Microsoft's assets are supported by strong equity positions with a very moderate use of debt liabilities. On the other hand, AMR's need to finance its large investment in aircraft requires it to use and manage a large amount of debt, particularly when its long-term, noncancelable operating leases are factored into the equation. The effect of off-balance sheet operating leases on a company's indebtedness is clearly seen in the adjusted capitalization ratios of several other companies. McDonald's makes heavy use of them for its restaurant facilities; and Albertson's and Wal-Mart both need lots of space for their retail trade. In the case of Manpower, operating leases must provide for the vast majority of its nationwide network of offices. The very high leverage positions of GE and Ford, and to a lesser degree IBM, are due, in the case of the former two, to the consolidation of their finance subsidiaries, and in the case of IBM to the financing used to support its significant sales-leasing program. The G20 sample is comprised of relatively large companies with established reputations and operating histories. In general, this type of company can take on more indebtedness than companies of lesser stature.

Astute use of leverage increases the financial resources available to a company for growth and expansion. It assumes that management can earn more on borrowed funds than it pays in interest expense and fees to use these funds. However successful this formula may seem, it does require a company to maintain a solid record of complying with its various borrowing commitments. A company considered too highly leveraged may find its freedom of action restricted by its creditors and/or may have its profitability hurt by high interest costs. Of course, the worst of all scenarios is having trouble meeting operating and debt liabilities on time and surviving adverse

EXHIBIT 2.5 • Sampling of Industry and Company Book Value per Common Share Data

INDUSTRY	COMPANY	FISCAL YEAR	YEAR END SHARES OUTSTANDING (millions)	SHAREHOLDERS' COMMON EQUITY (millions $)	BOOK VALUE PER SHARE	BOOK VALUE MULTIPLE (a) (x)
Airlines	AMR Corporation	12/31/97	86.6	6,216	$71.78	0.9
Aerospace	Boeing	12/31/97	973.5	12,953	$13.31	3.7
Automotive	Ford	12/31/97	1,203	30,734	$25.55	1.3
Beverage	Coca-Cola	12/31/97	2,470	7,311	$2.96	22.5
Computer	IBM	12/31/97	970.3	19,816	$20.41	5.1
Computer Software	Microsoft	6/30/97	1,204	10,777	$8.95	7.1
Conglomerate	GE	12/31/97	3,265	34,438	$10.55	7.0
Energy	Exxon	12/31/97	2,457	43,660	$17.77	3.4
Leisure Time	Disney	9/30/97	679	17,285	$25.46	1.1
Manufacturing	3M	12/31/97	404.7	5,926	$14.64	5.6
Media	Gannett	12/31/97	283.9	3,480	$12.26	2.4
Mining	Cyprus Amax	12/31/97	93.5	2,330	$24.92	0.6
Personal Care	Procter & Gamble	6/30/97	1,350.8	12,046	$8.92	7.9
Pharmaceutical	Merck	12/31/97	1,194	12,614	$10.57	10.03
Restaurant	McDonald's	12/31/97	685.7	8,852	$12.91	3.7
Retailing—Food	Albertson's	1/31/98	245.7	2,419	$9.85	4.9
Retailing—General	Wal-Mart	1/31/98	2,241	18,503	$8.26	4.8
Service	ManPower	12/31/97	80.4	618	$7.69	4.6
Technology	Intel	12/31/97	1,628	19,295	$11.85	5.9
Telecomunications	Ameritech	12/31/97	1,177	8,308	$7.06	5.7

Notes:

(a) Calculated using the company's stock price as of its 1997 fiscal year end date. (Stock price/ Book value per share).

economic conditions. Last, a company in a highly competitive business, if hobbled by high debt, will find its competitors taking advantage of its problems to grab more market share.

BOOK VALUE PER SHARE

Book value per share is generally calculated by dividing shareholders' equity at year-end by the number of common shares outstanding at year-end. Both numbers are found in the equity section of the balance sheet and/or in the statement of shareholders' equity. The book value per share of our G20 sample is shown in Figure 2.5. In the case of Procter & Gamble, its 1998 book value on a per share basis was $9.15 (1,337.4 million shares ÷ $12,236 million). Investors can compare this book value per share to P&G's year-end stock price of $90.06 to calculate one of the four most-used measurements of market valuation—price/book value. In this example, Procter & Gamble's stock was trading at a multiple of approximately 9.8 times ($90.06 ÷ $9.15 = 9.84). A comparison of a company's price/book value to its own historical performance as well as to current overall market, industry sector, and direct competitor price/book value ratios is considered a useful stock price valuation measurement.

CHAPTER 3

Understanding the Income Statement and Its Components

A company's income statement summarizes its sales/revenues and expenses over its fiscal year. Audited statements generally present three years of operating performance. The final net figure, either a gain or a loss, is transferred at year-end, net of any payment of dividends on preferred stock, to the retained earnings account in shareholders' equity in the balance sheet. The names used to identify what I refer to as the income statement vary—statement of income, statement of earnings, statement of operations, or statement of operating results. Many financial professionals, including myself, still use the phrase *P and L,* which stands for profit and loss, but the term is seldom used in written form to identify the income statement. We've already established in the introduction that the terms *profits, earnings,* and *income* all mean the same thing and are used interchangeably.

Two basic formats for the income statement are used in financial reporting presentations—multistep and singlestep. For investors, the former presentation allows one to pinpoint the results of operations at critical profit junctures as the flow of the business is viewed by management functions. Exhibit 3.1 illustrates the easy-to-understand multistep approach used in Albertson's 1997 consolidated earnings statement of income. This format reveals gross profit and operating income, which, as we discuss later, are two key profitability measurements. Gross profit and operating income aren't revealed with the singlestep income statement format; investors doing their own analysis have to work to get this information from that format. As illustrated in Merck's income statement in Exhibit 3.2, costs and income/expense items are aggregated and deducted as a sum total from the amount of sales/revenues, which results in income before taxes. You'll have to do some math to arrive at gross profit and operating income numbers.

The sum of Merck's materials and production ($11.8 billion) and research and development ($1.7 billion), for example, constitutes its cost of sales—$13.5 billion. Thus, in round numbers, we arrive at a gross profit figure of $10.1 billion by subtracting the cost of sales from sales of $23.6 billion. We calculate the operating income figure—$5.8 billion—by subtracting the marketing and

EXHIBIT 3.1 • Multistep Income Statement Format—Albertson's

Consolidated Earnings

(In thousands except per share data)	52 Weeks January 29, 1998	52 Weeks January 30, 1997	52 Weeks February 1, 1996
Sales	$ 14,689,511	$ 13,776,678	$ 12,585,034
Cost of sales	10,807,687	10,211,348	9,371,736
Gross profit	3,881,824	3,565,330	3,213,298
Selling, general and administrative expenses	2,990,172	2,715,776	2,406,082
Operating profit	891,652	849,554	807,216
Other (expenses) income:			
Interest, net	(82,563)	(64,569)	(55,633)
Other, net	17,814	9,862	6,918
Earnings before income taxes	826,903	794,847	758,501
Income taxes	310,089	301,068	293,540
Net Earnings	$ 516,814	$ 493,779	$ 464,961
Earnings Per Share:			
Basic	$ 2.09	$ 1.96	$ 1.84
Diluted	2.08	1.95	1.83
Weighted average common shares outstanding:			
Basic	247,735	251,710	253,080
Diluted	248,497	252,730	254,093

EXHIBIT 3.2 • Singlestep Income Statement Format—Merck

Consolidated Statement of Income

Merck & Co., Inc. and Subsidiaries

Years Ended December 31

($ in millions except per share amounts)	1997	1996	1995
Sales	$23,636.9	$19,828.7	$16,681.1
Costs, Expenses and Other			
Materials and production	11,790.3	9,319.2	7,456.3
Marketing and administrative	4,299.2	3,841.3	3,297.8
Research and development	1,683.7	1,487.3	1,331.4
Equity income from affiliates	(727.9)	(600.7)	(346.3)
Gains on sales of businesses	(213.4)	–	(682.9)
Other (income) expense, net	342.7	240.8	827.6
	17,174.6	14,287.9	11,883.9
Income Before Taxes	6,462.3	5,540.8	4,797.2
Taxes on Income	1,848.2	1,659.5	1,462.0
Net Income	$ 4,614.1	$ 3,881.3	$ 3,335.2
Earnings per Common Share	$3.83	$3.20	$2.70
Earnings per Common Share Assuming Dilution	$3.74	$3.12	$2.64

administrative expenses of $4.3 billion from the gross profit figure we just calculated. The other accounts listed are other income/expense items, which, after having been added to and/or subtracted from operating income, result in a pretax income amount.

We touched on the subject of accrual accounting in the introduction. Investors must remind themselves that the income statement recognizes revenues when they are realized (i.e., when goods are shipped, services rendered, and expenses incurred). With accrual accounting, the flow of accounting events through the income statement doesn't necessarily coincide with the actual receipt and disbursement of cash; the statement of income measures profitability, not cash flow.

INCOME STATEMENT ACCOUNTS

Procter & Gamble refers to its income statement as a statement of earnings and, for the most part, uses a multistep format, which provides a good example for reviewing an income statement's components; refer to Exhibit 3.3.

Net Sales

Even though a company's bottom line, its net income, gets most of the attention in investment commentaries, the top line is where the revenue process begins. Also, in the long run, profit margins on a company's existing products tend to eventually reach a maximum that is difficult

EXHIBIT 3.3 • Procter & Gamble Statement of Income

CONSOLIDATED STATEMENTS OF EARNINGS   The Procter & Gamble Company and Subsidiaries

Amounts in Millions Except Per Share Amounts	Years Ended June 30		
	1998	1997	1996
Net Sales	$37,154	$35,764	$35,284
Cost of products sold	21,064	20,510	20,938
Marketing, research and administrative expenses	10,035	9,766	9,531
Operating Income	6,055	5,488	4,815
Interest expense	548	457	484
Other income, net	201	218	338
Earnings Before Income Taxes	5,708	5,249	4,669
Income taxes	1,928	1,834	1,623
Net Earnings	$ 3,780	$ 3,415	$ 3,046
Basic Net Earnings Per Common Share	$ 2.74	$ 2.43	$ 2.14
Diluted Net Earnings Per Common Share	$ 2.56	$ 2.28	$ 2.01
Dividends Per Common Share	$ 1.01	$ .90	$ .80

See accompanying Notes to Consolidated Financial Statements.

to improve on. Thus, companies typically can grow no faster than the growth of their revenues. The terms *net sales, sales,* and *revenue(s)* all refer to the value of a company's sales of goods and services to its customers. For Procter & Gamble in 1998, its net sales exceeded $37 billion.

Four qualitative aspects of a company's sales warrant the attention of investors—how growth is achieved, sales mix, customer concentration, and the incidence of international sales. Obviously, a healthy sales growth rate generally defines a growing company and is considered a positive investment indicator. Therefore, even though all sales increases are good, some are qualitatively better than others. Information about sales growth is not always available to individual investors, but it should be looked for or requested in critical situations. Sometimes the basis for sales increases is disclosed and discussed in a company's management discussion and analysis section of its annual report. A good company investor relations contact can also be helpful. Sales grow through more unit volume from existing and/or new products, price increases, acquisitions, and the impact of foreign exchange rates on recorded international sales. There's no question that greater unit volume is the best growth factor. Price increases, especially those above the general level of inflation, have their limits, as does sales expansion from acquisitions. Exchange rate movements of a stronger or weaker U.S. dollar affect recorded sales from foreign operations but are outside the control of management. Over time the positive and negative effects of exchange rates usually are a wash. Quality sales growth comes from better unit volume and the maintenance of reasonable pricing.

A company's sales mix can affect its profitability. A company's products or product lines generally carry different profit margins. If a high-margin product accounts for a greater percentage of total sales than normal, the resulting boost to earnings is attributed to the sales mix.

Major customers should be looked at carefully to determine their long-term commercial and financial viability. Sales of more than 10 percent of a company's total sales to any one customer must be disclosed in a note to a company's financials. If there is evidence of a high concentration of sales to one or more customers, it follows that a company's sales performance becomes vulnerable, depending on the degree of concentration, to the fortunes of a single customer or group of customers. For example, a note in Procter & Gamble's 1998 financials indicates that Wal-Mart Stores accounted for 11 percent of its sales for that year. In this instance, the favorable status and performance of Wal-Mart as a major retailer would be interpreted, most likely, as a plus. However, if a customer lacked Wal-Mart's status, P&G's sales could be exposed to downside risk even with a relatively modest degree of sales concentration.

A healthy percentage of international sales is a positive sign for any company's revenue base. In today's global economy, international exposure is a plus. International business challenges management to think in global terms, which usually exposes a company to new ideas and competitive pressures that hone its production and marketing skills. For example, as this book was being written, a *Business Week* article mentioned how ice cream maker Haagen-Dazs discovered a new flavor, *Dulce de Leche,* that had its origin in the company's operations in Argentina. Introduced into the U.S. market, this flavor registered some of the highest monthly sales growth rates in the company's history. The author admits to contributing significantly to this success story!

Cost of Sales

The cost of sales is the expense incurred for raw materials, labor, and manufacturing overhead used in the production of a company's goods and services. This account may also be called the cost of goods sold or the cost of products sold, which is the caption Procter & Gamble uses in its income statement ($21,064 million in 1998). The definition above is easy to relate to a manufacturing company, but in the case of wholesalers and retailers, the cost of sales is basically the purchase cost of merchandise for resale; and for a service business it is the cost of services or cost of revenues.

Referring back to Chapter 1, we are reminded that a company's choice of inventory valuation methods—FIFO, LIFO, or average—influences the computation of its cost of sales. The use of the LIFO accounting method tends to overstate the cost of sales and is considered a more conservative approach because of its consequent understatement of earnings. FIFO works in an opposite fashion, and the average methodology represents a LIFO-FIFO compromise.

If depreciation expense is stated as a separate account in the income statement, it is safe to assume that virtually all of this amount relates to the production process. Therefore, for computing financial ratios and making intercompany comparisons, depreciation should be considered part of a company's cost of sales.

Gross Profit

A company's gross profit has more importance than simply representing the mathematical difference between net sales and the cost of sales. It is the first of four key measurements of a company's profitability as evidenced by its income statement. Gross profit provides the financial resources to cover all the other expenses of the company. Obviously, the greater and more stable a company's gross profit, the greater potential there is for positive bottom-line results. For whatever reason, Procter & Gamble doesn't have a gross profit account in its income statement, but it's easily calculated by subtracting its cost of sales of $21,064 million from its net sales of $37,154 million, which results in $16,090 million in gross profit for 1998.

Selling, General, and Administrative Expenses

Often referred to as SG&A, this account comprises a company's operational expenses; Procter & Gamble refers to SG&A as "marketing, research and administrative expenses" ($10,035 million in 1998). Financial analysts generally assume that management exercises a great deal of control over this category of expense. The trend of SG&A expenses as a percentage of sales is watched closely to detect signs of efficiency or inefficiency in the management of a company's operations. Stability and/or improvement (i.e., less relative expense) in this measurement are positive signs, particularly if the company is in a growth mode. It means management has a good grip on spending.

If selling expenses are broken out from SG&A in a separate account, which a few companies do, it allows the investor to pinpoint the effectiveness of a company's marketing efforts by making a specific comparison of selling expenses, in percentage terms, to sales performance. That is to say, the sales bang generated for the selling expense buck expended.

Research and development expenses are considered an operational item and are usually included in a company's SG&A account. However, because of the importance of R&D to technology-driven companies and others that depend on technological advancements in their products to enhance their competitive position, it may appear as a separate account in the income statement. If not, the item is sure to appear in a note to the financials. Financial analysts like to compare R&D expense to sales to determine a company's level of commitment to staying technologically fit. A steady or improving trend in a company's R&D expense/sales ratio is a positive sign for investors.

Operating Income

Deducting the cost of sales and operating expenses from a company's net sales produces operating income, the company's earnings from its normal operations before any nonoperating expenses, taxes, or special items. Income at this operating level is another key profitability indicator. Financial analysts often use the operating income figure, which is viewed as more reliable, rather than the net income figure in their measurements of a company's profitability. Procter & Gamble recorded an operating income of $6,055 million in 1998, the result of applying its SG&A expense of $10,035 against its gross profit of $16,090.

Interest Expense

Generally, the cost of a company's borrowings is shown separately in the income statement, and sometimes companies record a net figure for interest expense and interest income. The investor should be aware that because a company is allowed to capitalize certain interest costs, the interest expense item in the income statement may not reflect the true amount of interest actually paid. Any difference, however, is generally not material. Information about interest paid information is found either in the notes to the financials or as supplemental data to the cash flow statement. Procter and Gamble incurred $548 million in interest expense in 1998.

Other Income and Expense

These items are usually not material and may be expressed individually or netted out against each other. Procter & Gamble uses the latter approach in the account ($201 million in 1998) it captions "other income, net."

Earnings before Income Taxes, and Income Taxes

The pretax income figure is another key indicator of profitability. Once the costs of sales and operational and nonoperational expenses have all been deducted from revenues, the only remaining charge against revenue is income tax. The income tax amount as shown in the income statement has not been paid but is an estimate (i.e., a provision) to cover what a company expects to pay. Numerous and diverse techniques are available for companies to avoid and/or minimize taxes that consequently affect their reported net income. Therefore, many financial analysts choose to use pretax income in their profitability calculations rather than the net income, or after-tax, number. As a result, investors should track a company's effective tax rate—income taxes divided by earnings before income taxes. Interannual comparisons of a company's effective tax rate reveal the impact, both positive and negative, of income taxes on net income. Procter & Gamble's, effective tax rates for the 1996–1998 period, for example, were 34.8 percent, 34.9 percent, and 33.8 percent, respectively, indicating little distortion of its reported net income figures because of a tax impact.

Special Items

Procter & Gamble's income statements don't reflect any unusual or extraordinary items that can add to, but most often subtract from, income. A variety of events can occasion charges against income, and they are identified by a corresponding variety of captions; some of the more common include extraordinary expense, restructuring charges, unusual or nonrecurring items, and discontinued operations. These write-offs are supposed to be one-time events. When they are, investors must take these special items, which can distort evaluations, into account when making interannual profit comparisons.

A special item by definition should be an infrequent event, but recently some financial professionals have become concerned about the practice of companies taking so-called big-bath write-offs with such frequency that they are no longer extraordinary but rather commonplace. A highly visible, and egregious, example is Eastman Kodak's six major restructuring charges over the past seven years. A *Business Week* cover story (October 5, 1998) about several corporate financial reporting issues concluded that "huge multiyear write-offs are increasingly distorting corporate earnings—so much so, in fact, that some question whether the underlying meaning of profit numbers and their value as a true reflection of corporate performance is getting trampled." Special items are another reason why many financial analysts prefer to work with operating and pretax income numbers to evaluate a company's earnings, thereby eliminating the distortions of special items.

Net Income

We have finally arrived at the bottom line, the most commonly used indicator of a company's profitability. Net income, net profits, and net earnings all mean the same thing and, after the payment of preferred dividends, if any, represent the income that is transferred to retained earnings in a company's equity position. Of course, if the aggregate of costs, expenses, and special charges exceed revenues, this account caption changes to net loss. Then investors can follow the advice of Boomer Esaison, a former pro football quarterback and current ABC sports commentator. In a *New York Times* interview about his financial literacy, he provided this simple assessment of income statements: "All you have to do is look at the bottom of the page and see if there are parentheses," which is how losses are expressed. As an investor, this is not a symbol you want to see.

Supplemental data pertaining to net income per common share is also presented on both a basic (shares actually outstanding) and a diluted (reflecting the effect of the potential conversion of stock options, warrants, etc. into shares outstanding) basis as just described.

Procter & Gamble's net income in 1998 of $3,780 million is expressed as net earnings and is accompanied by supplemental earnings per common share data.

Comprehensive Income

As mentioned in Chapter 1, the Financial Accounting Standards Board has issued a new rule, SFAS No. 130, that requires companies to change the way certain income/expense items are reported in their financials. Comprehensive income is a new concept that appeared in company financial statements as of year-end 1998. It includes the traditional net income plus other comprehensive income, which, at year-end 1998, included foreign currency translation adjustments, minimum pension liability adjustments, and unrealized gains and losses on certain investments in debt and equity securities. The issue is not that these items aren't being reported but rather where they're being reported. Until the new FASB rule, these items weren't included in the income statement but were accounted for as adjustments to the equity section in the balance sheet. Some financial professionals felt that all income/expense items should be reflected in the income statement, and that is what SFAS No. 130 dictates.

Companies have been given three alternatives for presenting comprehensive income. It may appear as an extension of the income statement, as a separate statement, or as part of the shareholders' equity statement, although the third alternative is being discouraged by the FASB. Although proponents of this new approach view comprehensive income as an improvement in financial reporting, not all financial professionals agree. My guess is that financial analysts and the investment community will continue to focus on net income as a more stable, reliable measurement of profitability. All the items listed under other comprehensive income relate to volatile market and/or economic events that are out of the control of management. Their impact is real when they occur, but they tend to even out over an extended period of time.

Having covered the various components of the income statement, we can now move on to the next chapter where investors will learn how to use these components to evaluate a company's profitability.

CHAPTER 4

Key Investment Evaluators for the Income Statement

To a large degree, it is the quality and growth of a company's earnings that drive its stock price. Obviously, it is imperative, then, that investors be conversant with the various indicators used to measure profitability. The income statement is the principal source of data used for this purpose. The balance sheet also needs to be consulted for some of the figures needed in the computation of the return on equity and capital employed ratios. Therefore, as we continue to use Procter & Gamble's financials to illustrate our key investment evaluators, readers should consult P&G's balance sheet in Exhibit 1.2 and income statement in Exhibit 3.3 to identify the accounts from which the numbers used in the ratio calculations are taken. The same G20 sample of industries and companies used to illustrate the balance sheet ratios and financial indicators is used in this chapter for the income statement investment evaluators.

PROFIT MARGINS

In financial statement analysis, the term *margin* is used to express the comparison of the four levels of profit—gross profit, operating income, pretax income, and net income—to sales. Thus, the terms *gross margin, operating margin, pretax margin,* and *net margin* correspond, respectively, to these profit levels. They are expressed as a percentage or in the equivalent decimal form (100% = 1.00). As with all ratios, profit margins should be tracked over a minimum of three to five years. The objective is to detect consistency or positive/negative trends.

The calculation of profit margins is easy: simply divide the profit figure by the sales figure. If we use Procter & Gamble's 1998 income statement as an example, its profit margin analysis would look like this (figures in millions):

EXHIBIT 4.1 • Sampling of Industry and Company Profit Margins

(Expressed in decimals as a percentage of sales/revenues)

INDUSTRY	COMPANY	FISCAL YEAR	GROSS	OPERATING	PRETAX	NET
Airlines	AMR Corporation	12/31/97	0.44	0.10	0.09	0.05
Aerospace	Boeing (a)	12/31/97	0.11	(a)	(a)	(a)
Automotive	Ford	12/31/97	(b)	(b)	0.07	0.05
Beverage	Coca-Cola	12/31/97	0.68	0.27	0.32	0.22
Computer	IBM	12/31/97	0.39	0.12	0.12	0.08
Computer Software	Microsoft	06/30/97	0.90	0.45	0.47	0.30
Conglomerate	GE	12/31/97	0.55	0.10	0.13	0.09
Energy	Exxon	12/31/97	0.36	0.10	0.11	0.07
Leisure Time	Disney	09/30/97	0.19	0.20	0.15	0.09
Manufacturing	3M	12/31/97	0.43	0.18	0.23	0.14
Media	Gannett	12/31/97	0.50	0.28	0.26	0.15
Mining	Cyprus Amax	12/31/97	0.18	0.14	0.01	0.02
Personal Care	Procter & Gamble	06/30/97	0.43	0.15	0.15	0.10
Pharmaceutical	Merck	12/31/97	0.55	0.25	0.27	0.20
Restaurant	McDonald's	12/31/97	0.76	0.24	0.21	0.14
Retailing—Food	Albertson's	01/31/98	0.26	0.06	0.06	0.04
Retailing—General	Wal-Mart	01/31/98	0.20	0.04	0.05	0.03
Service	ManPower	12/31/97	0.18	0.04	0.03	0.02
Technology	Intel	12/31/97	0.60	0.36	0.43	0.28
Telecomunications	Ameritech	12/31/97	0.52	0.24	0.23	0.14

Notes:
(a) Negative.
(b) Net calculated because of the separate presentation of automotive and financial services figures.

Net sales	$37,154	1.00
Gross profit	$16,090	.43 = gross margin
Operating income	$6,055	.16 = operating margin
Pretax income	$5,708	.15 = pretax margin
Net income	$3,780	.10 = net margin

In the income statement, the absolute numbers don't tell us very much, so we must look to margin analysis for a company's true profitability. What do profit margins tell investors? They help investors keep score, as measured over time, of management's ability to manage costs and expenses. The success or lack of success of this important management function is what determines, to a large degree, a company's profitability. A large growth in sales will do little for a company's profitability if costs and expenses grow disproportionately. Besides monitoring a company's historical profit performance, these profit margin ratios can also be used to compare a company's results with those of its direct competitors, industry group companies, and the general market.

EXHIBIT 4.2 • Sampling of Industry and Company Expense Indicators

INDUSTRY	COMPANY	FISCAL YEAR	COST OF SALES	SG&A	EFFECTIVE TAX RATE (%) (a)
Airlines	AMR Corporation	12/31/97	0.56	0.34	40
Aerospace	Boeing	12/31/97	0.89	0.09	(b)
Automotive	Ford	12/31/97	N.A.	0.07	34
Beverage	Coca-Cola	12/31/97	0.32	0.42	32
Computer	IBM	12/31/97	0.61	0.21	33
Computer Software	Microsoft	06/30/97	0.10	0.28	35
Conglomerate	GE	12/31/97	0.45	0.23	27
Energy	Exxon	12/31/97	0.64	0.07	34
Leisure Time	Disney	09/30/97	0.81	0.02	42
Manufacturing	3M	12/31/97	0.57	0.25	36
Media	Gannett	12/31/97	0.50	0.16	41
Mining	Cyprus Amax	12/31/97	0.83	0.04	(c)
Personal Care	Procter & Gamble	06/30/97	0.57	0.28	35
Pharmaceutical	Merck	12/31/97	0.50	0.18	29
Restaurant	McDonald's	12/31/97	0.24	0.13	32
Retailing—Food	Albertson's	01/31/98	0.74	0.20	38
Retailing—General	Wal-Mart	01/31/98	0.80	0.16	37
Service	ManPower	12/31/97	0.18	0.15	34
Technology	Intel	12/31/97	0.40	0.12	35
Telecomunications	Ameritech	12/31/97	0.48	0.28	38

Notes:
(a) Income tax expense divided by pretax income.
(b) Negative earnings.
(c) Tax credit.

EXHIBIT 4.3 • Effective Tax Rates

COMPANY		1995	1996	1997
EFFECTIVE	American Stores (a)	42	43	46
TAX RATES	Kroger	38	38	38
(%)	Safeway	41	40	42
	Albertson's (a)	39	38	38

Note:
(a) Fiscal year's end in January 1996, 1997, and 1998.

Consistency and/or improvement in a company's profit margins are very positive signs for investors. Or, conversely, something for investors to worry about. For example, we see from our illustration of P&G's profit margins that for every dollar of sales, it is producing 43¢ (.43) of gross profit. Let's say, hypothetically, that P&G's next year's sales were to move upward from $37.2 billion to $41 billion, a healthy one-year increase of $3.8 billion. That looks good. Corresponding to increased sales activity, the company's cost of sales go up to $24 billion, resulting in a gross profit in 1999 of $17 billion in absolute terms—a seemingly positive result over its previous $16.1 billion gross profit in 1998. However, margin analysis would show us that P&G's 1999 gross margin would have fallen to 41.5 percent, or 41.5¢ on each sales dollar, of gross profit. At first glance, a 1.5 percent drop in gross margin does not seem like much, but it translates into $615 million ($41 billion x 0.15) less gross income. If, for the sake of this hypothetical discussion, everything else in P&G's income statement below the gross profit line stayed the same, net income would drop from $3.8 billion to $3.2 billion. That means a net margin of .078 or less than 8¢ on a dollar of sales compared with 10¢ for the previous year. Declining margins generally hurt a company's profitability.

The same technique used in profit margin analysis can be applied to key cost and expense items. This analysis involves the cost of sales, SG&A expenses, and taxes. Using Procter & Gamble's 1998 income statement figures, these cost and expense indicators would be calculated as follows (figures in millions):

Net sales	$37,154	1.00
Cost of sales	$21,064	.57
SG&A	$10,035	.27

With the tax number, the meaningful evaluator is the effective tax rate, which is calculated by dividing income tax expense by pretax income:

Pretax income	$5,708
Income taxes	$1,928
Effective tax rate	.34

The profit margins of the G20 companies in Exhibit 4.1 provide a graphic example of the wide diversity of results evidenced by companies in different lines of business.

The winners in the net profit margin category include such popular (with the investing public) companies as Coca-Cola, Microsoft, Merck, and Intel. As a group, these companies are earning between 20 to 30¢ on each dollar of their sales; low-margin retailing businesses like Albertson's and Wal-Mart, on the other hand, record net margins in the low single digits, which is typical of this industry sector. The expense indicators in Exhibit 4.2 reflect this diversity of performance.

Of particular interest is the wide range of effective tax rates. Once down to the pretax income level in the income statement, variances in effective tax rates of a few percentage points can have a material effect on the resulting net income figure. Exhibit 4.3 illustrates how intercompany comparisons of net income and net profit margins in the food supermarket sector would be problematical as a result of the impact of taxes. Obviously, in cases such as this, it would be more meaningful to use these companies' pretax income figures for comparative purposes.

PROFITABILITY RATIOS

In addition to profit margin ratios, there are two traditional profitability ratios that are widely used to measure a company's earnings performance. The return on equity (ROE) measures the profits being generated on the shareholders' investment. The higher the ratio, the greater the return, but there's a recognized weakness in this much used profitability indicator. Investors must also be aware of a company's use of financial leverage—debt liabilities—to accurately gauge the true value of a high ROE ratio. For example, Procter & Gamble's 1998 return on equity—remember that we use an average equity figure in this calculation—was a very high 30.1 percent. This level of ROE is well above the generally accepted favorable norm of 15 to 20 percent. Apart from P&G's solid profits, its effective use of leverage contributes significantly to its enviable return on equity.

The impact of leverage is picked up in another traditional profitability ratio—the return on capital employed (ROCE), also referred to as the return on invested capital. This indicator expands on the ROE ratio by adding borrowed funds to equity for a figure showing total capital employed. In this way a company's use of debt is factored into the equation. In the case of Procter & Gamble, the capital employed used to calculate its 1998 ROCE would be the average of the sum of its 1997–98 debt (debt due within one year and long-term debt) and total shareholders' equity (i.e., $18,660 million). With net income of $3,780 million in 1998, P&G's return on capital employed was 20.3 percent—still a very high return but about two-thirds of its return on equity. For this reason, conservative analysts prefer the ROCE ratio as a more comprehensive evaluation of how well management is using the debt and equity capital it has at its disposal.

The sample of G20 company ROEs and ROCEs in Exhibit 4.4 illustrates a variety of circumstances. Ford's and GE's major borrowings, which are needed to support their finance subsidiaries, substantially lower their relatively high returns on equity to low single-digit returns on capital employed. The low debt and strong profits of Coca-Cola, Microsoft, and Intel produce major returns on equity and capital employed for these companies.

EXHIBIT 4.4 • Sampling of Industry and Company Profitability Indicators

INDUSTRY	COMPANY	FISCAL YEAR	RETURN ON AVERAGE EQUITY (ROE) (%)	RETURN ON CAPITAL EMPLOYED (ROCE) (%)
Airlines	AMR Corporation	12/31/97	16.6	9.2
Aerospace	Boeing	12/31/97	(a)	(a)
Automotive	Ford	12/31/97	24.1	3.6
Beverage	Coca-Cola	12/31/97	61.3	37.8
Computer	IBM	12/31/97	29.3	13.3
Computer Software	Microsoft	06/30/97	38.9	38.9
Conglomerate	GE	12/31/97	25.0	4.8
Energy	Exxon	12/31/97	19.4	15.8
Leisure Time	Disney	09/30/97	11.7	6.9
Manufacturing	3M	12/31/97	34.7	25.4
Media	Gannett	12/31/97	22.2	14.2
Mining	Cyprus Amax	12/31/97	2.9	1.4
Personal Care	Procter & Gamble	06/30/97	28.7	19.8
Pharmaceutical	Merck	12/31/97	37.5	32.2
Restaurant	McDonald's	12/31/97	18.7	11.1
Retailing—Food	Albertson's	01/31/98	22.2	14.9
Retailing—General	Wal-Mart	01/31/98	19.8	12.4
Service	ManPower	12/31/97	26.9	20.4
Technology	Intel	12/31/97	38.4	37.2
Telecomunications	Ameritech	12/31/97	28.7	17.8

Notes:
(a) Negative net income.

EXHIBIT 4.5 • Sales and Net Income Interannual Growth Rates—Coca-Cola

YEAR	1992	1993	1994	1995	1996	1997	FIVE YEAR % INCREASE
SALES	13,119	14,030	16,264	18,127	18,673	18,868	-----
% Change	-----	+ 6.9	+ 15.9	+ 11.5	+ 3.0	+ 1.0	+ 43.8
NET INCOME	1,664	2,176	2,554	2,986	3,494	4,129	-----
% Change	-----	+ 30.8	+ 17.4	+ 16.9	+ 16.9	+ 18.2	+ 148.1

GROWTH RATES

Among other factors, the growth of a company's sales and net income are key indicators of investment quality. Logic tells us that growing, profitable companies are generally attractive investment opportunities. Companies whose earnings are growing at or above a rate of 15 percent annually usually represent growth stocks. Value stocks are not generally characterized by high growth rates but still must generate reasonable growth in sales and income to attract investor interest. It is possible to use multiyear average annual compounded growth rates, but interannual growth rates give the investor a clearer picture of a company's performance. In an average calculation, good years cover up bad ones. Simple math allows you to track the trend of a company's sales and net income. For example, to calculate Procter & Gamble's 1998 growth in sales, you simply subtract 1997's sales ($35,764) from 1998's sales ($37,154) and divide the difference ($1,390) by the 1997 base year's sales ($35764), which equals 3.9 percent. Exhibit 4.5 tracks Coca-Cola's sales and net income growth over a five-year period. Sales continue to grow, but the growth rates have been decreasing steadily since 1994. Nevertheless, over that same period the company's net income growth rates have stayed fairly consistent. This type of trend makes investors happy. The important point is that growth rates need to be viewed over extended periods to discern meaningful trends. Stock analysts prefer to look at ten years of performance. If you aren't up to ten years of number crunching, a five-year period is considered adequate.

EXHIBIT 4.6 • Sales and Earnings per Share Data—Coca-Cola

Year	1993	1994	1995	1996	1997
Average shares outstanding (millions)	2,603	2,580	2,525	2,494	2,477
Sales (millions)	$14,030	$16,264	$18,127	$18,673	$18,868
Net income (millions)	$2,188	$2,554	$2,986	$3,492	$4,129
Sales per share	$5.39	$6.30	$7.18	$7.49	$7.62
Earnings per share	$0.84	$0.99	$1.18	$1.40	$1.67
Share price (close Dec. 31)	$22.31	$25.75	$37.73	$52.63	$66.69
P/E Ratio (a)	26.6x	26.0x	31.5x	37.6x	39.9x
P/S Ratio (b)	4.1x	4.1x	5.3x	7.0x	8.8x

Note:
(a) The P/E ratio is calculated by dividing Price by Earnings per share.
(b) The P/S ratio is calculated by dividing Price by Sales per share.

PER SHARE DATA

In Procter & Gamble's 1998 financials, per share data on earnings, both basic and diluted, and dividends are provided. Sales per share information is usually not provided in company financial communications but is easily calculated. Continuing with Coca-Cola to illustrate the use of per share data, Exhibit 4.6 organizes per share data on sales and earnings into two of the most commonly used stock price valuation ratios—the price/earnings ratio (P/E) and the price/sales ratio (P/S). In the case of the latter, James O'Shaughnessy's best-selling investment book *What Works on Wall Street* has given a boost to the use of the P/S ratio. His extensive research indicated that P/S ratios work better than the more widely used P/E ratios. He found that stocks with low P/S ratios tend to be large, established businesses that are more likely to endure the test of time. What is a good P/S ratio? According to some investment professionals, stocks with a number greater than three are a bit pricey. O'Shaughnessy seems to be comfortable with a P/S ratio of less than two.

The calculation of the P/E and P/S ratios is simple—the price of the stock is divided by its earnings (net income) and sales, respectively. However, investors need to know what earnings figure is being used as the E in P/E. Are we talking about the last 12 months (trailing earnings), a combination of the past 6 months and an estimated future 6 months (Value Line uses this approach), or a forecast for the next 12 months (stock research analysts' forecasts)? There are more combinations than these; all of them have their proponents and can be considered valid. The conservative approach focuses on trailing earnings. As measured by the Standard & Poor's 500 index, the historical average for the P/E ratio has been around 14 (i.e., the S&P stocks have been selling for 14 times their earnings). However, in the bull markets of the 1990s, S&P 500 P/E ratios have been well above 20, even reaching 30 at one point.

Having completed our examination of the balance sheet and the income statement, we next discuss the important topic of cash flow and how a company's statement of cash flows can provide investors with some key insights to investment quality.

CHAPTER 5

Understanding the Cash Flow Statement and Its Components

If you believe in the old adage that "it takes money to make money," then you can grasp the essence of cash flow and what it means to a company. The statement of cash flows, or cash flow, reveals how a company spends its money (cash outflows) and where that money comes from (inflows). We learned in our discussion of the income statement that earnings and a company's profitability are important investment evaluators. It would be nice to be able to think of the net income figure as a quick and easy way to judge a company's performance. However, as we know, accrual accounting provides a basis for matching revenues and expenses, but the actual receipt and payment of funds means that profits can't be banked. Jonathan Moreland, in an August 1995 article in *Individual Investor*, makes the case for cash flow with this succinct assessment:

> At least as important as a company's profitability is its liquidity—whether or not it's taking in enough money to meet its obligations. Companies, after all, go bankrupt because they cannot pay their bills, not because they are unprofitable. Now, that's a rather obvious point. Even so, many investors routinely ignore it. How? By looking only at a firm's income statement and not its cash flow statement.

In addition, because the income statement is vulnerable to the impact of varying accounting policies, legitimate management manipulation, and tax decision maneuvers, many investment analysts believe that cash flow is a much more reliable indicator of a company's investment value. The cash flow statement is a straightforward, true accounting—a kind of "what you see is what you get" approach to financial accounting. In sum, the experts generally agree that cash flow is the single most important element to a company's survival and success. Because of this, investors need to have a solid understanding of how the cash flow statement works.

I use the term *cash flow* to mean a company's operating cash flow as it appears in the cash flow statement. This definition is widely accepted but is by no means universal. When reading about cash flow in investment reports and communications, it behooves investors to know how the term is defined. For example, to many financial professionals cash flow simply means the sum of a company's net income plus depreciation charges from the income statement. This number could approximate, or vary significantly from, a company's actual operating cash flow.

The statement of cash flows comes in two different formats—direct and indirect. The former is hardly ever seen as fewer than 2 percent of companies use it. Nevertheless, if someday it does appear on your analytical screen, its unfamiliarity need not complicate your cash flow analysis. I have provided an illustration of this form of presentation in Exhibit 5.1 for ABM Industries' statement of cash flows. The only real difference between the direct and the indirect format is in the presentation of the operating cash flow section. Otherwise, the formats are exactly alike; the number that investors need to work with is operating cash flow, which is clearly indicated in both formats.

THE STRUCTURE OF THE STATEMENT OF CASH FLOWS

Cash flow statements have three distinct sections, each of which relates to aspects of the cash flow of a particular component—operating, investing, and financing—of a company's business activities. Refer to Procter & Gamble's 1998 statements of cash flows in Exhibit 5.2 as our discussion guide. Readers less experienced in following company financials should note that one of the positive sides of working with cash flow statements is the use of literally descriptive account captions and the standardization of presentation formats among companies. P&G's cash flow statement is typical, but note that its use of the word *change* signifies an increase or decrease in the account entry, displayed as either a positive number or a negative one in parentheses.

Cash Flow from Operations

Cash flow from operating activities is the first and foremost source of a company's cash. In terms of types of cash flow, for investors this is the best because they are internally generated funds as opposed to those coming from investing and financing activities. You will recall from our review of the income statement that a company's net income is the end result of a variety of costs and expenses being offset against its revenues. Some of these costs and expenses are noncash charges (i.e., accounting expense entries that reduce income but don't represent an outflow of cash). In this section of the cash flow statement, the net income figure is adjusted, generally upward but sometimes downward to reconcile net income with net cash provided by operating activities.

Other adjustments appear as increases and decreases to working capital items in current assets and current liabilities. Sometimes, instead of being disclosed individually, these items are aggregated into a one-line entry as, for example, a "net change in operating assets and liabilities."

Let's now go through the various components of Procter & Gamble's 1998 operating cash flow to understand what the end result—cash flow from operations—is all about.

EXHIBIT 5.1 • Direct Format—Statement of Cash Flows

ABM Industries Incorporated and Subsidiaries

CONSOLIDATED STATEMENTS OF CASH FLOWS

Years Ended October 31 (in thousands of dollars)	1995	1996	1997
Cash flows from operating activities:			
Cash received from customers	$ 944,570	$ 1,055,112	$ 1,203,314
Other operating cash receipts	1,931	1,270	1,126
Interest received	489	449	552
Cash paid to suppliers and employees	(913,577)	(1,017,329)	(1,154,572)
Interest paid	(3,136)	(2,418)	(2,685)
Income taxes paid	(16,438)	(20,355)	(19,988)
Net cash provided by operating activities	13,839	16,729	27,747
Cash flows from investing activities:			
Additions to property, plant and equipment	(10,225)	(10,751)	(13,272)
Proceeds from sale of assets	590	777	660
Increase (decrease) in investments and long-term receivables	853	(5,657)	3,041
Intangible assets acquired	(12,499)	(13,044)	(28,606)
Net cash used in investing activities	(21,281)	(28,675)	(38,177)
Cash flows from financing activities:			
Common stock issued	5,297	8,022	8,778
Dividends paid	(6,061)	(7,235)	(8,597)
Increase (decrease) in bank overdraft	5,361	(426)	8,035
Increase (decrease) in notes payable	(4)	223	491
Long-term borrowings	89,000	110,777	115,654
Repayments of long-term borrowings	(91,679)	(99,688)	(113,715)
Net cash provided by financing activities	1,914	11,673	10,646
Net (decrease) increase in cash and cash equivalents	(5,528)	(273)	216
Cash and cash equivalents beginning of year	7,368	1,840	1,567
Cash and cash equivalents end of year	$ 1,840	$ 1,567	$ 1,783
Reconciliation of net income to net cash provided by operating activities:			
Net income	$ 18,219	$ 21,720	$ 27,239
Adjustments:			
Depreciation and amortization	11,527	13,651	16,118
Impairment of long-lived assets	—	—	2,700
Provision for bad debts	1,536	2,039	2,988
Gain on sale of assets	(127)	(314)	(257)
Deferred income taxes	(3,554)	(3,556)	(2,664)
Increase in accounts receivable	(18,823)	(26,890)	(50,312)
Decrease (increase) in inventories	(1,969)	516	(4,069)
Increase in prepaid expenses and other current assets	(6,906)	(1,170)	(5,628)
Decrease (increase) in other assets	(1,434)	(645)	1,580
(Decrease) increase in income taxes payable	309	(414)	2,401
Increase in retirement plans accrual	1,649	2,513	3,273
Increase in insurance claims liability	4,462	4,854	5,212
Increase in trade accounts payable and other accrued liabilities	8,950	4,425	29,166
Total adjustments to net income	(4,380)	(4,991)	508
Net cash provided by operating activities	$ 13,839	$ 16,729	$ 27,747
Supplemental Data:			
Non-cash investing activities:			
Common stock issued for net assets of business acquired	—	—	$ 6,100

The accompanying notes are an integral part of the consolidated financial statements.

17

EXHIBIT 5.2 • Procter & Gamble Statement of Cash Flows

CONSOLIDATED STATEMENTS OF CASH FLOWS   The Procter & Gamble Company and Subsidiaries

Amounts in Millions	Years Ended June 30		
	1998	1997	1996
Cash and Cash Equivalents, Beginning of Year	$ 2,350	$ 2,074	$ 2,028
Operating Activities			
Net earnings	3,780	3,415	3,046
Depreciation and amortization	1,598	1,487	1,358
Deferred income taxes	(101)	(26)	328
Change in accounts receivable	42	8	17
Change in inventories	(229)	(71)	202
Change in accounts payable, accrued and other liabilities	(3)	561	(948)
Change in other operating assets and liabilities	(65)	503	(134)
Other	(137)	5	289
Total Operating Activities	4,885	5,882	4,158
Investing Activities			
Capital expenditures	(2,559)	(2,129)	(2,179)
Proceeds from asset sales	555	520	402
Acquisitions	(3,269)	(150)	(358)
Change in investment securities	63	(309)	(331)
Total Investing Activities	(5,210)	(2,068)	(2,466)
Financing Activities			
Dividends to shareholders	(1,462)	(1,329)	(1,202)
Change in short-term debt	1,315	(160)	242
Additions to long-term debt	1,970	224	339
Reductions of long-term debt	(432)	(724)	(619)
Proceeds from stock options	158	134	89
Treasury purchases	(1,929)	(1,652)	(432)
Total Financing Activities	(380)	(3,507)	(1,583)
Effect of Exchange Rate Changes			
on Cash and Cash Equivalents	(96)	(31)	(63)
Change in Cash and Cash Equivalents	(801)	276	46
Cash and Cash Equivalents, End of Year	$ 1,549	$ 2,350	$ 2,074
Supplemental Disclosure			
Cash payments for:			
Interest, net of amount capitalized	$ 536	$ 449	$ 459
Income taxes	2,056	1,380	1,339
Liabilities assumed in acquisitions	808	42	56

See accompanying Notes to Consolidated Financial Statements.

Net income. For P&G, this is its net earnings figure, or bottom line, from its income statement ($3,780 million). Generally, this is the major source of operating cash flow, which is another reason investment professionals focus so intently on a company's earnings.

Depreciation, depletion, and amortization. These reductions in various asset values are usually major expenses for companies, particularly for those requiring a large investment in fixed assets, but they are only accounting entries—no cash leaves the company. As can be seen with P&G, as a large company with a substantial manufacturing infrastructure and purchased goodwill, its depreciation and amortization expenses ($1,598 million) are significant. As mentioned previously, it's not unusual for net income, depreciation, depletion, and amortization to represent the bulk of operating cash flow. For that reason, and as mentioned above, the sum of these two items is often used by financial professionals to express a company's cash flow.

Other adjustments. A variety of other noncash items can appear under this general category. Procter & Gamble has only one adjustment, a negative amount for deferred income taxes ($101 million). Other items typically found in this category, which are generally self-explanatory, are gains/losses on the sale of assets and securities, extraordinary or special gains/losses, discontinued operations, restructuring charges, effect of any change in accounting policies, retirement of assets, and so on. Most of the time these other adjustments are not material, but major amounts could be recorded, especially for discontinued operations and restructuring or under extraordinary special charges that can distort operating cash flow in a given year.

Changes in working capital assets and liabilities. Procter & Gamble's presentation provides a breakdown of these items. Of particular interest to investors is the behavior of accounts receivable and inventories over time as opposed to one-time annual results. A trend of positive contribution or low use of cash in these working capital items is a good sign. P&G's management appears to have done well over the period reviewed. Its position in accounts receivable is providing cash, albeit in modest amounts, as opposed to requiring the use of cash. Inventories seem to be going in the other direction, having been a provider of cash in 1996 but converting to a user in the last two years. This is a good illustration of the need to view these movements over time—I suspect that 1999 results will reflect a turnaround in this inventory behavior. Growing companies need to convert their receivables and inventories into cash as fast as possible; otherwise these major assets become big users of cash and a burden on operating cash flow.

Other items. This is a catchall category, usually not representing a material amount. P&G records a positive $137 million here.

Net cash provided (used) by operating activities. This subtotal is a key number for investors. It captures the adjustments to net income and measures a company's ability to manage its working capital assets to produce internally generated funds. The greater the amount of operating cash flow, the better. The more funds a company has for outlays of cash for essential assets, to avoid borrowing, to expand its business, or to withstand hard times, the greater its qualities as an investment opportunity. A stable, positive operating cash flow is a good indicator of a healthy company.

Cash Flows from Investing

The major components of investing activity usually involve the use of cash and are self-explanatory. Items such as capital expenditures for property, plant, and equipment; business acquisitions; and the purchase of marketable securities are common account entries that represent an outflow of funds. Conversely, the sale of businesses, assets, or marketable securities generate cash inflows. The capital expenditures number warrants the attention of investors; it's generally assumed that this use of cash is a prime necessity for ensuring the proper maintenance of, and additions to, a company's physical assets to support its operations and remain competitive.

Procter & Gamble's 1998 cash flow presentation for investing activities is fairly typical. P&G made consistently heavy outlays of cash for capital expenditures—$2.6 billion in 1998 and over $2 billion in the two previous years. An additional large outlay for business acquisitions also occurred in 1998 ($3.3 billion), which, when compared with previous years, obviously represents a major event for the company. As explained in a note in the company's financials, the acquisitions were multiple, involving the purchase of Tambrand, Inc., the maker of Tampax, and several ventures in Latin America and Asia. In the case of Asia, it is likely that P&G took advantage of the economic woes affecting the Asian market to expand its presence over the long term. Having the cash to make these kinds of moves makes P&G a stronger company. A small amount of cash was provided from some asset sales ($555 million) and the sale of investment securities ($63 million). The net result of P&G's investing cash flows is an outflow, or use of funds, of $5.2 billion, which is an unusually large amount because of the major acquisitions undertaken.

Cash Flow from Financing

A company's financing activities encompass both debt and equity transactions. Typically, it is the former rather than the latter that gets most of the action. Account entries will show the proceeds from, and the repayment of, both short-term and long-term debt. Companies are continuously taking on new debt and making payments on existing debt obligations in the regular course of business.

Two other items of specific interest to investors involve dividends and treasury stock purchases. If a company's stock carries a dividend, the dividends paid to shareholders are an outflow of cash. That explains why fast-growing companies, which need all the cash they can get for continued expansion, don't pay dividends, choosing rather to plough back all their earnings into the company. For dividend-paying companies, it's obvious that it takes cash, not profits, to pay cash dividends to shareholders. For investors interested in this aspect of a stock investment, a company's cash availabilities are an important factor in any investment decision.

Treasury stock purchases result from a company's declared purpose to repurchase its own stock, which, when effected, represents an outflow of cash. Why do companies do this? First, to satisfy employee stock purchase plans and attend to the exercise of stock options by management, companies may maintain a small position in treasury stock. More likely, large outlays of cash for treasury stock relate to stock repurchase plans. Stock buybacks are intended to shrink a company's equity base, making less stock available for investors to buy. The law of supply and demand is supposed to kick in and increase a company's stock price and, as a result of fewer shares outstanding, earnings per share tend to rise even on the same or a lesser amount of earnings. If a company is financially strong and experiencing a healthy operating cash flow, stock buybacks can have a positive effect on a company's stock price. However, if funds are being diverted from other corporate needs, or worse, being borrowed to finance stock purchases, then the practice becomes questionable.

Stock repurchase plans receive a lot of attention, usually positive, from the investment community, but history has shown that they mostly involve good intentions. The amount of stock actually bought back is often far below expectations. In a October 7, 1996, article in *Forbes,* investment guru Lazlo Birinyi described how Merck's announced billion-dollar buyback got sidetracked by an acquisition it paid for with stock during the same period. The result: While Merck was buying back shares on the one hand, it was issuing new shares for the acquisition on the other; as a consequence, the amount of Merck's shares outstanding actually increased. Birinyi concluded from his overall study of stock repurchase plans that "accepting buyback announcements is a little like predicting a fall in liquor and cigarette sales on the basis of New Year's resolutions."

A company's cash flow from financing activities can be either positive or negative. Looking at Procter & Gamble's 1998 results, we see a relatively small net outflow of cash from financing activities ($380 million). The company's large dividend payment ($1.5 billion) was a major item. It borrowed heavily on both a short-term and long-term basis compared with net repayments in the previous year for both types of debt. Why? The explanation comes from our discussion in the preceding section on the abnormally high cash outlay for P&G's acquisitions in its 1998 fiscal year. It is difficult to cover really big investment outlays, those that go beyond the routine level, from operating cash flow. So P&G had to borrow funds for this purpose. The lesson here for investors is to recognize that Procter & Gamble's strong balance sheet, steady profitability, and positive cash flows, from which these borrowings will be repaid, allowed it to act expeditiously on market opportunities the company deemed attractive.

The net increase (decrease) in cash and cash equivalents is applied to the balance at the beginning of the year (the same as the preceding year's ending balance) for a cash and cash equivalents amount at year-end. For obvious reasons, this bottom line for the statement of cash flows, unlike the income statement, is not that important. Investors need to keep their eyes focused on operating cash flow.

Let's look at Procter & Gamble's 1998 numbers for the net change in cash and cash equivalents. We arrive at this line as follows: $2,350 million at the beginning of the year less $801 million as the negative effect of all cash flows equals $1,549 million. If you check P&G's balance sheet in Exhibit 1.2, this last number is precisely the amount you will see recorded as cash and cash equivalents on the first line under current assets.

A company's cash flow pattern will vary according to its line of business and its stage of maturity. Whatever the case, if you come across a cash cow as an investment opportunity, chances are that as an investor you will also find a solid balance sheet and a solid profit performer. To prove my point, take a look at Microsoft's financials. Cash is truly king!

CHAPTER 6

Key Investment Evaluators for the Cash Flow Statement

An investor's analysis of the statement of cash flows is relatively easy. Terminology is generally not a problem and the standardization of the format among most companies facilitates the identification of the data needed to compute the relevant ratios. The figure for cash flow from operations is the critical element in all the investment evaluators that we discuss. Procter & Gamble's 1998 cash flow statement (figures in millions)—see Exhibit 5.2 in Chapter 5—will be used as our discussion guide for calculating the cash flow ratios. While it is important to use multiyear comparisons for all financial ratios, it is absolutely essential to apply this rule to the review of cash flow measurements. The dynamics of cash flow management can only be appreciated over an extended period of time.

OPERATING CASH FLOW/SALES RATIO

This ratio, which is expressed as a percentage comparison of a company's operating cash flow with its net sales or revenues, provides another angle of vision on the conversion of accounts receivable to cash. It would be worrisome to see a company's sales grow without a parallel growth in operating cash flow. Any trouble with this measure should be confirmed by the days sales outstanding indicator component of a company's operating cycle, which was discussed in Chapter 2. P&G's operating cash flow/sales ratio is calculated as follows:

> Operating cash flow ÷ Sales/Revenues (from the income statement) = %
> $4,885 ÷ $37,154 = 13.2 or 13 percent

There is no just right percentage with this investment evaluator. As you can see from the results in Exhibit 6.1, company experience varies widely. What is relevant for investors is to track this

EXHIBIT 6.1 • Sampling of Industry and Company Comparisons of Sales with Operating Cash Flow

INDUSTRY	COMPANY	FISCAL YEAR	SALES (Millions $)	OPERATING CASH FLOW (%) (a)
Airlines	AMR Corporation	12/31/97	2,920	16
Aerospace	Boeing	12/31/97	2,100	5
Automotive	Ford	12/31/97	27,634	18
Beverage	Coca-Cola	12/31/97	4,033	21
Computer	IBM	12/31/97	8,865	11
Computer Software	Microsoft	06/30/97	4,689	41
Conglomerate	GE	12/31/97	14,240	16
Energy	Exxon	12/31/97	14,676	12
Leisure Time	Disney	09/30/97	7,064	31
Manufacturing	3M	12/31/97	1,706	11
Media	Gannett	12/31/97	881	19
Mining	Cyprus Amax	12/31/97	481	14
Personal Care	Procter & Gamble	06/30/97	5,882	17
Pharmaceutical	Merck	12/31/97	6,317	27
Restaurant	McDonald's	12/31/97	2,442	21
Retailing—Food	Albertson's	01/31/98	865	6
Retailing—General	Wal-Mart	01/31/98	7,123	6
Service	ManPower	12/31/97	36	1
Technology	Intel	12/31/97	10,008	40
Telecomunications	Ameritech	12/31/97	4,510	28

Note:
(a) Operating cash flow divided by sales is expressed as a percentage.

indicator's performance historically to detect variances from what one can establish as the company's average cash flow/sales relationship.

CAPITAL EXPENDITURES RATIO/OPERATING CASH FLOW RATIO

For investors, this is a particularly important measurement of the adequacy of a company's cash flow. As we know, capital expenditures are considered a corporate necessity. Property, plant, and equipment must be continuously renewed and/or expanded to maintain a company's productivity and competitiveness. If operating cash flow is not adequate to cover capital expenditures, debt and/or equity capital must be found to provide the funds required. That is always possible, but it may take time, incur financing charges, and, in the case of debt, impose some restrictions as part of the borrowing agreement on a company's operational decision making. With this indicator, which is expressed as a percentage, the lower the number, the better. This means that capital expenditures are well covered and there is ample margin for other uses of cash. Procter & Gamble's capital expenditure/cash flow ratio would be calculated as follows:

> Capital expenditures (investing activities) ÷ Operating cash flow = %
> $2,559 ÷ $4,885 = 52.4 or 52 percent

P&G, even with its apparent major fixed asset commitments, had an operating cash flow level almost twice as large as its capital expenditures, a healthy sign for investors.

DIVIDENDS/OPERATING CASH FLOW RATIO

While not impossible, most companies that are presently paying a dividend would find it very difficult to suspend dividend payments. For many investors, the dividend payment is sacred.

Also, the investment community generally punishes the stock price of a company that lowers or drops its dividend payment. As you know, companies need cash to pay dividends. So here again, just like with capital expenditures, the more margin—that is, the lower the number of this ratio— the better. Procter & Gamble's dividend/cash flow ratio is calculated as follows:

> Dividends paid (financing activities) ÷ Operating cash flow = %
> $1,462 ÷ $4,885 = 29.9 or 30 percent

P&G's operating cash flow appears to provide a fairly high level of protection for its historical level of cash dividends paid.

CAPITAL EXPENDITURES PLUS DIVIDENDS PAID/OPERATING CASH FLOW RATIO

By combining the two most essential outlays of corporate cash, this formula represents what could be called the cash flow statement's equivalent of the balance sheet's acid test ratio. This is a tough test. Those companies that regularly generate internal funds sufficient to cover both capital expenditures and cash dividends should make investors smile. The greater the operating cash flow coverage of these two expenditures, the greater a company's ability to use debt on a discretionary basis and enjoy more freedom in the management of its affairs. Procter & Gamble's essential expenditure coverage ratio looks like this:

[Capital expenditures + Dividends paid] ÷ Operating cash flow = %
[$2,559 + $1,462] ÷ $4,885 = 82.3 or 82 percent

On the basis of this ratio level, P&G enjoys a fairly comfortable position with respect to funding its outlays for essential property, plant, and equipment as well as the payment of cash dividends.

FREE CASH FLOW/OPERATING CASH FLOW RATIO

Free cash flow is often defined as operating cash flow minus capital expenditures. I choose to use a more comprehensive definition by using the sum of capital expenditures and cash dividends paid as the amount to subtract from operating cash flow to arrive at free cash flow. As a practical matter, if a company has a history of dividend payments, it cannot easily suspend them without causing the company some pain. Therefore, a prudent investor will consider dividends in the same essential cash outlay category as capital expenditures. As a consequence, free cash flow as described here provides a company with a great deal of latitude in its application. It can be used to reduce debt, increase dividends, expand the business, or acquire other companies. A 1996 survey by investor relations firm Shelly Taylor & Associates confirmed that the 62 institutional investment firms questioned ranked free cash flow ahead of earnings as the most important piece of information companies should communicate. I would agree and suggest that investors focus on this investment evaluator to judge the investment quality of a company. Obviously, the larger the number the better.

In the case of Procter & Gamble, its free cash would be calculated as follows:

Operating cash flow—[Capital expenditures + Dividends paid] = Free cash flow
$4,885—[$2,559 + $1,462] = $824
Free cash flow ÷ Operating cash flow = %
$824 ÷ $4,885 = 16.9 or 17 percent

P&G's ability to generate free cash flow, albeit a modest amount, in a year of continued significant investments in fixed assets and the completion of a major acquisition program is admirable. The

EXHIBIT 6.2 • Sampling of Industry and Company Cash Flow Indicators

INDUSTRY	COMPANY	FISCAL YEAR	OPERATING CASH FLOW (millions $)	CAPITAL EXPENDITURES	CASH DVIDENDS	CE&CD TOTAL	FREE CASH FLOW
Airlines	AMR Corporation	12/31/97	2,920	0.48	0.00	0.48	0.52
Aerospace	Boeing	12/31/97	2,100	0.66	0.27	0.93	0.07
Automotive	Ford	12/31/97	27,634	0.32	0.07	0.39	0.61
Beverage	Coca-Cola	12/31/97	4,033	0.27	0.34	0.61	0.39
Computer	IBM	12/31/97	8,865	0.77	0.09	0.86	0.14
Computer Software	Microsoft	06/30/97	4,689	0.11	0.01	0.12	0.88
Conglomerate	GE	12/31/97	14,240	0.59	0.24	0.83	0.17
Energy	Exxon	12/31/97	14,676	0.50	0.30	0.80	0.20
Leisure Time	Disney	09/30/97	7,064	0.27	0.05	0.32	0.68
Manufacturing	3M	12/31/97	1,706	0.82	0.51	1.33	-0.33
Media	Gannett	12/31/97	881	0.25	0.23	0.48	0.52
Mining	Cyprus Amax	12/31/97	481	0.81	0.21	1.02	-0.02
Personal Care	Procter & Gamble	06/30/97	5,882	0.36	0.23	0.59	0.41
Pharmaceutical	Merck	12/31/97	6,317	0.23	0.32	0.55	0.45
Restaurant	McDonald's	12/31/97	2,442	0.86	0.10	0.96	0.04
Retailing—Food	Albertson's	01/31/98	865	0.78	0.18	0.96	0.04
Retailing—General	Wal-Mart	01/31/98	7,123	0.37	0.09	0.46	0.54
Service	ManPower	12/31/97	36	2.75	0.39	3.14	-2.14
Technology	Intel	12/31/97	10,008	0.45	0.02	0.47	0.53
Telecomunications	Ameritech	12/31/97	4,510	0.59	0.28	0.86	0.14

company's stellar free cash flow performance in 1997—$2.4 billion or 41 percent of operating cash flow—certainly helped P&G fill its coffers and position itself for the aggressive acquisition posture it assumed the following year.

Even though it is only a look at one year, the data for the G20 sample of companies in Exhibit 6.2 provide some interesting cash flow insights for investors to consider. AMR Corporation's heavy use of operating leases to fulfill its aircraft needs understates its capital expenditures, which in turn overstates its free cash flow number. Companies to which this circumstance applies are not as liquid as their free cash flow implies.

The term cash cow is not a very elegant expression, but it is certainly an appealing quality in the eyes of investors. A look at Microsoft's cash flow performance tells us why its corporate sound, if it has one, is moo! We saw in Exhibit 6.1 that Microsoft's sales produced significant operating cash flow—41 percent of sales in fiscal 1997. In terms of free cash flow, things get even better. With Microsoft's relatively small capital investment outlays and nominal dividend payment, it gets to keep 88 percent of its operating cash flow (i.e., almost $4 billion in free cash flow of its $4.7 billion in cash from operations). Compare this situation with that of Ameritech, which recorded a similar amount of operating cash flow to that of Microsoft in fiscal 1997—$4.5 billion. However, in its line of business as a telecommunications company, Ameritech has heavy capital investment requirements and more than nominal dividend payment requirements. As a consequence, it gets to keep only 14 percent of its cash from operations as free cash flow, which amounts to approximately $700 million, roughly one-sixth of Microsoft's take on similar operating cash flow amounts.

SHORT-TERM DEBT COVERAGE RATIO

This ratio compares a company's short-term debt—defined here as current borrowings and the current portion of long-term debt—with operating cash flow. The higher the ratio, the better the company's ability to meet its current debt obligations. This liquidity indicator is expressed as a times factor. Procter & Gamble's short-term debt coverage is calculated by picking up its current debt from its balance sheet, $2,281 million, and dividing this amount into operating cash flow, according to the following illustration:

Operating cash flow ÷ Short-term debt = Times factor (x)
$4,885 ÷ $2,281 = 2.1x

By this measurement, P&G's operating cash flow coverage is slightly more than two times the amount of its short-term debt.

The industry and company comparisons of short-term and long-term debt with operating cash flow are illustrated in Exhibit 6.3. Besides the usual diversity of debt/cash flow relationships revealed, the ratios tend to reinforce the logical connection of low debt and positive cash flow positions among the companies.

TOTAL DEBT COVERAGE RATIO

For purposes of this ratio, total debt is defined as the sum of a company's short-term debt, as described in the short-term debt coverage ratio, and its long-term debt, redeemable preferred stock, and two-thirds of the principal of noncancelable operating leases. On this basis, Procter & Gamble's total debt would be the sum of $2,281 million and $5,765 million, or $8,046 million. This ratio is expressed as a percentage in the following manner:

Operating cash flow ÷ Total debt = %
$4,885 ÷ $8,046 = 60.7 or 61 percent

A high percentage ratio is indicative of a significant operating cash flow in relation to a company's overall debt position. P&G's relatively high total debt coverage ratio is indicative of its ability to generate substantial cash flow.

PER SHARE DATA

Dividends per Share

This information is generally provided in a company's financial communications and/or by various investment information services. It can also be easily calculated by simply dividing the amount of cash dividends paid (financing section of cash flow statement) by the average weighted common shares outstanding, which is the same number we used to calculate sales and earnings per share from the income statement. Procter & Gamble's 1998 dividends per share would involve dividing the cash dividends paid of $1,426 million by 1,343.4 million shares outstanding, which results in a dividend per share figure of $1.09.

In her widely acclaimed book *The Dividend Connection,* Geraldine Weiss observes that "earnings are figures on an income statement ... but dividends are real money." Companies with a long history of paying dividends, especially those that provide a gradual but steady increase in the dividend per share, have been generally viewed as having considerable investment value. In the high-flying stock market of the 1990s, stock price appreciation has gotten all the attention. Dividends, as a stock investment quality, have been all but forgotten. Some investment professionals have even declared dividends to be irrelevant in the so-called new era. From my experience, it seems that eventually fundamentals have a way of reasserting themselves. Historically, dividends have comprised an important part of an equity investor's total return. So regardless of what is going on out there in the marketplace, it's likely that dividends will continue their role of providing support to the price of a stock and contributing in a meaningful way to an equity investment's total return.

EXHIBIT 6.3 • Sampling of Industry and Company Comparisons of Debt to Operating Cash Flow

INDUSTRY	COMPANY	FISCAL YEAR	SHORT-TERM DEBT (x) (a)	TOTAL DEBT (%) (b)
Airlines	AMR Corporation	12/31/97	5.5	66
Aerospace	Boeing	12/31/97	2.9	31
Automotive	Ford	12/31/97	N.M.	N.M.
Beverage	Coca-Cola	12/31/97	1.3	104
Computer	IBM	12/31/97	0.7	33
Computer Software	Microsoft	06/30/97	N.M.	738
Conglomerate	GE	12/31/97	N.M.	N.M.
Energy	Exxon	12/31/97	5.1	148
Leisure Time	Disney	09/30/97	2.5	64
Manufacturing	3M	12/31/97	1.1	68
Media	Gannett	12/31/97	48.9	50
Mining	Cyprus Amax	12/31/97	2.1	20
Personal Care	Procter & Gamble	06/30/97	6.9	118
Pharmaceutical	Merck	12/31/97	7.0	281
Restaurant	McDonald's	12/31/97	1.5	38
Retailing—Food	Albertson's	01/31/98	8.9	70
Retailing—General	Wal-Mart	01/31/98	6.2	66
Service	ManPower	12/31/97	0.5	14
Technology	Intel	12/31/97	31.1	1,300
Telecomunications	Ameritech	12/31/97	1.5	59

Note:

(a) Operating cash flow divided by short-term debt is expressed as a times. Short-term debt is comprised of the balance sheet's current borrowings and the current portion of long-term debt.

(b) Operating cash flow divided by the total debt is expressed as a percentage. Total debt is comprised of the balance sheet's shrt-term debt, as defined in (a), and long-term debt and capital leases.

EXHIBIT 6.4 • Cash Flow per Share Data—Coca-Cola

YEAR	AVERAGE SHARES OUTSTANDING (millions)	CASH FLOW FROM OPERATIONS (millions)	CASH FLOW PER SHARE
1993	$2,603	$2,508	$0.96
1994	$2,580	$3,361	$1.30
1995	$2,525	$3,328	$1.32
1996	$2,494	$3,463	$1.39
1997	$2,477	$4,033	$1.63

Cash Flow per Share

Just as many financial professionals prefer to focus on a company's cash flow as opposed to its earnings as a performance indicator, it is only logical that cash flow per share is presumed to be a better performance indicator than the traditional earnings per share. Cash flow per share is calculated by simply dividing operating cash flow by the weighted average of shares outstanding. Exhibit 6.4 illustrates the recent history of Coca-Cola as measured by its cash flow per share performance.

With Procter & Gamble's 1998 financials, computing its cash flow per share involves dividing its operating cash flow number, $4,885 million, by the number of weighted average shares outstanding, 1,343.4 million, which equals $3.64 of cash flow per share. The last of the market valuation ratios, the price/cash flow (P/CF) ratio, uses this monetary value in its calculation. As was the case with the previously discussed market valuation ratios—price–book value, price/sales, and price/earnings—the P/CF ratio is computed by dividing the price of its stock by cash flow per share.

Piecing together an array of reliable sources of information is the key to making informed investment decisions. The exercise is similar to solving a puzzle. One needs to look for clues in order to pick the right pieces that fit and complete the picture. How to select winning stocks—an investment puzzle—challenges investors to do the same. Financial statements, and the clues they contain to evaluating a company's investment qualities, are, without question, critical sources of information for investors. In Part IV I discuss some information sources that provide additional insights to using financial statements as investment indicators that were reviewed in the preceding pages.

CHAPTER 7

Managements' Discussion and Analysis—Managerial Insights

Management's discussion and analysis of a company's financial position is found in both annual reports and Form 10K. These managerial insights, often referred to by financial professionals as MD&A, generally carry the formal title of Management's Discussion and Analysis of Financial Condition and Results of Operations or Analysis of Operations and Financial Condition or simply Financial Review. Investors should be aware that the information presented in this report is not audited. The commentary focuses on three major aspects of a company's financial position: the income statement (results of operations), capital resources (debt and equity), and liquidity. If the presentation is done well, an investor can obtain some additional insights on a company's financials. Even a rather perfunctory MD&A narrative can provide some qualitative information that expands on the data provided by the financial statements.

The Securities and Exchange Commission (SEC) made the MD&A a corporate financial reporting requirement in the mid-1980s. A few years later, the SEC became concerned that companies were tending toward mechanistic, numbers-oriented presentations on year-to-year changes of material accounts in their financials as the main thrust of their commentary in the MD&A. Consequently, the SEC issued an interpretive release specifying the kind of disclosure it wanted to see. In brief, the recommendations encouraged companies to provide narrative explanations of their financial position and performance, with an emphasis on their prospects for the future. This emphasis on prospective information is very important for investors. As we have seen, a company's financial statements are historical; and while history is valuable as a basis for stock evaluations, it is a company's future prospects that are important to investment decisions. In the words of the SEC, "the MD&A is intended to give the investor an opportunity to look at the company through the eyes of management by providing both a short- and long-term analysis of the business of the company."

Unfortunately, the past ten years have shown little progress in turning the MD&A into a truly meaningful financial reporting disclosure tool. Hill & Knowlton, a major investor relations firm, undertook a survey in 1989 that concluded that "many companies are failing to meet investors' needs with the MD&A section of their annual reports." It is not very different today, even with the subsequent passage of safe harbor legislation that protects companies against lawsuits for management's actual results falling short of the statements it made regarding future performance.

PRESENTATION ASPECTS OF THE MD&A REPORT

While recognizing that a company's MD&A report may not measure up to its full potential as a source of investment information, there still are, in general, some helpful insights to be found. Also, some companies do a better job than others do, and in these cases it is worthwhile for investors to look for good analytical, forward-looking MD&A content. Before indicating what investors should be looking for in the report, readers who are less experienced with financial reporting matters should be warned about three problems concerning the format and content of MD&A presentations that are somewhat problematical.

The Blur Technique

Obviously, good qualitative commentary is the single most important aspect of any management and discussion analysis. Equally important to content, however, is the form of presentation (i.e., the format used to express the information that is being communicated). An easy-to-read presentation that utilizes tables, charts, and other graphic techniques to enhance the understanding of the text makes a big difference in comprehension for readers of all levels of financial expertise. It is not unusual, however, to find all of the MD&A text to be single-spaced, run together, with little in the way of graphics, and no paragraph headings to guide the reader from one topic to another. The pages are packed full of words, one almost indistinguishable from another. I refer to this formatting style as the blur technique. It is understandably hard reading, particularly for the financial novice. For investors faced with this situation, I can only advise them to persevere. Even the poorest of MD&A presentations offers some valuable clues to a company's financial position and performance.

Segmentation

Some companies segment their MD&A commentary, which covers their latest three-year operating period, into two distinct interannual reviews instead of viewing the period as a whole. For example, I think most people find it easier to evaluate a company's performance by looking at one period—let's say, 1996–98 review period—as opposed to breaking up the review period into two parts, 1996–97 and 1997–98. The narrative comes off as disjointed, and it is harder to pick up trends. Fortunately, not too many companies follow this latter approach. Here again, I have no solution to the problem other than to persevere!

Lack of Substantive Content

The content issue is the most serious MD&A problem for investors. Little valuable insight is provided if a company chooses to simply recite an assortment of historical quantitative data without explaining *why* changes occurred or indicating where a company is headed in the foreseeable future. I have been disappointed on numerous occasions by poor MD&A presentations, but I would advise investors, as I do myself, to keep looking for useful information. When mining for investment clues, you may not find a mother lode in the MD&A, but just discovering a few nuggets can make the exercise worthwhile.

MANAGERIAL INSIGHTS

The MD&A report, as I said before, focuses on three specific aspects of a company's financial position and performance:

- Results of operations
- Capital resources
- Liquidity

The commentary on the results of operations provides a fairly detailed analysis of a company's income and expense performance—its income statement—over a three-year period. It's hoped that some clues to future performance are also included. Investors should look for an explanation of why sales increased or decreased, which should include, for example, percentage changes as the result of volume, price, foreign currency fluctuations, and/or acquisitions. Often, specifics are provided on the individual performance of products or product lines if the company is a multiline operation. General economic and marketplace conditions may be cited as helping or hindering the prospects for a growth in sales.

Other factors affecting revenues and expenses may include comments on distribution systems, product improvements, manufacturing capacity, research and development efforts, tax legislation, and nonrecurring income and expense items. Generally, profit margins are stated and reasons given for variances. Of particular interest, among other items, is management's view on cost factors—the stability of raw material costs, interest expense, competition, and inflation. In sum, a narrative that provides answers or insights on why the numbers have changed and, even better, what might be the effects on the company's future operations is very valuable to investors.

Capital Resources

This commentary aims to assure the reader that the company is financially strong and is able to adequately fund its operations. In fact, a statement to that effect, in this section, seems to be routine for most companies:

> The Company believes its internally generated liquidity, together with access to external capital resources, will be sufficient to satisfy existing commitments and plans, and to provide adequate financial flexibility to take advantage of potential strategic business opportunities should they arise.

Suffice it to say, investors must make up their own minds in this regard after digesting considerably more information than just relying on an affirmative statement from management.

In addition to this customary affirmation of a company's strong financial condition, investors also will find information regarding the company's policy on indebtedness and a discussion of some relevant debt ratios. Capital expenditures usually warrant comment as well as acquisitions and expansion plans.

During the decade of the 1990s, many companies have been borrowing less from banks and are now, in today's market, relying increasingly on financial markets to provide their credit needs. Look for comments on ratings of the company's debt, principally bonds and commercial paper, from credit rating agencies, such as Moody's and Standard & Poor's, as shown in Exhibit 7.1. Corporate management is sensitive to these formal risk evaluations ratings, and for good reason. A downgrading of a rating can cost the debt-issuing company a considerable amount of money in interest and create problems with its creditors. Conversely, an upgrading can make it easier to borrow and at better rates. Investors should note that a credit rating pertains to the individual debt issue only and does not judge the overall credit quality of the company. As a practical matter, though, this is often not the general perception. The investing public tends to think of companies, not the debt, as being rated.

Liquidity

Management's comments on liquidity focus on a company's ability to have sufficient cash available to meet its short-term operational obligations. Items such as the current ratio, receivable and inventory turnover, and lines of credit are discussed to demonstrate the adequacy of a company's liquidity. You now know how these indicators work and can check your assessment against the company's. For example, AMR Corporation's 1997 annual report's MD&A contains this comment:

> AMR (principally American Airlines) historically operates with a working capital deficit as do most other airline companies. The existence of such a deficit has not in the past impaired the Company's ability to meet its obligations as they become due and is not expected to do so in the future.

EXHIBIT 7.1 • Credit Rating Agencies and Ratings (a)

Quality Ranking (b)	Standard & Poors (c)	Moody's (c)	Duff & Phelps	Fitch
Highest	AAA	Aaa	1	AAA
High	AA+ AA AA–	Aa	2 3 4	AA+ AA AA–
Upper Medium Grade	A+ A A–	A	5 6 7	A+ A A–
Medium Grade	BBB+ BBB BBB–	Baa	8 9 10	BBB+ BBB BBB–
Speculative/ Low Grade	BB/B	Ba/B	11	BB/B

Notes:

(a) The ratings in the exhibit are for long-term debt obligations. Short-term debt ratings (e.g., for commercial paper) are as follows:

	S&P	Moody's
Superior	A	P-1
Strong	A1, A2	P-2
Adequate	A3, B	P-3

(b) These descriptive captions are the author's and are meant to be indicative. They are not formally used by the credit rating agencies.

(c) Standard & Poor's uses plus and minus modifiers. Moody's refines their grades by using numerical modifiers (1, 2, and 3) to indicate high, middle and low levels, respectively.

You can refresh your memory on this point by referring back to Exhibit 2.2 showing liquidity/efficiency indicators. You will see that, yes, AMR's 1997 current liabilities did exceed its current assets, which means it had a negative working capital position. On the face of it, this does not sound very good. However, AMR turns over its accounts receivable in less than 4 weeks, a fast 27 days to be exact, and it has no salable inventory to worry about. A rough calculation of AMR's accounts payable turnover indicates an average payment period of over 30 days. So AMR is right about its working capital deficit! In addition, if you check Exhibit 6.1—a comparison of operating cash flow with sales—you see that AMR's cash flow/sales ratio at 16 percent puts it at the upper end of this cash availability indicator.

Investors should not let their expectations for managerial insight from the MD&A exceed what most companies actually deliver. Users of management's discussion and analysis information, particularly investors, would be better served if the historical performance of a company—hindsight—would be used as a basis to look forward—insight. Nevertheless, the MD&A material does contain qualitative observations on a company's financial and investment qualities that will help investors put together a more complete analytical profile.

CHAPTER 8

Notes to the Financial Statements— Essential Reading

It's difficult for the numbers in financial statements alone to provide adequate financial disclosure required by regulatory authorities and financial analysts. Also, as I mentioned in the introduction, financial accounting allows estimates, judgments, and alternative applications of accounting methods. The notes to the financial statements highlight and explain these management actions. Therefore, notes, often referred to in investment literature as footnotes, provide investors with additional, detailed information that helps to properly evaluate a company's financials. How many times in the preceding chapters have I suggested that you consult the notes to the financials as useful for further reference? The notes are essential reading.

Unfortunately, many corporate financial presentations have a low readability factor. A lot of technical financial jargon usually appears and the presentations are crammed into a less-than-stimulating format. You must not be deterred. You do not have to understand all the material presented to obtain valuable insights. In view of the complexity and diversity of note presentations, I am going to concentrate on seven fairly standard notes that generally include key informational inputs for investors.

ACCOUNTING POLICIES

A company's accounting policies will appear as the first note under a title called Summary of Significant Accounting Policies and will cover such items, among others, as:

Nature of Operations; Fiscal Year; Basis of Consolidation; Cash Equivalents; Inventories; Property, Plant, and Equipment; Depreciation, Amortization, Depletion; Research and Development; Intangible Assets; Earnings per Share; Income Taxes; Revenue Recognition; Foreign Currency Translation; Use of Estimates; New Accounting Standards; Derivatives; and Reclassifications.

The accounting policies note tends to look like boilerplate text, but investors need to know what these policies are and the consequences of any changes. Investors should look for three things that may be important. First, be aware of the impact of accounting policies and any changes on a company's financial position and performance. For example, a change in the estimated useful life applied to fixed assets would effect depreciation charges and, if material, have an impact on both earnings and cash flow. Such consequences are described in a note. I highly recommend Thorton O'glove's book *The Quality of Earnings* for its perspective on the influence of accounting changes on a company's profitability. O'glove states that "accountants know quite well and the general public, including investors, hardly at all, that according to the [accounting] methods used, a company can report a very wide range of earnings."

Second, the degree of conservatism in the presentation of a company's earnings depends, basically, on three accounting policies: revenue recognition, inventory valuation, and depreciation. Products or services that are completed and delivered to the customer generally constitute a completed sale. Recognizing a sale's total revenue on an uncompleted sale, which could involve any number of conditional circumstances, is not a conservative approach. As discussed in Chapter 1, the LIFO inventory valuation is more conservative than the FIFO valuation; and accelerated depreciation is more conservative than the straight-line method. However, with regard to depreciation, I have yet to see accelerated depreciation, which is generally used with tax reporting, applied to financial statement reporting.

Third, some companies use accounting practices that run counter to general practice but do conform to industry practice. For example, tobacco and alcoholic beverage companies classify leaf tobacco and bulk whiskey inventories as current assets. In reality, these products will not be sold (i.e., converted to cash) for several years. However, industry practice classifies these items as current assets and the companies do the same in their balance sheets.

ACQUISITIONS

The note on acquisitions, which is fairly self-explanatory, mentions the basis for a business combination—either the purchase method or the pooling of interests method. Historically, the former method has been the one most used, but with the high stock valuations of the 1990s, many companies have preferred to use their high-priced stock to undertake business combinations through a pooling of interests, which uses stock instead of cash for an acquisition.

In very simplified terms, here is what happens to a company's financial position according to these two different methods of accounting for acquisitions. The purchase approach means that the acquired company becomes part of the consolidated operations of the parent company as of the date of the purchase. The purchase price frequently exceeds the book value of the acquired company, which creates an intangible asset (refer back to Chapter 1) called goodwill or purchased goodwill in the parent company's balance sheet, and the amortization of this intangible asset will be charged against income.

The pooling of interests method, which requires conformity to a long list of conditions, unites two companies through an exchange of stock. Their recorded assets and liabilities are fused together in a new combined corporation. Two positive things happen from an accounting standpoint: First, earnings for the full fiscal year are attributed to the new entity regardless of the purchase date, which tends to inflate the surviving entity's true profit performance; and second, there are no intangible assets and consequently no amortization charges against income. In addition, any subsequent disposition of the pooled company's assets could produce additional profits in later years.

DEBT AND BORROWING ARRANGEMENTS

Debt is an important consideration for any company, so it follows logically that the note on debt and borrowing arrangements often contains critical information that investors can use in evaluating a company's debt position. Exhibit 8.1 illustrates the long-term debt note from Gannett Company's 1997 financials.

We see that the unsecured promissory notes, which constitute the bulk of the company's borrowings, are actually short-term (more flexible) borrowings, supported by a revolving credit agreement in the amount of $3 billion that extends to November 12, 2000. It is therefore classified as long-term debt. The weighted average interest rate (5.5 percent) on these borrowings was considerably below the prime rate (8.5 percent) for the dates in question. This relatively low cost of borrowing is indicative of Gannett's high credit quality and the de facto short-term structuring of these borrowings. Also, the note indicates that over the past three years, Gannett has not ever had to make maximum use of the credit available, which is another positive sign. Investors should carefully scrutinize restrictive covenants for their impact on a company's operations. It appears that the only restrictive covenant in place for Gannett is an obligation to maintain a net worth (shareholder's equity) position of at least $1.2 billion. In addition to the note's indication of compliance on this obligation, Gannett's balance sheet would also show us that its net worth at year-end 1997 was $3.5 billion, which provides ample margin to meet this condition.

The last piece of interesting data relates to the maturity profile on the debt. While its debt maturities are concentrated in the year 2000, the amount basically represents the revolving credit agreement mentioned above. It seems likely that Gannett will renew or restructure this debt with relative ease—a fairly safe bet based on Gannett's continued strong financial position, its use of the facility, and the general tendency to renew revolving credit facilities that have been properly handled, As an investor, I would like to know the institution(s) providing major credit facilities, but this information is seldom provided in a note. It should be; perhaps if enough of us ask, companies will be prompted to supply it.

A shelf registration, which does not appear in the Gannett note, is a liquidity and capital resources enhancement for a company. It means that the SEC has given prior approval to a company for the issuance of debt and/or equity securities to raise capital. A shelf registration of securities

EXHIBIT 8.1 • Note on Debt—Gannett Company

NOTE 4
Long-term debt
The long-term debt of the company is summarized below.

In thousands of dollars

	Dec. 28, 1997	Dec. 29, 1996
Unsecured promissory notes	$ 1,198,695	$ 1,339,078
Notes due 3/1/98, interest at 5.25%	274,920	274,401
Notes due 5/1/00, interest at 5.85%	249,787	249,695
Unsecured obligations	16,725	16,725
Other indebtedness	18,782	23,696
	1,758,909	1,903,595
Less amount included in current liabilities	(18,375)	(23,302)
Total long-term debt	$ 1,740,534	$ 1,880,293

The unsecured promissory notes at Dec. 28, 1997 were due from Dec. 31, 1997 to Jan. 27, 1998 with rates varying from 5.54% to 5.8%.

The unsecured promissory notes at Dec. 29, 1996 were due from Dec. 30, 1996 to Jan. 23, 1997 with rates varying from 5.35% to 5.65%.

The maximum amount of such promissory notes outstanding at the end of any period during 1997 was $1.3 billion and during 1996 was $2.2 billion. The daily average outstanding balance was $1.154 billion during 1997 and $1.873 billion during 1996. The weighted average interest rate was 5.5% for 1997 and 5.4% for 1996.

The unsecured obligations are due in 2008 to 2009 and bear interest at the PSA Municipal Index plus .25%. At Dec. 28, 1997 and Dec. 29, 1996 the weighted average interest rates were 4.4%.

At Dec. 28, 1997, the company had $3.0 billion of credit available under a revolving credit agreement. The agreement provides for a revolving credit period which permits borrowing from time to time up to the maximum commitment. The revolving credit period extends to Nov. 12, 2000.

EXHIBIT 8.1 • Note on Debt—Gannett Company, continued

The commitment fee rate may range from .07% to .175%, depending on Standard & Poor's or Moody's credit rating of the company's senior unsecured long-term debt. The rate in effect at Dec. 28, 1997 was .09%. At the option of the company, the interest rate on borrowings under the agreement may be at the prime rate, at rates ranging from .13% to .35% above the London Interbank Offered Rate or at rates ranging from .255% to .50% above a certificate of deposit-based rate. The prime rate was 8.5% at the end of 1997 and 8.25% at the end of 1996. The percentages that will apply will be dependent on Standard & Poor's or Moody's credit rating of the company's senior unsecured long-term debt.

The revolving credit agreement contains restrictive provisions that relate primarily to the maintenance of net worth of $1.2 billion. At Dec. 28, 1997 and Dec. 29, 1996, net worth was $3.5 billion and $2.9 billion, respectively.

At Dec. 28, 1997, the unsecured promissory notes and the notes due March 1, 1998 are supported by the $3.0 billion revolving credit agreement and, therefore, are classified as long-term debt.

Approximate annual maturities of long-term debt, assuming that the company had used the $3.0 billion revolving credit agreement as of the balance sheet date to refinance existing unsecured promissory notes and the notes due March 1, 1998, on a long-term basis, are as follows:

In thousands of dollars

1998	$ 18,375
1999	23
2000	1,723,404
2001	
2002	
Later years	17,107
Total	$ 1,758,909

For financial instruments other than long-term debt, including cash and cash equivalents, trade and other receivables, current maturities of long-term debt and other long-term liabilities, the amounts reported on the balance sheet approximate fair value.

The company estimates the fair value of its long-term debt, based on borrowing rates available at Dec. 28, 1997, to be $1.740 billion, compared with the carrying amount of $1.741 billion. At Dec. 29, 1996, the fair value of long-term debt was estimated at $1.877 billion, compared with a carrying amount of $1.880 billion.

allows a company to react quickly to unexpected needs or favorable capital market conditions to raise funds.

Last, if not mentioned in the MD&A report, commentary on a company's credit ratings are sometimes included in the debt note.

OPERATING LEASE COMMITMENTS

Operating leases allow a company to structure a lease so that it does not meet the definition of a capital lease, which is a type of long-term debt. Therefore, operating lease obligations don't appear in a company's balance sheet as a debt liability as do capital leases. It is what financial professionals refer to as off-balance sheet debt. Prudent determination of a company's long-term debt dictates that all or a portion of the future minimum payments required under noncancelable operating leases be considered as a component of a company's debt.

A note to a company's financials provides a way to assess a company's use of operating leases. Exhibit 8.2, for example, illustrates AMR Corporation's capital and operating lease information. Financial analysts use a rule of thumb that estimates approximately one-third of the total ($18.1 billion) for noncancelable operating leases relates to interest expense, and therefore the remaining two-thirds is considered long-term debt principal. Conservative analysis would include the whole amount as debt. Using AMR's note information and the two-thirds guideline, which is what I suggest investors use, the company's long-term debt would be adjusted to include an additional $12 billion in off-balance sheet debt to that formally recorded in its financials.

PENSION AND RETIREMENT BENEFITS

It has been estimated that companies owe more to their employees and retirees in health and pension obligations than they do to creditors. The difference between these obligations, if one assumes that a company is a going concern, is that pension and retirement benefits are a part of doing business. They will never go away or be completely paid off as long as companies have employees and continue to operate. Although they certainly constitute a corporate liability, most financial analysts would distinguish this type of obligation from a true debt liability. The note or notes on pension and retirement benefits are quite complex. I suggest, as a practical matter, that investors focus their attention on four fundamental aspects of employee benefits.

First, in recent years, companies, for the most part, have changed their employee benefit packages from a defined benefit to a defined contribution plan. The distinction between the two is subtle but important. The defined benefit package made it difficult to ascertain its liability obligation (how much will the benefit cost in the future) and consequently the future impact on its financial position. In contrast, the defined contribution approach (a specific dollar amount is predetermined) allows a company to exercise control over the extent of its liability and its subsequent financial impact.

EXHIBIT 8.2 • Note on Operating Leases—AMR Corporation

4. Leases

AMR's subsidiaries lease various types of equipment and property, including aircraft, passenger terminals, equipment and various other facilities. The future minimum lease payments required under capital leases, together with the present value of net minimum lease payments, and future minimum lease payments required under operating leases that have initial or remaining non-cancelable lease terms in excess of one year as of December 31, 1997, were (in millions):

Year Ending December 31,	Capital Leases	Operating Leases
1998	$ 255	$ 1,011
1999	250	985
2000	315	935
2001	297	931
2002	247	887
2003 and subsequent	1,206	13,366
	2,570[1]	$ 18,115[2]
Less amount representing interest	806	
Present value of net minimum lease payments	$ 1,764	

[1] Future minimum payments required under capital leases include $192 million guaranteed by AMR relating to special facility revenue bonds issued by municipalities.

[2] Future minimum payments required under operating leases include $6.2 billion guaranteed by AMR relating to special facility revenue bonds issued by municipalities.

At December 31, 1997, the Company had 186 jet aircraft and 44 turboprop aircraft under operating leases, and 82 jet aircraft and 63 turboprop aircraft under capital leases. The aircraft leases can generally be renewed at rates based on fair market value at the end of the lease term for one to five years. Most aircraft leases have purchase options at or near the end of the lease term at fair market value, but generally not to exceed a stated percentage of the defined lessor's cost of the aircraft or at a predetermined fixed amount.

During 1996, American made prepayments totaling $565 million on cancelable operating leases it had on 12 of its Boeing 767-300 aircraft. Upon the expiration of the amended leases, American can purchase the aircraft for a nominal amount. As a result, the aircraft are recorded as flight equipment under capital leases.

Rent expense, excluding landing fees, was $1.2 billion for 1997 and 1996 and $1.3 billion for 1995.

Second, investors should review the annual behavior of the pension expense amount. A fairly self-explanatory table is presented within the note and provides this information. Accelerating increases may be cause for concern in the future; otherwise, move on.

Third, determine if a company's plan assets at fair value exceed its projected benefit obligation. There is a table for this status. Obviously, an underfunded status, depending on the magnitude, could be cause for concern.

Fourth, look for consistency in the company's application of the actuarial assumptions for the discount rate, rate of return on assets, and the rate of compensation increases. You could also make intercompany comparisons in this regard. Management's selection of these rates directly affects the final outcome of its pension expense and liability. Reasonableness and consistency are the only practical guides for investors' evaluation of these assumptions.

BUSINESS SEGMENT INFORMATION

Until fiscal year 1997, diversified businesses with multilines or products have provided a breakdown of segments of the company by sales, operating profits, depreciation, and capital expenditures. In addition, if applicable, this same information has been provided on a geographic basis.

The Financial Accounting Standards Board's Statement No. 131, issued in June 1998, requires companies with fiscal years ending after December 15, 1998, to expand the income statement information they had been reporting previously in their business segment note. As this book is being written, no new business segment formats are as yet available. Nevertheless, the old format, which is used in Exhibit 8.3 for the business segment information from the 1997 notes to the financials for United Technologies, serves as a sufficient guide to illustrate the usefulness of this information for investors. We hope, the new format will be even better.

Among other helpful insights, being able to distinguish the strong and weak performers in a company's product line is valuable, and especially so if different industry sectors are involved. Obviously, an expansion of a low-margin market segment would contribute relatively little to a company's overall profitability. Growth rates in sales and earnings can be compared to the allocation of capital expenditures. Finally, profit margins and the return on assets can be identified for a company's various business segments.

COMMITMENTS AND CONTINGENCIES

Commitments differ materially from contingencies, although often they are discussed as one and the same. Commitments generally are quantifiable and represent proactive, positive positions of company management (e.g., proposed capital expenditures for the expansion of operating facilities). Contingencies, on the other hand, are much more uncertain in their ultimate consequences and, if they do occur, tend to adversely affect the company. The most common of these

EXHIBIT 8.3 • Business Segment Information—United Technologies

Business segment information for the three years ended December 31, 1997 follows:

BUSINESS SEGMENTS

IN MILLIONS OF DOLLARS	Total Revenues			Operating Profits		
	1997	1996	1995	1997	1996	1995
Otis	$ 5,548	$ 5,595	$ 5,287	$ 465	$ 524	$ 511
Carrier	6,056	5,958	5,456	458	422	354
UT Automotive	2,987	3,233	3,061	173	196	180
Pratt & Whitney	7,402	6,201	6,170	816	637	530
Flight Systems	2,862	2,651	2,947	285	234	209
Corporate items and eliminations	(142)	(126)	(119)	(23)	(21)	2
Total segment	$24,713	$23,512	$22,802	2,174	1,992	1,786
General corporate expenses and other				(215)	(211)	(198)
Interest expense				(195)	(221)	(244)
Consolidated income before income taxes and minority interests				$1,764	$1,560	$1,344

IN MILLIONS OF DOLLARS	Identifiable Assets			Capital Expenditures			Depreciation and Amortization		
	1997	1996	1995	1997	1996	1995	1997	1996	1995
Otis	$ 2,434	$ 2,712	$ 2,613	$143	$132	$115	$134	$116	$108
Carrier	3,618	3,387	2,959	143	169	151	148	145	134
UT Automotive	1,875	1,856	1,875	163	138	140	128	128	122
Pratt & Whitney	4,165	4,261	4,215	285	248	240	286	296	314
Flight Systems	1,544	1,416	1,425	92	86	106	121	123	127
Corporate items and eliminations	3,083	3,113	2,871	17	21	28	31	45	39
Total	$16,719	$16,745	$15,958	$843	$794	$780	$848	$853	$844

GEOGRAPHIC AREAS

IN MILLIONS OF DOLLARS	Total Revenues			Intergeographic Revenues			External Revenues		
	1997	1996	1995	1997	1996	1995	1997	1996	1995
United States operations	$15,127	$14,007	$13,968	$ 559	$ 592	$ 534	$14,568	$13,415	$13,434
International operations:									
Europe	4,961	4,977	4,769	173	177	170	4,788	4,800	4,599
Asia Pacific	3,330	3,395	3,024	378	353	317	2,952	3,042	2,707
Other	2,809	2,668	2,463	429	430	421	2,380	2,238	2,042
Corporate items and eliminations	(1,514)	(1,535)	(1,422)	(1,539)	(1,552)	(1,442)	25	17	20
Total	$24,713	$23,512	$22,802	$ —	$ —	$ —	$24,713	$23,512	$22,802

IN MILLIONS OF DOLLARS	Operating Profits			Identifiable Assets		
	1997	1996	1995	1997	1996	1995
United States operations	$1,176	$ 965	$ 773	$ 7,752	$ 7,252	$ 7,110
International operations:						
Europe	453	461	457	2,596	2,749	2,540
Asia Pacific	225	272	235	1,814	2,171	2,078
Other	343	310	321	1,467	1,454	1,357
Corporate items and eliminations	(23)	(16)	—	3,090	3,119	2,873
Total	$2,174	$1,992	$1,786	$16,719	$16,745	$15,958

events of potential liability relate to litigation, which is a routine circumstance for most companies given the litigious legal environment so prevalent in the United States.

A standard phrase in the contingency note states that the circumstance in question "will, in the opinion of management, result in no material loss to the company," or words to that effect. Investors should read this note carefully, however, and use their common sense. Environmental liability is a particularly sensitive area with some potentially large risks. As a rule of thumb, the longer and more complicated a note, the more likely that the contingency is a serious one. For example, 3M's contingency note in its 1997 financials has a split personality—the first part is routine, which is typical for most companies, and runs to three short paragraphs. The second part on breast implant litigation, runs more than two whole, single-spaced pages! In most instances like the latter, it is virtually impossible to quantify the risk described. And while it may appear to be self-serving, companies are rightfully reluctant to make estimates, particularly monetary ones, without full and complete information on the risk. For investors, evaluating the consequences of potentially damaging contingent liabilities becomes a judgment call: you can simply practice avoidance and look at other investment opportunities without these complications.

CHAPTER 9

The Independent Auditors' Report— What to Look For

Financial statements provide essential information about a company's financial position and performance. Because the preparation and presentation of this information is the responsibility of management, an audit lends credibility to a company's financial statements. Publicly listed companies must have audited financials. Suffice it to say that investors should only look at companies with audited statements. When a company's financials are accompanied by an auditors' report, you can be reasonably sure that management's accounting representations and the numbers in the financials are reliable. It is equally important, however, for investors to understand what an auditors' report does not represent. It is not

- an endorsement of a company's financial position;
- a 100 percent guarantee against material misstatement; or
- any indication that the company is a good investment or financially sound.

Do auditors sometimes make mistakes? Sure, and in instances involving large, highly visible companies, those mistakes make headlines. But, by and large, the accounting profession does a good job in the vast majority of its audits in providing reasonable assurance that a company's financial statements are reliable.

The auditors' reports illustrated in Exhibit 9.1 are conventional presentations, referred to as standard reports. Price Waterhouse, which just recently merged with Coopers Lybrand to become PricewaterhouseCoopers, has used a single-paragraph format instead of the more widely used three-paragraph format. With the merger, PricewaterhouseCoopers will be using both formats but with a stated preference for the single-paragraph approach. Both formats carry the same information as follows:

- The audited financial statements are identified.
- Management's and auditors' responsibilities are defined.

EXHIBIT 9.1 • Examples of Auditors' Reports

Report of Independent Public Accountants

To the Stockholders and
Board of Directors of Merck & Co., Inc.:

We have audited the accompanying consolidated balance sheet of Merck & Co., Inc. (a New Jersey corporation) and subsidiaries as of December 31, 1997 and 1996, and the related consolidated statements of income, retained earnings and cash flows for each of the three years in the period ended December 31, 1997. These financial statements are the responsibility of the Company's management. Our responsibility is to express an opinion on these financial statements based on our audits.

We conducted our audits in accordance with generally accepted auditing standards. Those standards require that we plan and perform the audit to obtain reasonable assurance about whether the financial statements are free of material misstatement. An audit includes examining, on a test basis, evidence supporting the amounts and disclosures in the financial statements. An audit also includes assessing the accounting principles used and significant estimates made by management, as well as evaluating the overall financial statement presentation. We believe that our audits provide a reasonable basis for our opinion.

In our opinion, the financial statements referred to above present fairly, in all material respects, the financial position of Merck & Co., Inc. and subsidiaries as of December 31, 1997 and 1996, and the results of their operations and their cash flows for each of the three years in the period ended December 31, 1997, in conformity with generally accepted accounting principles.

Arthur Andersen LLP

New York, New York   ARTHUR ANDERSEN LLP
January 27, 1998

EXHIBIT 9.1 • Examples of Auditors' Reports, continued

Report of Independent Accountants

Price Waterhouse LLP

To the Board of Directors and Shareholders
of The Goodyear Tire & Rubber Company

In our opinion, the accompanying consolidated balance sheet
and the related consolidated statements of income, shareholders' equity and cash flows present fairly, in all material
respects, the financial position of The Goodyear Tire &
Rubber Company and Subsidiaries at December 31, 1997
and 1996, and the results of their operations and their cash
flows for each of the three years in the period ended
December 31, 1997, in conformity with generally accepted
accounting principles. These financial statements are the
responsibility of the Company's management; our responsibility is to express an opinion on these financial statements
based on our audits. We conducted our audits of these statements in accordance with generally accepted auditing
standards which require that we plan and perform the audit
to obtain reasonable assurance about whether the financial
statements are free of material misstatement. An audit
includes examining, on a test basis, evidence supporting the
amounts and disclosures in the financial statements, assessing
the accounting principles used and significant estimates made
by management, and evaluating the overall financial statement presentation. We believe that our audits provide a
reasonable basis for the opinion expressed above.

Price Waterhouse LLP

Cleveland, Ohio
February 2, 1998

- The auditors attest to the accounting standards applied and that their audit results provide a reasonable basis for an opinion.
- The auditors provide an opinion of fair presentation of a company's financials based on generally accepted accounting principles (GAAP).

The vast majority of companies obtain a standard report like those for Merck and Goodyear in Exhibit 9.1. Any modification of, or addition to, the wording in a standard report is by definition a nonstandard report. In the "old days," the term *auditors' opinion* was used interchangeably with the term *auditors' report*. Today, the former now applies only to the third paragraph of the auditors' report; for PricewaterhouseCoopers, the opinion is the opening sentence. This apparently trivial distinction is important to investors.

In previous financial parlance, if the auditors gave a company a clean bill of health , their report was considered an unqualified (in accounting jargon, without any impairing, qualifying remarks) or clean opinion. If there was a problem, the auditors' report contained qualifying language such as "subject to" (the resolution of a problematical circumstance). This type of report was considered a qualified (in accounting jargon, with impairing, qualifying remarks) opinion and readily alerted the reader to a potential financial uncertainty or danger. Under the accounting profession's new opinion structure, which has been around for almost ten years, the explicit "subject to" qualifying language has been dropped. The auditors now simply disclose a company's problem (s) in the body of their report.

What does all this mean to investors? They should read the auditors' report more carefully. The auditors may issue an unqualified opinion—paragraph three or PricewaterhouseCoopers' first sentence—but add modifying language in an additional paragraph. Simply put, any nonstandard auditors' report requires reading additional remarks to assess their impact on a company's financials. Thus, my advice to investors is to read the auditors' report before digging into the financials; if it's in standard report form, it will take you less than 60 seconds. You can then move on to more serious analysis and number crunching with a high degree of confidence. Nonstandard report forms mandate further scrutiny.

THE NONSTANDARD AUDITORS' REPORT

Reference to the Report of Another Auditor

This type of reference occurs when a material portion of the audit work is performed by another auditing firm. Generally speaking, such nonstandard language shouldn't be a major concern because it's a rather benign qualifying remark. You will notice, however, that the original auditor always remains anonymous. While a change of auditors is seldom explained in corporate financial communications, investors should definitely find out why a change occurred.

Changes in Accounting Policies

This type of nonstandard wording implies that the company had reasonable justification for the change and that the auditors concur. If the auditors don't approve, they issue a qualified opinion because of the departure from GAAP. Changes in and/or additions to accounting policies are generally benign, but they can affect a company's financial condition and performance. In particular, profits can be affected, either beneficially or adversely, by such changes. Investors need to be alert to these effects, which usually are explained in the notes to the financials.

Material Uncertainties

A company or its auditors can't always reasonably estimate the financial consequences of material uncertainties. This additional language highlights such circumstances as unresolved lawsuits, debt arrangements, violations of or the loss of a major customer and/or market share. The prudent investor should view a material uncertainty paragraph as a definite red-flag warning that requires thorough investigation. Again some clues to the magnitude of the problem should be revealed in the notes to the financials.

Going-Concern Problems

This type of problem casts doubt on the ability of a company to stay in business. As a practical matter, investors generally will have read about any serious problem in the financial press long before the matter is dealt with in the auditors' report. Needless to say, investors should consider this language as a large black cloud over a company's future and proceed accordingly, which is to say, head for the exit!

Emphasis of a Matter

The auditors may wish to emphasize a matter in the financial statements but still wish to issue an unqualified opinion. Thus, an explanatory paragraph is added that discloses the matter to be emphasized. Generally speaking, this nonstandard wording doesn't indicate a problem and should normally not be of concern to investors.

Qualified Opinions

A number of circumstances can prompt auditors to use nonstandard language in the opinion part of their report A limitation in the scope of an audit, if the monetary consequence is not material, would be an example of a circumstance of little concern to investors. On the other hand, auditor disclaimers, departures from generally accepted accounting principles, and a material misstatement of a company's financial position are, obviously, grounds for serious concerns. It is most likely, here again, that these circumstances will have been known to the investing pubic long before reading about them in the auditors' report.

In sum, as a general rule an auditors' report, in its standard form, will provide investors with a reasonable assurance that a company's financials can be relied on. The report is not an unconditional guarantee of financial soundness; investors have to judge that for themselves. A nonstandard auditors' report requires some careful reading to determine what the underlying circumstances are that occasioned the additional language and their impact on a company's financial position and performance.

CHAPTER 10

Analyzing Modine Manufacturing Company's Financials

Modine Manufacturing Company manufactures and sells heat transfer equipment. Its line of products includes radiators; radiator cores; charge-air coolers and oil coolers for all types of engines; transmissions; auxiliary hydraulic equipment; air-conditioning components used in cars, trucks, farm, and construction equipment; and heating and cooling equipment for residential and commercial buildings. Its principal markets are automobile, truck, and bus manufacturers; construction contractors; wholesalers of plumbing and heating equipment; radiator repair shops; and wholesalers of auto repair parts.

I have chosen Modine for applying the investment evaluators discussed in the previous chapters to give you a different look. Modine is a medium-size company, a departure from Procter & Gamble and the other very large companies that comprise the G20 sample. Its financial statement presentations are uncomplicated and mainstream, and its smaller numbers are easier to work with than those of the G20 giants. For economy, I have included only Modine's most recent financials, as they appeared in its 1997–98 annual report, in Exhibits 10.1 to 10.3, even though our statement analysis goes back to the company's 1994 fiscal year. I include Modine's original financial statements to familiarize you with the origin of the numbers that go into the analytical worksheets presented in Exhibits 10.4 to 10.6. You'll notice that Modine's financial statement numbers are expressed in thousands, which I have further simplified to be expressed in millions in the worksheets. The accounts in Modine's balance sheets, income statements, and cash flow statements are coded with the line numbers from the worksheets as a guide to where the numbers go on a year-to-year comparative basis.

The analytical worksheets are often referred to by financial professionals as spreadsheets. Analysts use this type of worksheet to standardize the analysis of diverse financial statements of all different types of companies. These worksheets are a handy tool to organize financial statement information into a format that permits calculating any number of financial ratios and indicators to determine a company's financial position and performance over an extended period.

EXHIBIT 10.1 • Modine's Balance Sheet

Consolidated balance sheets

	(In thousands, except per-share amounts)	
March 31	**1998**	*1997*

Assets

Current assets:

Cash and cash equivalents **1**	**$ 36,410**	$ 34,822
Trade receivables, less allowance for doubtful accounts of $4,585 and $4,140 **3**	**162,177**	149,800
Inventories **5**	**152,674**	142,115
Deferred income taxes and other current assets **6**	**41,922**	39,405
Total current assets	**393,183**	366,142

Noncurrent assets:

Property, plant, and equipment — net **9**	**248,253**	210,115
Investment in affiliates **10**	**8,376**	9,497
Intangible assets — net **11**	**59,355**	62,948
Deferred charges and other noncurrent assets **10**	**49,857**	46,253
Total noncurrent assets	**365,841**	328,813
Total assets	**$759,024**	$694,955

Liabilities and shareholders' investment

Current liabilities:

Short-term debt **13**	**$ 20,878**	$ 2,962
Long-term debt — current portion **14**	**2,835**	14,061
Accounts payable **15**	**84,345**	72,173
Accrued compensation and employee benefits **16**	**48,081**	44,497
Income taxes **16**	**10,073**	7,535
Accrued expenses and other current liabilities **16**	**26,516**	28,771
Total current liabilities	**192,728**	169,999

Noncurrent liabilities:

Long-term debt **19**	**89,587**	85,197
Deferred income taxes **21**	**14,258**	13,331
Other noncurrent liabilities **21**	**39,976**	40,740
Total noncurrent liabilities	**143,821**	139,268
Total liabilities	**336,549**	309,267

Shareholders' investment:

Preferred stock, $0.025 par value, authorized 16,000 shares, issued — none	—	—
Common stock, $0.625 par value, authorized 80,000 shares, issued 30,342 shares	**18,964**	18,964
Additional paid-in capital	**12,384**	9,760
Retained earnings	**423,001**	378,740
Foreign currency translation adjustment	**(8,102)**	(3,016)
Treasury stock at cost: 678 and 509 common shares	**(20,977)**	(14,949)
Restricted stock — unamortized value	**(2,795)**	(3,811)
Total shareholders' investment **24**	**422,475**	385,688
Total liabilities and shareholders' investment	**$759,024**	$694,955

The notes to consolidated financial statements are an integral part of these statements.

EXHIBIT 10.2 • Modine's Income Statement

Consolidated statements of earnings

(In thousands, except per-share amounts)

For the years ended March 31	1998	1997	1996
Net sales **33**	$1,040,418	$999,046	$990,493
Cost of sales **34**	739,619	721,626	735,120
Gross profit	300,799	277,420	255,373
Selling, general, and administrative expenses **39**	183,323	176,552	161,082
Income from operations	117,476	100,868	94,291
Interest expense **41**	(4,010)	(4,972)	(6,825)
Other income — net **42**	2,506	1,887	11,683
Earnings before income taxes	115,972	97,783	99,149
Provision for income taxes **45**	43,501	34,020	37,750
Net earnings	$ 72,471	$ 63,763	$ 61,399
Net earnings per share of common stock			
Basic **49**	$2.44	$2.14	$2.07
Assuming dilution **50**	$2.39	$2.10	$2.03

The notes to consolidated financial statements are an integral part of these statements.

With a little bit of practice and patience, you can apply what you learned in previous chapters to this real-life financial statement analysis of Modine's balance sheet strength, profitability, and cash flow generation. It's this type of analysis that provides clues to a company's investment qualities. Whether you are a do-it-yourselfer or use investment information services, being conversant with this form of number crunching will help you develop keener investor insights and facilitate more informed investment decisions.

I have included blank forms of the worksheets in Appendix B that you can copy and use for your own purposes. In addition, instructions for computing various aggregate numbers, ratios, and indicators are provided. Computer-literate investors can set up their own computer-driven worksheets with this information. However, unless you have a high volume of analytical work, a standard calculator and a number-three pencil will also get the job done. As a way to get a feel for the task, I especially recommend this hands-on approach to those less experienced and without a financial background. One last word for beginners: there's a lot to learn about financial statement analysis, so you may not recognize or understand every account in a company's financials. Focus on the big numbers and don't worry about lesser accounts that you may have trouble classifying (e.g., placing them in the correct column) in the worksheets. You may make some mistakes, but they probably won't be fatal.

EXHIBIT 10.3 • Modine's Cash Flow Statement

Consolidated statements of cash flows

			(In thousands)
For the years ended March 31	**1998**	*1997*	*1996*
Cash flows from operating activities:			
Net earnings	**$ 72,471**	$ 63,763	$61,399
Adjustments to reconcile net earnings with cash provided by operating activities:			
Depreciation and amortization	**41,767**	41,504	39,641
Gain on sale of business	**—**	—	(5,009)
Pensions	**(2,256)**	(2,275)	(3,000)
Loss/(gain) from disposition of property, plant, and equipment	**837**	1,038	(1,852)
Deferred income taxes	**(91)**	(1,452)	(1,759)
Provision for losses on accounts receivable	**497**	(866)	(1,477)
Undistributed earnings of affiliates, net of dividends received	**679**	51	(1,202)
Other — net	**2,884**	1,184	1,421
	116,788	102,947	88,162
Change in operating assets and liabilities excluding acquisitions:			
Trade receivables	**(16,526)**	(7,851)	12,303
Inventories	**(13,236)**	3,889	(3,706)
Deferred income taxes and other current assets	**(2,781)**	(2,725)	(6,286)
Accounts payable	**13,855**	(1,819)	(2,716)
Accrued compensation and employee benefits	**3,724**	2,611	1,447
Income taxes	**3,081**	(1,000)	(1,996)
Accrued expenses and other current liabilities	**(1,977)**	4,178	(2,628)
Net cash provided by operating activities 53	**102,928**	100,230	84,580
Cash flows from investing activities:			
Expenditures for property, plant, and equipment 54	**(80,682)**	(54,529)	(55,689)
Acquisitions, net of cash acquired 57	**(2,604)**	(1,629)	(56,798)
Proceeds from sale of business	**—**	—	9,117
Proceeds from dispositions of assets	**1,927**	881	3,895
Investments in affiliates	**—**	(4,236)	—
Increase in deferred charges and other noncurrent assets	**(1,003)**	(1,805)	(296)
Other — net	**(200)**	(62)	13
Net cash (used for) investing activities	**(82,562)**	(61,380)	(99,758)
Cash flows from financing activities:			
Increase/(decrease) in short-term debt — net	**18,597**	(8,330)	(2,007)
Additions to long-term debt	**27,102**	25,925	69,967
Reductions of long-term debt	**(28,607)**	(15,681)	(45,861)
Issuance of common stock, including treasury stock	**4,567**	4,265	5,275
Purchase of treasury stock	**(16,990)**	(6,832)	(8,740)
Cash dividends paid 55	**(22,605)**	(20,292)	(17,802)
Other — net	**—**	(347)	(9)
Net cash (used for)/provided by financing activities	**(17,936)**	(21,292)	823
Effect of exchange-rate changes on cash	**(842)**	(694)	(378)
Net increase/(decrease) in cash and cash equivalents	**1,588**	16,864	(14,733)
Cash and cash equivalents at beginning of year	**34,822**	17,958	32,691
Cash and cash equivalents at end of year	**$ 36,410**	$ 34,822	$17,958
Cash paid during the year for:			
Interest, net of amounts capitalized	**$ 4,434**	$ 5,035	$ 6,849
Income taxes	**$ 37,715**	$ 34,428	$37,716

The notes to consolidated financial statements are an integral part of these statements.

GETTING STARTED

Let's say you had some general knowledge of Modine Manufacturing Company from Value Line and Standard & Poor's reports as well as from the company's latest annual report. By calling Modine's investor relations department, you obtained a recent history of press releases and the additional annual reports you needed to cover the five-year financial period you wanted to review. Modine's Form 10Ks would also contain this same information. You read the 1998 annual report's narrative text on the company's operations to get a feel for the business. Next, you checked the auditors' reports and found that except for some nonmaterial auditor comments in fiscal 1994, all the other annual audits were standard reports. Then you focused on the financials covering the most recent period, fiscal 1996–98, to get a general impression of the numbers in the balance sheet, income statement, and the cash flow statement, shown in Exhibits 10.1 through 10.3. Reading the relevant notes to the financial statements was an integral part of this exercise. You then coded the various accounts in Modine's financials with the appropriate line numbers from the worksheets, entering the amounts from the financial statements in the corresponding numbered lines in the worksheets for the balance sheet, income statement, and cash flow statement in Exhibits 10.4 through 10.6. After some adding, subtracting, multiplying, and dividing, the worksheets are completed.

WHAT DO ALL THESE NUMBERS TELL US ABOUT MODINE?

Using the investment evaluators we discussed in previous chapters, we are able to measure the company's balance sheet strength, profitability, and cash flow capacity over a sufficient period to make these measurements meaningful. To facilitate summary remarks on various financial indicators, I suggest using a point system to help you rank your overall financial evaluation. Don't get hung up on the preciseness of the ranking, which is meant to be a helpful guide and not some technically correct quantification of investment quality. Although based on quantitative data, the rankings are undeniably a subjective judgment. Here is the system I use in a review of Modine: excellent = 5; satisfactory plus = 4; satisfactory = 3; satisfactory minus = 2; and poor = 1. You can use a decimal with the ranking (e.g., 3.5) to indicate gradations of quality.

The Balance Sheet

The worksheet for Modine's balance sheet is found in Exhibit 10.4. For the period reviewed, Modine's balance sheet has grown almost 50 percent, from total assets of $510 million in 1994 to $759 million in 1998. Supporting this asset growth, the company's equity position has grown (68 percent) at more than double the rate of its liabilities (31 percent). As a consequence, and as we see later, the company has a very strong equity position with little debt to service. This circumstance, obviously, sends a positive message to investors.

EXHIBIT 10.4 • Balance Sheet Worksheet—Modine Manufacturing Co.

AMOUNTS IN: Millions (Except per share amounts)
FISCAL YEAR-END: March 31

CODE	BALANCE SHEET FISCAL YEAR	A 1994	B 1995	C 1996	D 1997	E 1998
	ASSETS					
1	Cash and Equivalents	39	33	18	35	36
2	Temporary Invested Funds					
3	Accounts Receivable	110	145	148	150	162
4	**Total Quick Assets**	149	178	166	185	198
5	Inventories	104	136	150	142	153
6	Other Current Assets	19	26	35	39	42
7	**Total Current Assets**	272	340	351	366	393
8	Noncurrent Invested Funds					
9	Property, Plant & Equipment	164	171	201	210	248
10	Other Noncurrent Assets	41	45	49	56	59
11	Intangible Assets	33	34	71	63	59
12	**Total Assets**	510	590	672	695	759
	LIABILITIES					
13	Short-Term Borrowings	11	14	12	3	21
14	Current Portion Long-Term Debt	11	11	13	14	3
15	Accounts Payable	56	74	77	72	84
16	Accrued Expenses	62	71	79	81	85
17	Other Current Liabilities					
18	**Total Current Liabilities**	140	170	181	170	193
19	Long-Term Debt	78	62	88	85	90
20	Redeemable Preferred Stock					
21	Noncurrent Liabilities	40	50	53	54	54
22	**Total Liabilities**	258	282	322	309	337
23	Minority Interest					
	EQUITY					
24	**Total Shareholders' Equity**	252	308	350	386	422
25	**Total Liabilities & Equity**	510	590	672	695	759
	INVESTMENT EVALUATORS					
26	Days Sales Outstanding (days)		51	54	55	54
27	Inventory Turnover (days)		68	72	73	74
	Operating Cycle (days)		119	116	128	128
	Fixed Asset Turnover (x)		5.4	5.3	4.9	4.5
	Return on Assets (%)		12.4	9.7	9.4	9.9
	Liability/ Asset Ratio (dcml)	.51	.51	.48	.45	.44
	Liability/ Equity Ratio (x)	1.0	1.0	.9	.8	.8
	Capitilazation Ratio (dcml)	.26	.26	.22	.20	.18
	Adj. Capitalization Ratio (dcml)	.29	.29	.25	.23	.20
	Book Value per Share ($ amt)	8.40	8.40	11.67	12.87	14.07
	NOTATIONAL DATA					
28	Operating Leases	14	14	14	14	12
29	Number of Common Shares	30	30	30	30	30
30	Net Sales	670	913	990	999	1,040
31	Cost of Sales	467	645	735	722	740
32	Net Income	44	68	61	64	72

Liquidity/efficiency indicators. To make a comprehensive judgment on Modine's liquidity, it's necessary to compare its operating cycle with competitor companies and/or industry standards. In general, Modine, for a manufacturer, appears to have a fairly good conversion of its accounts receivable and inventories to cash. (Refer to Exhibit 2.2 for comparisons of this indicator with other manufacturing companies in the G20 sample.) The consistency of its operating cycle results indicates efficient management of accounts receivable and inventories. On the other hand, this positive performance has taken place during a period of relatively slow growth in sales. Periods of fast growth are what really test management's capabilities in handling these important corporate assets. Also, the trend, while mild over the four-year period reviewed, has pushed the operating cycle upward. For now, I would give Modine a rank of 4 on liquidity/efficiency, and watch this measurement's performance closely in the coming years.

Indicator	1994	1995	1996	1997	1998
Days sales outstanding (days)	——	51	54	55	54
Inventory turnover (days)	——	68	72	73	74
Operating cycle (days)	——	119	116	128	128

Asset productivity. Modine's fixed asset turnover is quite good, particularly considering the restraining effect on this ratio of a relatively slow growth in sales and a fairly significant investment in property, plant, and equipment, particularly the 1995–98 period. It is not surprising, therefore, that the fixed asset turnover ratio has declined. Nevertheless, at the ratio's present level, Modine appears to be getting excellent productivity from its fixed asset investment. As a manufacturer, it again compares very favorably with companies of a somewhat similar nature shown in Exhibit 2.3, and very well over all.

Modine's asset growth has significantly outpaced its growth in earnings for the period reviewed, which, as a consequence, has tended to lower its return on assets. Nevertheless, the company's ROA ratio is quite respectable, better than the average registered by the G20 companies in Exhibit 2.3. I would rank Modine a 4 in asset productivity.

Ratio	1994	1995	1996	1997	1998
Fixed asset turnover (x)	——	5.4	5.3	4.9	4.5
Return on assets (%)	——	12.4	9.7	9.4	9.9

Leverage. Modine's very strong equity position and, as we will see further on, cash flow generation have amply supported the company's growth over the past five years. Its modest use of debt means that it has a very low leverage factor. All of Modine's leverage ratios are at the low end of the indebtedness scale and compare favorably with those of the prime name companies in the G20 sample in Exhibit 2.4. As a relatively debt-free company, Modine is extremely well positioned to undertake additional growth from a solid base that would permit it to tap debt capital, if needed, to finance acquisitions and/or a major expansion of its operations. For investors, this is a very positive aspect of Modine's balance sheet and one that warrants an excellent ranking—5—on the leverage factor.

Ratio	1994	1995	1996	1997	1998
Liability/Asset (%)	51	51	48	45	44
Liability/Equity (x)	1.0	1.0	0.9	0.8	0.8
Capitalization (dcml)	.26	.26	.22	.20	.18
Adjusted capitalization (dcml)	.29	.29	.25	.23	.20

Last, while book value per share is not a measurement used to judge the strength of a company's balance sheet, shareholders certainly like to see the intrinsic value, as opposed to the market value, of their investment increase. Even though Modine's profit generation has not been spectacular over the period reviewed, its shareholder base has remained stable, which has produced close to a 68 percent increase in book value per share from 1994 to 1998. This level of performance is quite good, particularly when considering Modine's relatively conservative financial position.

Indicator	1994	1995	1996	1997	1998
Book value per share ($ amt)	8.40	8.40	11.67	12.87	14.07

Summary Balance Sheet Evaluation

Assigning more weight to Modine's low leverage than to its liquidity and asset productivity indicators, I would rank its overall balance strength at the 4.5 level. The company has maintained a consistently strong balance sheet and is very well positioned to withstand adversity and/or take advantage of new opportunities—all positive investment qualities.

The Income Statement

The worksheet for Modine's income statement is found in Exhibit 10.5.

Sales and income growth. For the period reviewed, Modine's major growth in sales basically took place in one year, fiscal 1995. In the ensuing years, 1996–98, sales increases have been nominal. In the company's 1998 annual report, the management discussion and analysis section reveals that over 40 percent of Modine's sales are foreign, and they have suffered because of the foreign currency translation effect of the strong U.S. dollar. Over time, these foreign exchange impacts even out. What a company loses in one period (strong U.S. dollar), it gains in another (weak U.S. dollar). Nevertheless, the reasons for the general slowness in sales are not found in the income statement, which will only tell us what happened, not why. Investors will have to look to investment information services like Value Line and Standard & Poor's reports as well as company

EXHIBIT 10.5 • Income Statement Worksheet—Modine Manufacturing Co.

AMOUNTS IN: Millions (Except per share amounts)
FISCAL YEAR-END: March 31

CODE	INCOME STATEMENT FISCAL YEAR	A 1994	B 1995	C 1996	D 1997	E 1998
33	Sales/Revenues	670	913	990	999	1,040
34	Cost of Sales	-467	-645	-735	-722	-739
35	Gross Profit	203	268	255	277	301
36	Selling Expenses					
37	General & Administrative					
38	Research & Development					
39	Total Operating Expenses	-127	-156	-161	-176	-184
40	Operating Profit	76	112	94	101	117
41	Interest Expense	-6	-6	-7	-5	-4
42	Other Income	3	2	12	2	3
43	Other Expense					
44	Pretax Income	73	108	99	98	116
45	Provision for Taxes	-30	-40	-38	-34	-44
46	Minority Interest					
47	Special Items	1				
48	Net Income	44	68	61	64	72
49	Per Share—Basic	1.44	2.24	2.07	2.14	2.44
50	Per Share—Diluted	N.A.	N.A.	2.03	2.10	2.39
51	Number of Average Shares	30.5	30.5	30.3	30.4	30.3
	INVESTMENT EVALUATORS					
	Gross Profit Margin (%)	30	29	26	28	29
	Operating Profit Margin (%)	11	12	9	10	11
	Pretax Profit Margin (%)	11	12	10	10	11
	Net Margin (%)	7	7	6	6	7
	Return on Equity (ROE) (%)		24	19	17	18
	Return on Capital Empl.(ROCE) (%)		19	15	14	14
	Sales Growth (%)		+36	+8	+1	+4
	Net Income Growth (%)		+55	-10	+5	+13
	Sales per Share ($ amt)	21.97	29.93	32.67	32.86	34.32
	Earnings per Share ($ amt)	1.44	2.23	2.01	2.11	2.38

financial communications and the financial press for the whys of slow sales. Weak sales have meant weak growth in income.

As we will see in the following remarks, margin improvements have helped income to grow, which reflects well on management, but, in general, Modine has underperformed in the growth of its sales and earnings. The investment community likes to see earnings grow at a 10 to 15 percent annual rate. Accordingly, a ranking of 2.5 corresponds to this performance.

Indicator	1994	1995	1996	1997	1998
Sales growth (%)	——	+36	+8	+1	+4
Net income growth (%)	——	+55	−10	+5	+13

Profit margins. During the period, Modine's gross and operating profit margins dipped and then recovered to their previous historical levels. The behavior of the company's cost of sales and operating expenses (SG&A) indicates that management did a fairly good job in controlling costs, which allowed Modine to restore its return on sales (i.e., its net margin) to previous years' levels after losing ground for a couple of years.

Ratio	1994	1995	1996	1997	1998
Gross margin (%)	30	29	26	28	29
Operating margin (%)	11	12	9	10	11
Pretax margin (%)	11	12	10	10	11
Net margin (%)	7	7	6	6	7
Cost of sales (%)	70	71	74	72	71
Operating expenses (%)	19	17	16	18	18

Although Modine would not be considered a high-tech company, technological advances in its field are important to the company. It does not break out its research and development costs, which are part of its operating expenses, in its income statement. But investors who do their homework can find R&D expenses in the notes to Modine's financials. As you can see from the following illustration, Modine appears to have a strong commitment to its research and development activities, which is a positive sign for investors (amounts in millions):

Indicators	1994	1995	1996	1997	1998
R&D expense	9.5	10.9	14.5	16.8	16.8
Sales	670	913	990	999	1,040
R&D/Sales ratio (%)	1.4	1.2	1.5	1.7	1.6

Modine management has done a good job in squeezing as much profit as possible out of revenues. But the company's struggle for greater profitability is a classic example of the influence of the top line (i.e., sales) on the more familiar bottom line (i.e., net income). Investors need to be aware that because of the magnitude of the sales number, a small percentage improvement in the gross profit margin generates a lot of income, which, if operating expenses are managed well, passes through to the bottom line. Modine is not a high-margin business. It has managed to recoup its return on sales (net margin) within the context of a sluggish sales environment and merits a ranking of 4 in this component of profitability.

Last, the impact of taxes on net income is well illustrated by the Modine experience, which also provides a good example of why multiyear comparisons of performance are necessary. As can be seen in the calculation of Modine's effective tax rate, 1997's net income improved, albeit only slightly, entirely as a result of the change in the provision for taxes. Pretax income in 1997 was $98 million compared with $99 million in 1996, but the effective tax rate dropped from 38 percent in 1996 to 35 percent in 1997, producing a positive year-to-year performance for net income. If the 38 percent rate had been applied to 1997's pretax income, that year's net income would have dropped to $61 million, which would have been a flat year-to-year earnings comparison. In the sports world, the breaks are supposed to even out; and maybe the same happens to companies. In 1998, Modine's effective tax rate popped back up to 38 percent. If the 1997 effective tax rate of 35 percent had been operative, the company would have netted $75.4 million instead of $72 million. This may not seem like much of a difference, but earnings per share would have been improved from the recorded $2.38 to $2.49—a big difference that would attract interest from the investment community.

Ratio	1994	1995	1996	1997	1998
Effective tax rate (%)	41	37	38	35	38

Return on equity and on capital employed. Even though Modine's ROE and ROCE ratios have declined over the past five years, they still register enviable percentages. The company's return on equity is especially impressive because of its very low use of leverage. Qualitatively, Modine's ROE is very strong and is confirmed by its relatively high ROCE ratios, which combine debt and equity as the base for measuring profitability. Investors are well served with ROE and ROCE ratios in the range of 15 to 20 percent and 10 to 15 percent, respectively. Modine's otherwise excellent ranking in these profitability indicators gets clipped to 4.5 because of the declining trend evidenced in the 1994–98 period.

Ratios	1994	1995	1996	1997	1998
Return on equity (%)	——	24	19	17	18
Return on capital employed (%)	——	19	15	14	14

Sales and earnings per share. Everyone likes to see sales and earnings per share increase. It is important for investors, however, to take note how this increase is accomplished. If stock buybacks shrink the number of shares outstanding and revenue/earnings stay the same, these indicators show improvement. There's nothing wrong with that, and it generally helps boost a company's stock price. However, it is far better to witness a real growth in sales and earnings as opposed to a managed decrease of shares outstanding. Modine's share base has remained relatively stable, which means that it has not materially affected the company's per share profitability indicators.

From what we already know about Modine's sales performance in the past four years, it's not surprising that its sales per share performance has been somewhat flat. The same can be said about earnings and earnings per share. A ranking here of 2.5 simply parallels that for the overall weak performance of sales and earnings growth discussed above.

Indicator	1994	1995	1996	1997	1998
Sales per share ($ amt)	21.97	29.93	32.67	32.86	34.32
Earnings per share ($ amt)	1.44	2.23	2.01	2.11	2.38

Summary Income Statement Evaluation

Modine's profitability indicators are generally positive, and the company appears to be poised for better performance, having recouped its margin positions as of fiscal 1998. Assuming that it maintain this status, a little help from increased sales would do wonders for future profits. For now, Modine's income statement profitability indicators warrant a ranking of 3.5.

The Cash Flow Statement

The worksheet for Modine's cash flow statements is found in Exhibit 10.6.

Operating cash flow. The Modine's operating cash flow evidences steady annual increases since 1995 and a fairly stable percentage of total sales, which is a positive indicator of the stability of its cash conversion capability and operating cycle.

Ratio	1994	1995	1996	1997	1998
Operating cash flow/Sales ratio (%)	11	7	9	10	10

Capital expenditures. From 1994 to 1999, Modine invested $255 million in new property, plant, and equipment. In the previous five-year period, 1989 to 1993, its capital expenditures, as reported in its 1998 annual report, amounted to just $104 million. A high level of capital investment, coupled with a commitment to research and development, generally pays off for investors down the road. Operating cash flow always covered capital expenditures, even at Modine's relatively high level of investment.

EXHIBIT 10.6 • Cash Flow Statement Worksheet—Modine Manufacturing Co.

AMOUNTS IN: Millions (Except per share amounts)
FISCAL YEAR-END: March 31

CODE	CASH FLOW STATEMENT FISCAL YEAR	A 1994	B 1995	C 1996	D 1997	E 1998
52	Sales	670	913	990	999	1,040
53	Operating Cash Flow	75	67	85	100	103
54	Capital Expenditures	-29	-34	-56	-55	-81
55	Dividends Paid	-14	-15	-18	-20	-23
56	Free Cash Flow	32	18	11	25	-1
57	Business Acquisitions	-19	0	9	0	0
58	Short-Term Debt	22	25	25	17	24
59	Total Debt	114	101	127	116	126
	INVESTMENT EVALUATORS					
	Operating Cash Flow/Sales (%)	11	7	9	10	10
	Cap. Expenditures/ Op. Cash Flow (%)	39	51	66	55	79
	Dividends/ Op. Cash Flow (%)	19	22	21	20	22
	Cap. Expd.+ Div./ Op. Cash Flow (%)	57	73	87	75	101
	Free Cash Flow/ Op. Cash Flow (%)	43	27	13	25	N.M.
	Op. Cash Flow/ Short-term Debt (x)	3.4	2.7	3.4	5.9	4.3
	Op. Cash Flow/ Total Debt (%)	66	66	67	86	82
	Cash Flow per Share ($ amt)	2.46	2.20	2.81	3.29	3.40
	Dividends per Share ($ amt)	0.46	0.49	0.66	0.66	0.76

Ratio	1994	1995	1996	1997	1998
Capital expenditures/Operating cash flow (%)	39	51	66	55	79

Dividends paid. Modine has paid dividends since 1959. A long history of dividend payments, in this case a near 40-year record qualifies, and a steadily increasing rate of payment, as evidenced in the period reviewed, are very positive investment qualities. The company's dividend payment has been amply covered by operating cash flow.

Ratio	1994	1995	1996	1997	1998
Cash dividends paid (%)	19	22	21	20	22

Free cash flow. Modine barely missed racking up five straight years of positive free cash flow. Here again, its performance is impressive. It has spent heavily on capital improvements and increased its dividend payments, all of which have been covered until a minor shortfall in 1998, by internally generated funds.

Ratio	1994	1995	1996	1997	1998
Cap. expd. + Div/Operating cash flow (%)	57	73	87	75	101
Free cash flow/Operating cash flow (%)	43	27	13	25	−1

Operating cash flow and debt. As a function of good cash flow and low debt, Modine's operating cash flow coverage of both short-term and total debt is considered to be at the high end of the scale.

Ratio	1994	1995	1996	1997	1998
Operating cash flow/ Short-term debt (x)	3.4	2.7	3.4	5.9	4.3
Operating cash flow/Total debt (%)	66	66	67	86	82

Cash flow and dividends per share. Modine's stable balance of shares outstanding and its record of paying dividends and generating good cash flows, as discussed above, have produced positive cash flow and dividend per share performance for investors.

Indicator	1994	1995	1996	1997	1998
Cash flow per share ($ amt)	2.46	2.20	2.81	3.29	3.40
Dividends per share ($ amt)	0.46	0.49	0.66	0.66	0.76

Summary Cash Flow Evaluation

Modine's 1994–98 cash flow statements send investors a most positive message. The company is internally generating a considerable amount of cash, which explains a very low use of debt capital. At the same time, it is paying a decent dividend and investing heavily in its physical plant. Once capital expenditures level off, and even if sales only increase modestly, the company will generate significant free cash flow, which it can use for acquisitions and further expansion of its business. Both past and expected future cash flows qualify Modine for a high overall cash flow 4.5 ranking.

Market Valuation Indicators

Market valuation ratios are not generally related to financial statement analysis. And this information is generally accessed by investors from various investment information services. Investors can, however, calculate their own market valuation indicators from the per share data in the worksheets and by obtaining year-end stock price quotes directly from the company or Internet online sources. Here are the calculations for Modine (price data are fiscal year-end):

Ratio	1994	1995	1996	1997	1998
Price/Earnings per share	17.2	15.0	13.2	11.6	14.6
Price/Sales per share	1.1	1.1	0.8	0.7	1.0
Price/Cash flow per share	10.1	15.2	9.4	7.5	10.2
Price/Book value per share	2.9	4.0	2.3	1.9	2.5

SUMMARY ANALYSIS OF MODINE'S FINANCIALS

In the beginning of this chapter, I posed the question, "What do all these numbers tell us about Modine?" Using the worksheets, we have completed an analysis of the company's financial statements and have uncovered a number of financial ratios and indicators that tell us quite a bit about its operations and investment qualities. Applying the qualifying rankings I have used to measure Modine's financials, the summary evaluation is very positive. In brief, Modine has a strong balance sheet. There is room for improvement in the income statement, but there is some fundamental strength in its margin positions, which, if maintained, could improve profitability with only a modest increase in sales. Last, the quality of Modine's cash flow performance matches its balance sheet strength and provides a solid foundation to the company's plans for growth and expansion. An investment decision on a company's stock involves more elements than just an appraisal of its financials. Nevertheless, a highly ranked financial position is an essential starting point for identifying quality companies that have long-term investment potential.

CHAPTER 11

Bank Financial Statements

Banks are an important part of the universe of corporate investment opportunities. Financial institutions make up 17 percent of the total amount of companies in the Standard & Poor's 500 Index. Investment legend and author Peter Lynch popularized the concept of common knowledge as a tool for individual investors to identify investing opportunities. I would venture to guess that most, if not all, of the investing public is familiar with a bank and how it functions, at least in a general way. Residents in market areas with local and community banks who have an interest in financial services have a unique investment opportunity. I refer to the direct access they have to and/or the acquaintance with the owners and managers of these institutions as well as firsthand knowledge of the bank's market and customer base. According to a *Forbes* article (May 18, 1998), money manager David Harvey of Everest Partners, L.P., has made a career of finding obscure bank stocks. His advice to individual investors is to "look at the banks within an hour's drive of your home" and "avoid paying more than 15 times earnings or 2 times book value."

Investors will find that bank financial statements are radically different from those of manufacturers, retailers, wholesalers, or service providers. If, after struggling with all the material in the preceding chapters, that seems like bad news, the good news is that bank financial statements have a fairly standardized format, are much easier to understand, and require readers to be concerned with only two statements—the balance sheet and the income statement. Because the business of banks is cash flow (i.e., the intermediation of funds between borrowers and depositors), the cash flow statement is not used in the financial analysis of banks. So compared with a nonfinancial company, an investor's analytical workload is reduced by one-third! Nevertheless, when investors are evaluating banks, they need to read the notes to the financials, the commentary in the MD&A section, and the auditors' report just as they do with nonfinancial companies.

Bank financial statement analysis is not just for investors. Large depositors and/or businesses that are dependent on bank loans to support their operations can use the investment evaluators, which are discussed in Chapter 12, to determine the strength and dependability of the financial institutions they work with.

I have chosen the financials of Boston-based Fleet Financial Group, a major regional bank and diversified financial services company operating principally in the northeastern part of the United States, to explain the components of bank balance sheets and income statements. Exhibits 11.1 and 11.5 use Fleet's statements as they appeared in its 1997 annual report. Investors should be aware that bank annual reports and Forms 10-K contain a wealth of supplemental information that is valuable for financial statement analysis purposes. I've coded the statements in the figures because the code numbers are a reference for completing the bank financial statement worksheets in the next chapter.

A BANK'S BALANCE SHEET

Assets

Cash, due from banks and interest-bearing deposits. Fleet recorded $4,983 million in this account in 1997. Cash, for obvious reasons, is a major holding for banks. In addition, for correspondent banking purposes, as well as for maintaining regulatory cash reserve requirements, banks maintain accounts with other banks. These accounts with other banks in banking parlance are referred to as due from as opposed to the due to accounts (i.e., other banks' accounts with Fleet) that we find in Fleet's liabilities. Due from accounts are generally maintained on an as-needed basis with prime banks in major cities located regionally, nationally, and internationally. If a bank is experiencing a period of excess liquidity, funds will be placed in interest-bearing deposits rather than leaving the money idle (i.e., unproductive) in a bank account.

Federal funds sold and securities purchased under agreements to repurchase. On a day-to-day basis, a bank can experience a deficit or surplus of *federal funds,* the term applied to the cash reserves a bank must maintain on all or portions of its deposits. The Federal Reserve Bank sets the rules, which currently call for a 10 percent reserve on demand deposits (checking accounts). According to their reserve needs and availabilities, banks trade these funds between themselves for short periods, generally a matter of days, on a regular basis and earn interest on these placements. The same sort of thing happens with securities when a bank has short-term liquidity and wants to earn interest on the funds. It purchases a security, which could be a 90-day Treasury bill, for 15 days and agrees to sell it back to the provider, generally another bank. The bank on the other end of the transaction may have needed some cash for 15 days, which prompted its sale for that period. Repurchase agreements, or "repos" as bankers call them, work both ways and are a commonly used mechanism to help banks manage their liquidity positions. Just like federal funds, securities are bought and sold under agreements to resell and purchase. And as is the case with Fleet, both types of transactions can go on at the same time. As of its 1997 year-end, Fleet's net position on

EXHIBIT 11.1 • Bank Balance Sheet—Fleet Financial Group

Consolidated Balance Sheets

December 31
Dollars in millions, except share amounts

	1997	*1996*
Assets		
Cash, due from banks and interest-bearing deposits **1**	$ 4,983	$ 7,243
Federal funds sold and securities purchased under agreements to resell **2**	498	1,772
Securities (market value: **$9,367** and $8,675) **2**	9,362	8,680
Loans **4**	61,179	58,844
Reserve for credit losses **5**	(1,432)	(1,488)
Net loans **6**	59,747	57,356
Mortgages held for resale **8**	1,526	1,560
Mortgage servicing rights **8**	1,768	1,566
Premises and equipment **7**	1,184	1,347
Intangible assets **8**	2,137	1,699
Other assets **8**	4,330	4,295
Total assets **9**	$85,535	$85,518
Liabilities		
Deposits:		
Demand	$13,148	$ 17,903
Regular savings, NOW, money market	30,485	27,976
Time	20,102	21,192
Total deposits **10**	63,735	67,071
Federal funds purchased and securities sold under agreements to repurchase **11**	3,635	2,871
Other short-term borrowings **11**	3,268	756
Accrued expenses and other liabilities **12**	2,363	2,291
Long-term debt **14**	4,500	5,114
Total liabilities **15**	77,501	78,103
Stockholders' equity		
Preferred stock	691	953
Common stock (**263,239,019** shares issued in 1997 and 263,395,054 shares issued in 1996)	3	3
Common surplus	3,242	3,145
Retained earnings	4,105	3,342
Net unrealized gain on securities available for sale	97	31
Treasury stock, at cost (**1,922,334** shares in 1997 and 1,402,930 shares in 1996)	(104)	(59)
Total stockholders' equity **16**	8,034	7,415
Total liabilities and stockholders' equity **17**	$85,535	$85,518

See accompanying Notes to Consolidated Financial Statements.

federal funds bought/sold and securities resold/repurchased was that of a user of funds to bolster its liquidity—$498 million sold compared with $3,635 million purchased.

Securities. Banks invest in a variety of securities, mainly debt instruments issued by the U.S. government and by state and municipal authorities, from concern about liquidity, asset/liability management, and risk strategies. The investment of a portion of the funds at a bank's disposal in high-grade securities, which can be quickly converted to cash, is considered a prudent bank management practice. Loan assets, however good their quality, don't enjoy that level of dependability. The lower the percentage of securities as a component of a bank's total assets, the higher the risk of the bank's asset position. However, the downside of extreme safety, a large position in securities, is lower earnings. Loans generate much more income with interest and fees than do the securities generally found in a bank's portfolio.

Securities are classified in a bank's balance sheets according to how management intends to use these investments. At the time of purchase, securities are categorized as "available for sale" (to be held for an indefinite period and used as an asset/liability management tool), "held to maturity" (to be held for pure investment return), and "trading account" (held for sale for trading profits). In Fleet's balance sheet, securities are stated in the aggregate, $9,362 million, and broken down in a note to the financials. The notation for market value ($9,367 million in 1997) acknowledges an accounting rule that requires banks to record available-for-sale and trading securities at fair market value, while held-to-maturity securities are recorded at cost. The notation simply provides information on any valuation differences, which normally shouldn't be great but could be.

In banking parlance, the sum of a bank's cash and due from bank's, federal funds sold, securities purchased under agreements to resell, and amounts for the sale, trading, and investment of securities are referred to as primary assets—the equivalent of a nonfinancial company's quick assets. They represent cash or holdings that are presumed to be readily convertible to cash with little or no loss in value as recorded in the balance sheet. For banks, primary assets are generally considered to be no-risk assets and/or very low risk assets.

Loans, reserve for credit losses, and net loans. As these account captions imply, they summarize the carrying values of a bank's lending activities. In some instances, just the net loan figure is provided and the breakdown is provided in a note to the financials. Also, there is usually a note like the one in Exhibit 11.2 that provides a profile of the various aspects of a bank's consumer and commercial lending activities.

Fleet's approximately $61.2 billion gross loans are reduced by a reserve or allowance for potential loan losses ($1.4 billion) to a net figure of $59.7 billion. As we learned previously, in the world of commerce some customers don't pay, and companies anticipate these circumstances by creating a cushion to absorb real losses on money owed them. In the lending business, loan losses are a fact of life, but don't confuse a bank's reserve/allowance for credit losses, as it appears in its balance sheet, with actual losses. An important note to every bank's financials provides critical information to explain its actual loan loss experience.

EXHIBIT 11.2 • General Note on Loan Portfolio—Fleet

Note 4.

Loans

December 31
Dollars in millions

	1997	1996	1995	1994	1993
Loans:					
Commercial and industrial	**$32,238**	$ 29,278	$23,251	$ 19,675	$19,031
Residential real estate	**10,019**	8,048	11,475	8,529	7,378
Consumer	**9,869**	12,454	9,556	10,893	10,229
Commercial real estate:					
Construction	**890**	1,074	606	666	637
Interim/permanent	**4,787**	5,379	4,414	4,789	5,279
Loans, net of unearned income	**57,803**	56,233	49,302	44,552	42,554
Lease financing:					
Lease receivables	**3,342**	2,587	2,267	1,765	1,291
Estimated residual value	**936**	688	520	212	165
Unearned income	**(902)**	(664)	(564)	(494)	(297)
Lease financing, net of unearned income[a]	**3,376**	2,611	2,223	1,483	1,159
Total loans net of unearned income	**$61,179**	$58,844	$51,525	$46,035	$43,713

[a] The corporation's leases consist principally of full-payout, direct financing leases. The corporation's investment in leverage leases totaled $935 million and $644 million for 1997 and 1996, respectively. For federal income tax purposes, the corporation has the tax benefit of depreciation on the entire leased unit and interest on the long-term debt. Deferred taxes arising from leverage leases totaled $503 million in 1997 and $344 million in 1996. Future minimum lease payments to be received are $575 million in 1998; $488 million, 1999; $426 million, 2000; $320 million, 2001; $244 million, 2002; $1,289 million, 2003, and thereafter.

Total loans increased $2.3 billion from $58.8 billion at December 31, 1996 to $61.2 billion at December 31, 1997. Excluding the sale of the $2.2 billion indirect auto lending portfolio, loans and leases increased $4.5 billion, or 8.0%, over December 31, 1996, due primarily to growth in the commercial and industrial portfolio, lease financings and purchases of residential mortgages.

Concentrations of Credit Risk. Although the corporation is engaged in business nationwide, the lending done by the banking subsidiaries is primarily concentrated in New England, New York and New Jersey.

EXHIBIT 11.3 • Note on Reserve for Loan Losses—Fleet

Note 5.

Reserve for Credit Losses

Year ended December 31 *Dollars in millions*	**1997**	*1996*	*1995*
Balance at beginning of year	**$1,488**	$1,321	$1,496
Provision charged to income	**322**	213	101
Loans charged off	**(514)**	(484)	(418)
Recoveries of loans charged off	**138**	114	116
Acquisitions/other	**(2)**	324	26
Balance at end of year	**$1,432**	$1,488	$1,321

The reserve for credit losses decreased $56 million from December 31, 1996, to $1.432 billion at December 31, 1997. The 1997 provision for credit losses was $322 million, $109 million higher than the prior year level of $213 million. The increase in the provision for credit losses was due primarily to a higher level of bankruptcies and delinquencies related to the consumer loan portfolio.

EXHIBIT 11.4 • Note on Nonperforming Assets—Fleet

Note 6.

Nonperforming Assets

December 31 *Dollars in millions*	**1997**	*1996*	*1995*	*1994*	*1993*
Nonperforming loans and leases:					
Current or less than 90 days past due	**$216**	$264	$ 157	$186	$ 254
Noncurrent	**176**	432	283	480	584
OREO	**24**	27	59	95	200
Total NPAs[a]	**$416**	$723	$499	$761	$1,038
NPAs as a percent of outstanding loans and OREO	**.68%**	1.23%	0.97%	1.65%	2.35%
Accruing loans contractually past due 90 days or more	**$202**	$247	$198	$139	$ 120

[a] Excludes $214 million, $265 million, and $317 million of NPAs classified as held for sale or accelerated disposition at December 31, 1997, 1996, and 1995, respectively.

Nonperforming assets (NPAs) decreased $307 million from December 31, 1996 to December 31, 1997, due primarily to declining levels of nonperforming assets in all loan and OREO portfolios as a result of the successful resolution of certain commercial and industrial and commercial real estate loans, as well as $231 million of nonperforming assets transferred to assets held for sale or accelerated disposition.

Fleet's note, as illustrated in Exhibit 11.3, is typical and can be easily understood. You will see that the bank ended 1996 with a balance in its reserve for credit losses of $1.5 billion, which logically becomes 1997's beginning balance for the reserve. In 1997 Fleet charged, or provisioned, $322 million against income and added this amount to the reserve. Why $322 million? Because in management's view, after a close look at its loan portfolio, the general credit environment, and its existing reserve balance, this amount was the appropriate one. It is a management judgment call, albeit one that involves a considerable amount of time and effort. Next come the actual loan write-offs that as loans charged off reduce the reserve by $514 million. Banks work hard at recovering loans that have been previously written off; sometimes it takes years, but when borrowers finally make good or guaranties and collateral provide repayment amounts, these amounts are added back to the reserve as recoveries of loans charged off ($138 million). After possible other adjusting entries, positive or negative, an end-of-year loan loss reserve balance ($1,432) remains.

Another note to the financials that is important for understanding the quality of a bank's loan assets is the note on nonperforming assets, as illustrated for Fleet in Exhibit 11.4, that discloses a bank's problem loans. These loans are classified as such by the bank itself and/or by direction of state and federal bank examiners that make periodic, unannounced reviews of a bank's operations, particularly the credit function. Nonperforming loans are loans that are not accruing interest, and payment in full is in doubt. They can be past due or current, but if the credit quality of the borrower is materially impaired, the loan will be classified as nonperforming. You don't have to be a banking expert to recognize that loan charge-offs come from this category of asset. So fewer and/or a declining proportion of nonperforming loans to total loans is what an investor wants to see. As with loan charge-offs, it is the trend of nonperforming loans that is important to monitor.

Related to nonperforming loans is real estate owned, which is also captioned as OREO for other real estate owned. This asset sometimes appears as a balance sheet asset account. There's nothing yummy about these OREOs—they represent real estate that was used by borrowers as loan collateral and subsequently acquired by the bank through foreclosure proceedings when borrowers defaulted on their loan payments. OREOs are the kind of asset that you don't want to see too much of in a bank's balance sheet.

A number of ratios use nonperforming loan information to evaluate the asset quality of a bank's loan portfolio. It's easy to do, and for investors in bank stocks, it's a key investment evaluator. A bank's loan portfolio is its single largest asset and, in essence, the key to its financial position and performance.

Other asset accounts. Generally, the balance sheet accounts following the loan data are not consequential and have no particular impact on any evaluative considerations. In the case of Fleet, these accounts cover its mortgage resale and servicing business, its premises and equipment, intangibles, and miscellaneous assets.

Total assets. The sum of primary, net loan, and other assets.

Liabilities

Deposits. A breakdown is usually provided by the type of deposit—demand (checking accounts), savings, interest-bearing (NOW and money market accounts), certificates of deposit (CDs), and other forms of time deposits—and summed up as total deposits. For Fleet, this amounts to $63.7 billion.

Federal funds purchased and securities sold under agreements to repurchase. This is the flip side of the asset account whereby a bank is obtaining funds to boost its liquidity and/or for asset/liability management purposes.

Other short-term borrowings. As the account caption implies, borrowings other than those represented by the use of "fed" funds purchased and securities sold are recorded here. Many of the larger banks tap the financial markets (commercial paper) to raise flexible, short-term funds at relatively low interest rates. Fleet has obtained $3.3 billion from such sources.

Long-term debt. Here again, typically, the larger banks have access to longer-term capital under a variety of borrowing mechanisms, and it is in this account that such obligations are recorded. Fleet records $4.5 billion in its balance sheet. A look at Chase Bank's balance sheet in Exhibit 12.1 in Chapter 12 shows one of the all-time great examples of financial jargon used to describe one of Chase's long-term debt obligations—"Guaranteed Preferred Beneficial Interests in Corporation's Junior Subordinated Deferrable Interest Debentures." The acronym—GPBICJSDID—looks like someone's forced attempt at a triple word score in a Scrabble game!

Accrued expenses and other liabilities. Fleet's $2.4 billion in this entry represents a catch-all account for a variety of operational obligations.

Total liabilities. For a bank, total liabilities cover major obligations to depositors and creditors for borrowed funds and, to a much lesser degree, to employees/vendors for goods and services needed to run the bank.

Shareholders' Equity

There is little difference between the equity section of a nonfinancial company and that of a financial institution. Capital stock, additional paid-in capital, and retained earnings comprise the major components of equity. These accounts are followed by adjustments, typically involving treasury stock and unrealized gain (loss) on securities available for sale. As mentioned previously, the latter account records the effect of adjusting the cost of the securities in this category to market value.

Investors should note that in the language of banking, the terms *equity* and *capital,* or capital funds, are synonymous. Evaluations of a bank's equity position use such terms as *capital adequacy* and *capital ratios* to measure various equity relationships with other financial statement elements (discussed in Chapter 12).

EXHIBIT 11.5 • Bank Income Statement—Fleet Financial Group

Consolidated Statements of Income

Year ended December 31 Dollars in millions, except per share amounts	1997	1996	1995
Interest and fees on loans	$5,259	$5,087	$4,721
Interest on securities	589	755	1,304
Total interest income **18**	5,848	5,842	6,025
Interest expense:			
Deposits	1,654	1,754	1,726
Short-term borrowings	229	295	801
Long-term debt	338	390	478
Total interest expense **19**	2,221	2,439	3,005
Net interest income **20**	3,627	3,403	3,020
Provision for credit losses **23**	322	213	101
Net interest income after provision for credit losses	3,305	3,190	2,919
Noninterest income:			
Service charges, fees and commissions	633	537	442
Investment services revenue	418	372	322
Mortgage banking revenue, net	327	372	321
Student loan servicing fees	101	98	72
Trading revenue	74	55	39
Venture capital revenue	71	106	36
Securities gains	33	43	32
Net gains on sales of business units	175	–	–
Other	415	430	401
Total noninterest income **21**	2,247	2,013	1,665
Noninterest expense:			
Employee compensation and benefits **24**	1,591	1,607	1,448
Occupancy	282	284	250
Equipment	274	266	209
Intangible asset amortization	163	135	105
Legal and other professional	112	131	102
Marketing **25**	97	97	93
Merger and restructuring-related charges	–	–	490
Loss on assets held for sale or accelerated disposition	–	–	175
Other	862	752	678
Total noninterest expense **26**	3,381	3,272	3,550
Income before income taxes **27**	2,171	1,931	1,034
Applicable income taxes **29**	868	792	424
Net income **30**	$1,303	$1,139	$ 610
Diluted weighted average common shares outstanding (in millions)	261.8	268.2	264.3
Net income applicable to common shares	$1,241	$1,067	$ 416
Basic earnings per share	4.89	4.06	1.71
Diluted earnings per share	4.74	3.98	1.58

See accompanying Notes to Consolidated Financial Statements.

The Income Statement

Fleet's income statement for 1997 is shown in Exhibit 11.5, which we'll follow to understand the dynamics of Fleet's income.

Interest income. Bank income statements begin by recording interest and fee income on loans and, separately, interest income on securities. The total of these two items, which sometimes are broken down into more detail, is total interest income; for obvious reasons, total interest income is a major component of a bank's total income. For Fleet, this meant more than $5.8 billion in 1997.

Interest expense. Apart from capital funds and noninterest-bearing checking accounts, a bank has to pay for the funds it uses to lend to customers and invest for its own account in securities. This account records the interest expense on interest-bearing deposits and borrowed funds, which, for Fleet, amounted to a 1997 interest expense of $2.2 billion.

Net interest income. A key component of a bank's profitability, net interest income is simply the difference between the interest a bank earns and that which it pays out. This is one of those the-bigger, the-better numbers, which is a product of a bank's asset/liability management (i.e, the effective pricing of loans and deposits to maximize net interest income). Fleet recorded $3.6 billion in this account in 1997.

Provision for credit losses. Actual write-offs of bad loans are made against a bank's reserve for loan losses, not against its income statement. However, to create and maintain this reserve, a general charge or "provision" is made against income and fed into a reserve for credit losses. As illustrated in Exhibit 11.3, Fleet's 1997 provision figure of $322 million is the same one you saw as an addition to its loan loss reserve in 1997.

Noninterest income. Banks, particularly the larger ones with more complex business structures, generate additional income, or noninterest income, from a variety of fees, commissions, services, and ventures. Fleet has been very successful in this aspect of the banking business. Its noninterest income amounted to almost $2.3 billion in 1997, a significant 38 percent of the bank's total income of $5.9 billion. With regard to total income, which is simply the sum of net interest income and noninterest income, this figure is not usually recorded in bank income statements. You have to do the math. The investment community likes to see banks generate a healthy amount of noninterest income on the premise that it represents an additional boost to a bank's profit potential. Also, in problematical interest rate environments that make it difficult for banks to maintain their rate spreads, noninterest income acts as a cushion to earnings.

Noninterest expense. This item is the equivalent of a nonfinancial company's SG&A expense. The most critical component of these operational expenses is the one for personnel. In spite of significant advances in technology, the banking business is still fairly labor intensive. Generally, employee compensation and benefits are about 50 percent of total operating expenses. Fleet's 1997 operational expenses amounted to $3.4 billion, with personnel costs of $1.6 billion accounting for approximately 47 percent of the total.

Pretax income. In a bank income statement, noninterest income is added to net interest income after the provision for credit losses and noninterest expense is subtracted to arrive at income before income taxes.

Taxes. Applicable income taxes can be compared with pretax income for calculating the effective tax rate. For Fleet, taxes of $868 million were paid on taxable income of $2,171 million—an effective tax of almost 40 percent.

Net income. Fleet recorded after-tax net income of $1,303 million, its bottom line results for 1997.

As in the case of nonfinancial companies, additional data are provided at the end of the income statement showing the weighted average of shares outstanding and the period's earnings per share on a basic and diluted basis.

Having explained the components of a bank's balance sheet and income statement, we move to Chapter 12 to discuss how to use this financial statement data to evaluate financial institutions as investment opportunities.

CHAPTER 12

Key Investment Evaluators for Bank Financials

The business of banks is to take risk. Nonfinancial companies also take risks in their commercial endeavors; but if they make mistakes, their customers and suppliers generally demonstrate a level of patience not seen with banks. Nonfinancial businesses usually have time to work their way out of problems. Not so with banks. As leveraged institutions, banks need to have the continuous confidence of their depositors and creditors, to whom they "owe" large sums of money, in order to keep functioning. On rumor alone, let alone fact, a financial institution can be crippled in a matter of days if there is a public perception that it has a serious problem. A so-called run on a bank is not a pretty picture, literally or figuratively, and is one of the basic reasons why financial institutions are tightly regulated, monitored closely through quarterly call (information) reports, and examined periodically by state and federal banking authorities.

The reputation, experience, and the actual performance of its owners and managers build confidence in a bank. The results of these collective efforts can be measured, to a large degree, through various indicators formulated from information found in a bank's financial statements. For investors seeking investment opportunities in quality institutions, it's fairly easy to work with a bank's financials. Investors can use the bank worksheets to develop a framework of evaluative ratios and indicators to help with their investment decisions. Banks that do well in five areas—capital adequacy, loan asset quality, management efficiency, earnings, and liquidity—generally evidence positive investment qualities. In the following we discuss various measurements of these five basic elements of a bank's financial condition and performance.

In addition to Fleet's 1997 financial statements, shown in Exhibits 11.1 and 11.5, I have included at the end of this chapter the 1997 balance sheets and income statements of three other banks—Chase Manhattan (Chase), TrustCo Bank Corp NY (TrustCo), and Crazy Woman Creek Bancorp (CWCB)—in Exhibits 12.4, 12.5, and 12.6, respectively. These financial institutions differ greatly operationally and in size, which is not untypical in today's banking environment. Many larger financial institutions are becoming much more involved in financial services that go beyond

EXHIBIT 12.1 • Comparative Bank Financial Statements

CODE	BALANCE SHEET	CHASE	FLEET	TRUSTCO	CWCB
1	Cash & Banks	18,590	4,983	43	1.3
2	Invested Funds	156,059	9,860	997	28.2
3	Total Primary Assets	174,649	14,843	1,040	29.5
4	Gross Loans	168,454	61,179	1,298	29.2
5	Loan Loss Reserve	-3,624	-1,432	-53	-.3
6	Net Loans	164,830	59,747	1,245	28.9
7	Premises & Equipment	3,780	1,184	19	.4
8	Other Assets	22,262	9,761	68	1.1
9	Total Assets	365,521	85,535	2,372	59.9
10	Total Deposits	193,688	63,735	2,022	29.5
11	Borrowings	67,731	6,903	128	15.7
12	Accrued Expenses	12,526	2,363	43	.4
13	Other Liabilities	54,157	0	0	.1
14	Long-Term Debt	15,677	4,500	0	0
15	Total Liabilities	343,779	77,501	2,193	45.7
16	Shareholders' Equity	21,742	8,034	179	14.2
17	Total Liabilities & Equity	365,521	85,535	2,372	59.9
	INCOME STATEMENT				
18	Interest Income	21,756	5,848	172	3.9
19	Interest Expense	-13,598	-2,221	-87	-2.0
20	Net Interest Income	8,158	3,627	85	1.9
21	Fees, Commisions & Other	8,625	2,247	17	.1
22	Total Income	16,783	5,874	102	2.0
23	Provision for Loan Losses	-804	-322	-5	0
24	Employee Expense	-5,437	-1,591	-23	-.5
25	General Operating Expense	-4,632	-1,790	-23	-.5
26	Total Operating Expense	-10,069	-3,381	-46	-1.0
27	Pretax Income	5,910	2,171	51	1.0
28	Special Item	0	0	0	0
29	Taxes	-2,202	-868	-19	-.3
30	Net Income	3,708	1,303	32	.7
	SUPPLEMENTAL DATA				
31	Dividends Paid	1,212	529	22	.4
32	Employees (actual year-end)	69,000	36,000	459	12
33	Average Earning Assets	329,306	76,281	2,278	55
34	Average Total Assets	350,081	85,527	2,317	56
35	Average Total Equity	21,368	7,725	171	14.9
36	Average Gross Loans	161,773	60,012	1,271	27.5
37	Nonperforming Loans	1,018	416	11	.2
38	Loan Charge-Offs	1,096	514	7	n.m.

EXHIBIT 12.2 • Bank Financial Statement Investment Evaluators

RATIOS	CHASE	FLEET	TRUSTCO	CWCB
CAPITAL ADEQUACY				
Tier 1 Capital (%)	7.9	7.3	13.4	18.2
Total Capital (%)	11.6	10.9	14.7	45.6
Leverage (%)	6.0	7.7	7.0	n.a.
Equity/ Assets (%)	5.9	9.4	7.5	23.7
Dividends/ Net Income (%)	32.7	40.6	68.8	57.1
LOAN ASSET QUALITY				
Loan Loss Reserve/ Gross Loans (%)	2.2	2.3	4.1	1.0
Nonperforming Loans/ Gross Loans (%)	.6	.7	.8	.7
Nonperforming Loans/ Loan Loss Reserve (%)	28.1	29.1	20.8	66.7
Loan Charge-Offs/ Average Gross Loans (%)	.7	.9	.6	n.m.
MANAGEMENT EFFICIENCY				
Net Margin (%)	2.5	4.8	3.7	3.5
Efficiency (%)	60.0	57.6	45.1	50.0
Gross Loans per Employee (amt millions)	2.4	1.7	2.8	2.4
Total Income per Employee (amt millions)	.2	.2	.2	.2
PROFITABILITY				
Return on Assets (%)	1.1	1.5	1.4	1.3
Return on Equity (%)	17.4	16.9	18.7	4.7
LIQUIDITY RATIOS:				
Gross Loans/ Total Deposits (%)	87.0	96.0	64.2	99.0
Total Primary Assets/ Total Deposits (%)	90.2	23.3	51.4	100.0

the traditional activities generally associated with commercial banks. Nevertheless, for our purposes the comparisons of these disparate institutions help to explain balance sheet and income statement relationships that are used to analyze a bank's financial position. Exhibit 12.1 presents the four banks' individual financial positions and Exhibit 12.2 their financial statement evaluators. Both of these presentations use the bank financial statement worksheets provided in Appendix B. The banks' financials have been coded to reconcile their numbers to the line classifications and ratios/indicators used in the worksheets.

Exhibit 12.3—Banking Industry Ratios—contains excerpted data from the investment banking firm of Keefe, Bruyette & Woods' *Quarterly Bankbook* (June 1998). The ratios are developed from the reports of 184 banks of all sizes and are useful comparative benchmarks. In this chapter's discussion of various bank ratios, I refer, when appropriate, to a KBW industry ratio to provide additional perspective on the meaning of these indicators.

Chase is a large, multinational money center bank based in New York City with a sophisticated range of financial services provided both domestically as well as in many foreign markets. Fleet, as we know, is, in addition to its position as a major regional bank, a diversified financial services company based in Boston. It serves both the Northeast and national U.S. markets. TrustCo is a relatively small institution based in Schenectady, New York, that provides traditional commercial banking services to the upstate capitol region of New York State. The Crazy Woman Creek Bancorp—what a great name!—is the holding company for the Buffalo Federal Savings Bank, a very small (12 employees) savings and loan institution located in Buffalo, Wyoming.

I now look at the financial statements of these institutions to show investors how to measure bank financial condition and performance. For illustrating the computation of the various ratios and indicators, I continue to use Fleet's 1997 figures in the examples. Also, remember that to be meaningful, ratio analysis must cover an extended period and comparisons must be made within peer groups.

CAPITAL ADEQUACY

Equity/Assets Ratio

Capital adequacy is defined by the degree of protection provided by a bank's equity capital against losses in asset values, principally loans. Such losses, in the extreme, could affect the return of depositors' funds as well as the safety of shareholders' investment. Capital adequacy is measured by comparing a bank's equity (capital) with its assets, which is expressed as a percentage. In the equity/assets ratio, a bank's assets are not risk-adjusted and the figure used for equity is simply that figure recorded in the balance sheet under shareholders' equity. As such, it is easy to calculate and provides a fair indication of a bank's capital adequacy. But it does not conform to regulatory requirements, discussed in the next section.

EXHIBIT 12.3 • Banking Industry Ratios

RATIOS	DECEMBER 1996	DECEMBER 1997	JUNE 1998
Return On Assets (%)	1.25	1.31	1.29
Return On Equity (%)	14.52	16.60	15.09
Tier 1 Capital(%)	11.20	11.65	11.65
Equity/ Assets (%)	8.54	8.34	8.57
Loss Reserve/ Loans (%)	1.55	1.57	1.49
Net Charge-Offs (a) (%)	0.31	0.34	0.26
Nonperforming Assets/ Loans (%)	0.66	0.62	0.63
Nonperforming Assets/ Loss Reserve (%)	33.70	31.70	33.40
Net Interest Margin (%)	4.56	4.53	4.41
Efficiency Ratio (b) (%)	59.45	59.06	59.16
Dividend Payout (%)	35.66	34.94	35.35

SOURCE: Keefe, Bruyette & Woods' Quarterly Bankbook. Data excerpted, with permission.

NOTES:
(a) Loan charge-offs are netted against loan recoveries.
In this form, the net loan charge-off ratio will be lower than when using total loan charge-offs.
(b) OREO related expenses excluded, which is not a material adjustment.

Equity/Assets Ratio (%):
Line 16 ÷ Line 9 = %
$8,034 ÷ $85,535 = .0939 or 9.4%

Even by this rough measurement, Fleet's equity/assets ratio, as well as those of the other banks in the group, reflect fairly strong capital positions. The KBW industry average for this ratio is around 8.5 percent. CWCB's capital position is extremely strong, so much so that one can safely assume that this relatively new bank has a very solid base on which to expand its activities.

Regulatory Capital Ratios

The Federal Reserve Board has established a regulatory framework for capital ratios, which conforms to international standards for national banks, and state banking authorities have followed suit. This framework establishes three types of capital and views assets as having different degrees of risk. A bank's capital is viewed from three different perspectives:

- Tier 1 or core capital: shareholders' equity + noncumulative perpetual preferred stock + minority interest

- Tier 2 or supplementary capital: tier 1 capital + reserve for loan losses + cumulative perpetual preferred stock + long-term subordinated debt

- Total capital: tier 1 capital + tier 2 capital

In simple terms, Tier 1 capital basically amounts to a bank's equity, as stated in its balance sheet, and Tier 2 capital amounts to a bank's equity plus any long-term subordinated debt. The other more exotic securities mentioned as capital items are seldom seen.

In calculating a bank's assets, so-called risk weighting involves applying a risk percentage factor to different asset types according to the degree of risk involved. Here are a few examples, which are self-explanatory, of risk-weighted assets:

Cash and due from banks	0 percent
Securities of U.S. government agencies	20 percent
Real estate loans with first mortgages	50 percent
Commercial and consumer loans	100 percent

A bank's regulatory risk-based capital ratios result from the application of its three capital computations to its risk-weighted assets. There are five categories of regulatory capital ratios—well capitalized, adequately capitalized, undercapitalized, significantly undercapitalized, and critically undercapitalized. As defined by the Federal Reserve Board, the Federal Deposit Insurance Corporation (FDIC), and the Comptroller of the Currency (OCC), the minimum capital and well-capitalized ratios for banks are as follows:

	Tier 1 Capital	**Total Capital**	**Tier 1 Leverage**
Well capitalized	6%	10%	5%
Minimum	4%	8%	3%

In the Tier 1 leverage ratio, a bank's risk-weighted assets are adjusted to include off-balance sheet risks associated with such items, among others, as bid bonds, performance bonds, direct guarantees, standby letters of credit, and commercial letters of credit.

The Tier 1 capital, total capital, and Tier 1 leverage ratios cannot be computed by investors from information publicly available. But these ratios are always included in a bank's annual report in the MD&A section and/or in the notes to the financials. Suffice it to say that investors should stick to those banks with capital ratios that qualify them as well capitalized. All our Exhibit 12.2 banks easily fall into this category. KBW's June 1998 industry average for Tier 1 capital is in the area of 11.7 percent. There's no doubt that the larger, well-established banks are more aggressive in their use of leverage and tend to register lower capital ratios than the banking industry as a whole.

Dividends/Net Income Ratio (%)

A bank's growth in assets must be matched by a proportional growth in equity. Internally generated earnings, left in the company, can be used for this purpose. This ratio measures the percentage of earnings paid out to shareholders with the balance retained to build the bank's capital base. Investors need to take a rational view of this issue. Obviously, dividend payouts need to be balanced against maintaining a healthy capital position. Well-run banks can both reward shareholders with reasonable dividends and build their capital through retained earnings.

Fleet's dividend payout ratio for 1997 was as follows (dividends are found in a bank's cash flow statement):

Line 31 ÷ Line 30 = %
$529 ÷ $1,303 = .4060 or 40.6%

The KBW industry average for this dividend payout ratio is approximately 35 percent.

LOAN ASSET QUALITY

Loan Loss Reserve/Gross Loans (%)

A bank's loan loss reserve is its first line of defense against loans that go bad. Tracked over time, this ratio indicates the cushion a bank has created to absorb loan charge-offs. During periods of relatively good credit quality, the ratio should remain stable in the range of between 2 to 3 percent. Material increases or decreases in the ratio are cause for concern, and material variances from peer bank ratios should be questioned. The KBW industry average for this ratio is about 1.5 percent. Fleet's loan loss reserve/gross loans ratio is calculated as follows:

Line 5 ÷ Line 4 = %
$1,432 ÷ $61,179 = .0234 or 2.3%

Nonperforming Loans/Gross Loans (%)

A bank's nonperforming loans will generally run about 1 percent of its total loan portfolio. Because these problem loans don't accrue interest and require extra management attention, their unproductive nature is a drag on earnings. The lower the ratio the better. A growing trend could be an indicator of a bank's entry into a riskier market area or a lowering of credit standards. Even with the great disparity in size and scope of operations of the banks shown in the exhibits, this key credit quality measurement is close to being the same for all four institutions. The KBW industry average ratio is virtually the same—0.6 percent. The ratio calculation for Fleet is as follows:

Line 37 ÷ Line 4 = %
$416 ÷ $61,179 = .0068 or .7%

Nonperforming Loans/Loan Loss Reserve (%)

In this instance, the ratio measures the adequacy of a bank's existing loan loss reserve vis-à-vis its problem loans, which theoretically could all go bad but usually don't. The lower the nonperforming loans/loan loss reserve ratio, the more margin there is to handle problems loans that become actual charge-offs. The KBW industry average for the equivalent of this ratio is about 33 percent. Fleet's ratio provides ample margin:

Line 37 ÷ Line 5 = %
$416 ÷ $1,432 = .2905 or 29.1%

Loan Charge-Offs/Average Gross Loans (%)

After all attempts at collection of a problem loan have failed and collateral proceeds, if any, are applied to the amount due, a bank will make a determination to write off the loan against its loan loss reserve. These actual loan charge-offs, when compared with a bank's loan portfolio, are the clearest indicator of credit quality. The nature and mix of a bank's lending activities will affect this ratio. For example, in 1997 the Crazy Woman Creek Bancorp had a loan charge-off of only $4,000 on a loan portfolio that had an average outstanding balance for the year of $27.5 million. The close lender-borrower relationship typical of a very small community bank and the secured nature of its loans explain the insignificant amount of the charge-off. In general, banks like to keep this ratio below the 1 percent level, at least during periods of relatively good credit conditions. Fleet's loan charge-offs/average gross loans ratio is as follows:

Line 38 ÷ Line 36 = %
$514 ÷ $60,012 = .0086 or .9%

Loan charge-off data are often presented on a net basis—loan recoveries are offset against loan charge-offs. This is the basis for Keefe, Bruyette & Woods's ratio. I disagree with this methodology, which tends to conceal the true extent of a bank's actual bad loan experience, and thus caution investors against using net loan charge-offs in loan quality ratios.

Loan asset loan quality is of paramount importance in evaluating the financial condition of a banking institution. Deteriorating loan quality detracts management from more productive endeavors, hurts earnings, and can potentially put a bank out of business. Monitoring and evaluating a bank's lending position, its core business, through asset quality ratios is a must for any prudent investor.

MANAGEMENT EFFICIENCY

Net Margin Ratio (%)

The net margin ratio is a comparison of net interest income with average earning assets. The latter, as its name implies, are a bank's income-producing assets, which for the most part consist of interest-bearing deposits with other banks, federal funds and securities placements, and loans. In the bank worksheet, earning assets consist of the sum of lines 2 and 4, which may overstate true earning assets somewhat because of the noninterest-bearing character of a bank's cash holdings and interest-free deposit accounts. But the figure is a close approximation and is used for its ease of calculation. The net margin ratio is an indicator of a bank's ability to successfully manage its asset and liability rates (i.e., its pricing of loans and deposits). The KBW industry average net margin ratio has ranged from 4.6 percent to 4.4 percent for the period of 1996 to June 1998. The upward and downward trends, or stability, in this indicator provide clues to management's performance on a year-to-year basis.

The mix of a bank's earning assets, basically the relative percentage of securities and loans, makes a difference in this ratio's outcome. Banks usually earn considerably more in interest and fees from loans than they do from securities. A comparison of Chase and Fleet on this factor illustrates the point. From the 1997 balance sheet data in Exhibit 12.1, you see that Chase's invested funds and its gross loans were almost even in amount, whereas Fleet's gross loans are approximately six times the amount of its invested funds. It's safe to assume that these two prime banks pay about the same for deposits and borrowed funds and that their lending rates are comparable. Fleet's 4.8 percent net margin is almost twice that of Chase (2.5), most likely because of its generation of higher-yielding interest and fee income on its proportionately larger loan position compared with that of its securities. The following calculation is Fleet's net margin ratio:

Line 20 ÷ Line 33 = %
$3,627 ÷ $76,281 = .0475 or 4.8%

Efficiency Ratio (%)

This indicator compares a financial institution's total operating expenses—what it costs to run the bank—with its total income. As a rule of thumb, banks like to keep this ratio under 60 percent, which is confirmed by the KBW industry average. Fleet has done well in this regard, as measured by its 1997 results:

Line 26 ÷ Line 22 = %
$3,381 ÷ $5,874 = .5756 or 57.6%

Gross Loans and Total Income per Employee (%)

You will recall that salaries and benefits generally account for about one-half of all bank operating expense. Because personnel costs have such an important impact on income, these two indicators (for gross loans and total income per employee) measure productivity in terms of a bank's loan portfolio and its total income. For Fleet in 1997, employee productivity meant gross loans per employee of $1.7 million and total income per employee of approximately $0.2 million. Employee counts are not always easily obtained from bank financial communications. However, these data can be obtained from a bank's investor relations department or from Internet investment information sources, such as Hoover's Online. The calculation of Fleet's per-employee productivity ratios are as follows:

Line 4 ÷ Line 32 = $ amount per employee
$61,179 ÷ 36,000 = $1.7 million

and

Line 22 ÷ Line 32 = $ amount per employee
$5,874 ÷ 36,000 = $0.2 million

PROFITABILITY

Return on Assets (%) and Return on Equity (%)

Of the two profitability ratios, it's a bank's return on assets (ROA) that gets the most attention. A bank's ROA is a key evaluator of investment quality. Generally, a return on assets above 1 percent is satisfactory—the typical banking industry range usually falls between 1 and 2 percent.

KBW's industry average for ROA shows itself close to a fairly consistent 1.3 percent mark. A bank's return on equity (ROE) is looked at in the same way as that of a nonfinancial company. Here again, the KBW industry average for ROE is in a very respectable 15 to 17 percent range. By way of explanation, Crazy Woman Creek Bancorp's nominal ROE of under 5 percent is a consequence of its highly underleveraged financial position, evidenced by its jumbo capital ratios. CWCB's relatively large equity base and underutilization of leverage provides an extremely high degree of safety for depositors and creditors but penalizes the results of the ROE ratio because of its highly underleveraged position. Fleet's ROA and ROE are calculated as follows:

ROA:

Line 30 ÷ Line 34 = %

$1,303 ÷ $85,527 = .0152 or 1.5%

ROE:

Line 30 ÷ Line 35 = %

$1,303 ÷ $7,725 = .1687 or 16.9%

LIQUIDITY

Loan/Deposit Ratio (%)

Given the dynamics of today's financial markets, traditional liquidity measurements don't carry the same weight they did in the past. Banks can raise funds quickly through a variety of money market mechanisms. Nevertheless, the traditional loan/deposit and primary asset ratios still have some value as general indicators of overall bank liquidity.

In the loan/deposit ratio, gross loans are compared with total deposits, which is a traditional indicator of how "loaned up" a bank is at a given point in time. A high ratio is an indicator that a bank has little lending capacity left. However, by only looking at deposits, the ratio doesn't take into account borrowed funds, which have increasingly become a part of many banks' funding base. For example, Chase, Fleet, and CWCB all use a significant amount of borrowed funds to support their operations. If these funds are factored into the deposit side of their loan/deposit ratios, the banks become much more liquid than they appear by traditional standards. For example, let's calculate Fleet's position both ways:

Loan/Deposit Ratio:

Line 4 ÷ Line 10 = %

$61,179 ÷ $63,735 = .9599 or 96.0%

Adjusted Loan/Deposit Ratio:

Line 4 ÷ [Line 10 + Line 11] = %

$61,179 ÷ [$63,735 + $6,903]

$61,179 ÷ $70,638 = .8661 or 86.1%

Total Primary Assets/Total Deposits (%)

Just as the loan/deposit ratio measures a bank's liquidity from the perspective of borrowers—a bank's ability to meet its loan commitments—the primary assets/deposits ratio measures a bank's ability to meet the withdrawals of its depositors. Generally, a bank's inflow of funds—loan repayments, maturing investments, and new or renewing deposits—is sufficient to meet its lending commitments and deposit withdrawals. It is the sensitivity of meeting its loan commitments and deposit withdrawals that requires a bank to maintain an adequate level of liquidity. A bank cannot afford even the perception of illiquidity. A ratio in the range of 15 percent is usually considered adequate. Fleet's primary assets/deposits ratio is calculated as follows:

Line 3 ÷ Line 10 = %
$14,843 ÷ $63,735 = .2329 or 23.3%

As a general rule, a company's profitability is what drives its stock price and attracts the attention of investors. However, with banks as opposed to nonfinancial companies, the concept of profitability is more complex, and it is a mistake to think of profitability to be the same as profits. First, for a bank to be profitable and warrant the interest of investors, it must be well capitalized. Second, it must prudently manage its risk assets and vast sums of money provided by depositors and creditors. Prudent management means taking risks and making money at the same time, which is not always an easy task. Finally, a bank can never afford to lose the confidence of its funding sources, either institutional or individual. If a bank can make these three elements work together, it will be profitable and represent, most likely, a positive investment opportunity.

EXHIBIT 12.4 • Financial Statements—Chase Manhattan Corporation

CONSOLIDATED BALANCE SHEET

December 31, (in millions, except share data)	1997	1996
ASSETS		
Cash and Due from Banks **1**	$ 15,704	$ 14,605
Deposits with Banks **1**	2,886	8,344
Federal Funds Sold and Securities Purchased Under Resale Agreements **2**	30,928	28,966
Trading Assets:		
Debt and Equity Instruments **2**	34,641	30,377
Risk Management Instruments, Net of Allowance for Credit Losses of $75 in 1997 and 1996	37,752	29,579
Securities:		
Available-for-Sale **2**	49,755	44,691
Held-to-Maturity (Market Value: $2,995 in 1997 and $3,849 in 1996)	2,983	3,855
Loans **4**	168,454	155,092
Allowance for Credit Losses **5**	3,624	3,549
Net Loans **6**	164,830	151,543
Premises and Equipment **7**	3,780	3,642
Due from Customers on Acceptances **8**	1,719	2,276
Accrued Interest Receivable **8**	3,359	3,020
Other Assets **8**	17,184	15,201
Total Assets **9**	$ 365,521	$ 336,099
LIABILITIES		
Deposits:		
Domestic:		
Noninterest-Bearing	$ 46,603	$ 42,726
Interest-Bearing	71,576	67,186
Foreign:		
Noninterest-Bearing	3,205	4,331
Interest-Bearing	72,304	66,678
Total Deposits **10**	193,688	180,921
Federal Funds Purchased and Securities Sold Under Repurchase Agreements **11**	56,126	53,868
Commercial Paper **11**	4,744	4,500
Other Borrowed Funds	6,861	9,231
Acceptances Outstanding **11** **13**	1,719	2,276
Trading Liabilities	52,438	38,136
Accounts Payable, Accrued Expenses and Other Liabilities, Including the **12** Allowance for Credit Losses of $170 in 1997 and $70 in 1996	12,526	12,309
Long-Term Debt **14**	13,387	12,714
Guaranteed Preferred Beneficial Interests in Corporation's Junior **14** Subordinated Deferrable Interest Debentures	1,740	600
Total Liabilities **15**	343,229	314,555
Commitments and Contingencies (See Note Twenty Four)		
PREFERRED STOCK OF SUBSIDIARY **14**	550	550
STOCKHOLDERS' EQUITY		
Preferred Stock	1,740	2,650
Common Stock (Authorized 750,000,000 Shares, Issued 440,753,296 Shares in 1997 and 440,747,317 Shares in 1996)	441	441
Capital Surplus	10,360	10,459
Retained Earnings	11,103	8,627
Net Unrealized Gain (Loss) on Available-for-Sale Securities	95	(288)
Treasury Stock, at Cost (19,788,820 Shares in 1997 and 9,936,716 Shares in 1996)	(1,997)	(895)
Total Stockholders' Equity **16**	21,742	20,994
Total Liabilities, Preferred Stock of Subsidiary and Stockholders' Equity **17**	$ 365,521	$ 336,099

The Notes to Consolidated Financial Statements are an integral part of these Statements.

EXHIBIT 12.4 • Financial Statements—Chase Manhattan Corporation, continued

CONSOLIDATED STATEMENT OF INCOME

Year ended December 31, (in millions, except per share data)	1997	1996	1995
INTEREST INCOME			
Loans	$ 12,826	$ 12,359	$ 12,842
Securities	3,028	2,862	2,591
Trading Assets	2,770	1,898	1,385
Federal Funds Sold and Securities Purchased Under Resale Agreements	2,607	2,135	1,889
Deposits with Banks	525	537	824
Total Interest Income **18**	• 21,756	19,791	19,531
INTEREST EXPENSE			
Deposits	6,561	6,038	6,291
Short-Term and Other Borrowings	5,903	4,630	4,175
Long-Term Debt	1,134	901	942
Total Interest Expense **19**	13,598	11,569	11,408
Net Interest Income **20**	8,158	8,222	8,123
Provision for Credit Losses **23**	804	897	758
Net Interest Income After Provision for Credit Losses	7,354	7,325	7,365
NONINTEREST REVENUE			
Corporate Finance and Syndication Fees	1,136	950	810
Trust, Custody, and Investment Management Fees	1,307	1,176	1,018
Credit Card Revenue	1,183	1,063	834
Service Charges on Deposit Accounts	376	394	417
Fees for Other Financial Services	1,607	1,529	1,453
Trading Revenue	1,323	1,371	1,065
Securities Gains	312	135	132
Revenue from Equity-Related Investments	806	726	626
Other Revenue	575	286	482
Total Noninterest Revenue **21**	8,625	7,630	6,837
NONINTEREST EXPENSE			
Salaries **24**	4,598	4,232	4,208
Employee Benefits	839	926	899
Occupancy Expense	767	824	897
Equipment Expense	792	724	755
Foreclosed Property Expense **25**	12	(16)	(75)
Restructuring Costs	192	1,814	15
Other Expense	2,869	2,640	2,691
Total Noninterest Expense **26**	10,069	11,144	9,390
Income Before Income Tax Expense and Effect of Accounting Change **27**	5,910	3,811	4,812
Income Tax Expense **29**	2,202	1,350	1,842
Income Before Effect of Accounting Change	3,708	2,461	2,970
Net Effect of Change in Accounting Principle	—	—	(11)
Net Income **30**	$ 3,708	$ 2,461	$ 2,959
Net Income Applicable to Common Stock	$ 3,526	$ 2,242	$ 2,732
EARNINGS PER SHARE:			
Basic:			
Income Before Effect of Accounting Change	$ 8.30	$ 5.13	$ 6.36
Net Income	$ 8.30	$ 5.13	$ 6.33
Diluted:			
Income Before Effect of Accounting Change	$ 8.03	$ 4.94	$ 6.07
Net Income	$ 8.03	$ 4.94	$ 6.04

The Notes to Consolidated Financial Statements are an integral part of these Statements.

EXHIBIT 12.5 • Financial Statements—TrustCo Bank Corp NY

Consolidated Statements of Condition

(dollars in thousands, except share data)

	As of December 31,	
	1997	1996
ASSETS		
Cash and due from banks. 1	$ 42,740	45,779
Federal funds sold . . 2	395,000	310,000
Total cash and cash equivalents.	437,740	355,779
Securities available for sale 2	601,899	618,670
Loans . . . 4	1,299,492	1,243,335
Less: Unearned income . . 8	1,216	1,453
Allowance for loan losses . 5	53,455	51,561
Net loans . . 6	1,244,821	1,190,321
Bank premises and equipment. 7	18,609	23,098
Real estate owned 8	9,309	6,518
Other assets 8	59,887	67,394
Total assets. 9	$2,372,265	2,261,780
LIABILITIES AND SHAREHOLDERS' EQUITY		
Deposits:		
Demand	$ 130,345	123,553
Savings	650,601	661,915
Interest-bearing checking accounts	240,699	236,264
Money market deposit accounts.	57,021	61,131
Certificates of deposit (in denominations of $100,000 or more).	112,599	89,793
Other time accounts	830,598	780,490
Total deposits . 10	2,021,863	1,953,146
Short-term borrowings 11	127,850	111,662
Accrued expenses and other liabilities. 12	43,727	34,572
Total liabilities . . . 15	2,193,440	2,099,380
Shareholders' equity:		
Capital stock; $1 par value. 50,000,000 shares authorized; 24,257,382 and 20,959,376 shares issued at December 31, 1997 and 1996, respectively	24,257	20,959
Surplus	112,702	114,228
Undivided profits.	32,119	23,221
Net unrealized gain on securities available for sale.	15,851	5,239
Treasury stock; 855,850 and 571,142 shares, at cost, at December 31, 1997 and 1996, respectively	(6,104)	(1,247)
Total shareholders' equity. 16	178,825	162,400
Total liabilities and shareholders' equity. 17	$2,372,265	2,261,780

See accompanying notes to consolidated financial statements.

EXHIBIT 12.5 • Financial Statements—TrustCo Bank Corp NY, continued

Consolidated Statements of Income

(dollars in thousands, except per share data)	Years Ended December 31,		
	1997	1996	1995
Interest income:			
Interest and fees on loans	$109,346	107,111	107,060
Interest and dividends on:			
U.S. Treasuries and agencies	27,356	31,466	28,193
States and political subdivisions	5,637	4,254	2,902
Mortgage-backed securities	10,094	4,114	8,602
Other	1,811	2,068	2,252
Interest on federal funds sold	17,761	17,634	12,543
Total interest income **18**	172,005	166,647	161,552
Interest expense:			
Interest on deposits	80,946	77,749	78,355
Interest on short-term borrowings	5,574	4,593	1,776
Interest on long-term debt	—	—	69
Total interest expense **19**	86,520	82,342	80,200
Net interest income **20**	85,485	84,305	81,352
Provision for loan losses **23**	5,414	6,577	12,698
Net interest income after provision for loan losses	80,071	77,728	68,654
Noninterest income:			
Trust department income	6,554	5,556	4,890
Fees for services to customers	7,671	6,981	7,003
Net gain/(loss) on securities transactions	(166)	(4,536)	243
Other	3,163	2,312	1,931
Total noninterest income **21**	17,222	10,313	14,067
Noninterest expense:			
Salaries and employee benefits **24**	23,162	21,532	19,895
Net occupancy expense	5,270	4,178	4,562
Equipment expense	4,165	3,289	3,403
FDIC insurance expense **25**	246	7	2,101
Professional services	3,489	3,676	3,585
Other real estate expenses	1,056	718	3,120
Other	8,838	8,615	7,774
Total noninterest expense **26**	46,226	42,015	44,440
Income before income taxes **27**	51,067	46,026	38,281
Income taxes **29**	18,892	17,327	12,754
Net income **30**	$ 32,175	28,699	25,527
Basic earnings per share	$ 1.37	1.23	1.10
Diluted earnings per share	1.33	1.20	1.07

Per share data has been adjusted for a 15% stock split in 1997 and 1996, and a 6 for 5 stock split in 1995.

See accompanying notes to consolidated financial statements.

EXHIBIT 12.6 • Financial Statements—Crazy Woman Creek Bancorp

CRAZY WOMAN CREEK BANCORP INCORPORATED AND SUBSIDIARY

Consolidated Balance Sheets

September 30, 1997 and 1996

Assets	1997	1996
Cash and cash equivalents **1** **2**	$ 1,193,775	451,445
Interest bearing deposits	99,000	99,000
Investment and mortgage-backed securities available-for-sale **2**	19,154,984	13,364,698
Investment and mortgage-backed securities held-to-maturity (estimated market value of $9,066,836 in 1997 and $10,180,716 in 1996) **2**	9,009,175	10,302,645
Stock in Federal Home Loan Bank of Seattle, at cost **8**	801,500	399,900
Loans receivable, net **6**	28,636,220	25,858,760
Accrued interest receivable **8**	558,782	495,750
Premises and equipment, net **7**	443,323	502,055
Other assets **8**	55,518	42,664
9	$ 59,952,277	51,516,917

Liabilities and Stockholders' Equity

Liabilities:	1997	1996
Deposits **10**	$ 29,506,343	29,370,985
Advances from Federal Home Loan Bank **11**	15,700,000	6,113,438
Advances from borrowers for taxes and insurance **13**	54,388	53,427
Federal income taxes payable **12**	155,103	14,953
Deferred income taxes **12**	115,346	80,925
Dividends payable **13**	95,485	105,800
Accrued expenses and other liabilities **12**	115,273	269,381
Total liabilities **15**	45,741,938	36,008,909

Stockholders' equity:	1997	1996
Preferred stock, par value $.10 per share, 2,000,000 shares authorized; none issued and outstanding	–	–
Common stock, par value $.10 per share, 5,000,000 shares authorized; 1,058,000 issued	105,800	105,800
Additional paid-in capital	10,041,629	10,027,393
Unearned ESOP/MSBP shares	(809,272)	(617,143)
Retained earnings	6,377,093	6,057,879
Unrealized gain (loss) on securities available-for-sale, net	77,007	(65,921)
Treasury stock, shares at cost	(1,581,918)	–
Total stockholders' equity **16**	14,210,339	15,508,008
17	$ 59,952,277	51,516,917

See accompanying notes to consolidated financial statements.

EXHIBIT 12.6 • Financial Statements—Crazy Woman Creek Bancorp, continued

CRAZY WOMAN CREEK BANCORP INCORPORATED AND SUBSIDIARY

Consolidated Statements of Income

Years ended September 30, 1997 and 1996

	1997	1996
Interest income:		
Loans receivable	$ 2,277,142	2,043,167
Mortgage-backed securities	589,004	485,571
Investment securities	1,001,049	627,593
Interest bearing deposits	5,047	26,452
Other	68,471	90,975
Total interest income **18**	3,940,713	3,273,758
Interest expense:		
Deposits	1,422,732	1,438,562
Advances from Federal Home Loan Bank	560,672	263,155
Total interest expense **19**	1,983,404	1,701,717
Net interest income **20**	1,957,309	1,572,041
Provision for loan losses **23**	–	–
Net interest income after provision for loan losses	1,957,309	1,572,041
Non-interest income:		
Customer service charges	41,803	41,213
Other operating income	30,015	31,605
Gain (loss) on sale of securities, net	(7,875)	30,198
Gain on sale of other real estate owned	–	13,599
Total non-interest income **20**	63,943	116,615
Non-interest expense:		
Compensation and benefits **24**	526,865	440,771
Occupancy and equipment	101,091	107,820
FDIC/SAIF deposit insurance premiums	26,703	66,684
Special assessment by the SAIF **25**	–	186,569
Advertising	40,184	37,349
Data processing services	94,195	150,162
Other	199,493	193,036
Total non-interest expense **26**	988,531	1,182,391
Income before income taxes **27**	1,032,721	506,265
Income tax expense **29**	341,826	151,420
Net income **30**	$ 690,895	354,845
Net income per share	$ .73	.36
Average common and common equivalent shares	942,515	995,143

See accompanying notes to consolidated financial statements.

CHAPTER 13

Electric Utility Financial Statements and Their Investment Evaluators

In 1992 federal deregulation of the electric utility industry kicked in and is still a work in progress today, but it is definitely moving forward. Legislative restructuring at the state level varies fairly evenly from fast to slow in all 50 states. But as Daniel Goldfarb points out in his article, "Are Electric Utilities Finally Seeing the Light?" (*Better Investing,* October 1998), electric utilities are no longer investment opportunities for widows and orphans: "From what was once a staid, sleepy, club-like industry, the rules of the game are being transformed so that the industry may turn out to be a higher-growth, less-regulated business with an improving capital structure. And that, for investors, may be the catalyst to drive the valuations of electric utility stocks higher."

In the old days, electric utilities were considered safe-haven investments with generous dividend payouts. Deregulation and competition have changed all that and the way investors go about selecting utility stocks. What do investors need to do? They need to carefully evaluate these stocks or, better yet, the companies they represent just as they would any industrial, commercial, or service company. Electric utilities with strong balance sheets, quality profits, and good cash flow are the ones that will prosper in the future. Some will do well in the new competitive environment and grow while others are likely to fade and become, at best, mediocre investments. Picking winning electric utility stocks will become a selective process and one that will require investors to become conversant with the clues to investment quality found in their financial statements. A number of aspects of an electric utility's balance sheet and income statement—the cash flow statement is a standard one—are different from your mainstream company. As a consequence, several of the conventional financial ratios used in financial analysis don't apply, and some electric utility industry-specific indicators are required.

Before digging into the financials of our example company, the FPL Group, investors need to appreciate the value of nonfinancial statement information when considering investing in the new version of an electric utility company. Among others, key items that need to be researched are the following:

- *The dollar cost of production on a per kilowatt basis.* Only low cost producers are going to survive and prosper.
- *The breakdown of the customer base between residential and commercial.* The industry average for the commercial component is around 35 percent. This segment of the market is more likely to shop around for suppliers of power and put the squeeze on rates, thus impacting revenues and profits.
- *The regulatory and political climate.* This element is still a factor in cost recovery on capital investments and rate setting.
- *The company's credit agency ratings.* Utilities are big users of borrowed funds. A quality ranking from Standard & Poor's means better access to capital markets and lower borrowing costs.
- *The company's projected construction program.* The business is very capital intensive, but the old days of spending somewhat freely on capital expenditures and recuperating the costs is no longer a sure thing.
- *The breakdown of power and fuel sources* (nuclear, oil, gas, and coal). Also their supply reliability and price stability.

The FPL Group's Florida Power & Light is one of the largest publicly owned electric utilities in the United States. This Florida-based company provides electricity for more than 3.6 million customers on Florida's eastern and lower western coasts (about half the state's population). FPL Group's other subsidiaries include ESI Energy (independent energy projects), Turner Foods (one of Florida's largest developers and operators of citrus groves), and FPL Group International, which was formed to invest in power projects overseas. We will use FPL Group's 1997 balance sheet, income statement, and cash flow statement to develop an understanding of what these financials can tell us about an electric utility's financial condition and performance.

THE BALANCE SHEET

The balance sheet of a utility company is fairly easy to understand. As is the case with the FPL Group, shown in Exhibit 13.1, its most important assets are concentrated in property, plant, and equipment. Its capitalization is the most relevant component of the liability/equity side of the balance sheet.

Assets

The presentation of an electric utility's assets is in reverse order to that of a regular business. As you can see, FPL Group's fixed assets come first and amount to roughly $9.4 billion out of approximately $12. 5 in total assets. That means that 75 percent of the company's asset total is

EXHIBIT 13.1 • Balance Sheet—FPL Group

Consolidated Balance Sheets

	(Millions of Dollars)	
December 31,	**1997**	**1996**
Property, Plant and Equipment		
Electric utility plant in service and other property	**$17,430**	$16,593
Nuclear fuel under capital lease	**186**	182
Construction work in progress	**204**	258
Less accumulated depreciation and amortization	**(8,466)**	(7,649)
Total property, plant and equipment – net	**9,354**	9,384
Current Assets		
Cash and cash equivalents	**54**	196
Customer receivables, net of allowances of $9 million and $12 million . .	**501**	462
Materials, supplies and fossil fuel inventory – at average cost	**302**	268
Deferred clause expenses	**122**	127
Other	**122**	120
Total current assets	**1,101**	1,173
Other Assets		
Special use funds of FPL	**1,007**	806
Other investments	**282**	327
Other	**705**	529
Total other assets	**1,994**	1,662
Total Assets	**$12,449**	$12,219
Capitalization		
Common shareholders' equity	**$ 4,845**	$ 4,592
Preferred stock of FPL without sinking fund requirements	**226**	290
Preferred stock of FPL with sinking fund requirements	**—**	42
Long-term debt	**2,949**	3,144
Total capitalization	**8,020**	8,068
Current Liabilities		
Short-term debt	**134**	—
Current maturities of long-term debt and preferred stock	**198**	155
Accounts payable	**368**	308
Customers' deposits	**279**	268
Accrued interest and taxes	**180**	259
Other	**340**	284
Total current liabilities	**1,499**	1,274
Other Liabilities and Deferred Credits		
Accumulated deferred income taxes	**1,473**	1,531
Deferred regulatory credit – income taxes	**166**	129
Unamortized investment tax credits	**229**	251
Storm and property insurance reserve	**252**	223
Other	**810**	743
Total other liabilities and deferred credits	**2,930**	2,877
Commitments and Contingencies		
Total Capitalization and Liabilities	**$12,449**	$12,219

invested in property, plant, and equipment. In general, this is typical of most utility companies, which by their nature are some of the most capital-intensive industries in the United States.

It is important for investors to note what percentage of the fixed asset total is comprised of construction work in progress (CWIP). The lower this percentage the better. A high percentage over an extended period of time can result in considerable financial strain. The issue of how much of a company's rate base is represented by CWIP is a critical one. Mishaps or delays in completion could occasion all, or a percentage of, the construction work to be removed from the rate base and could have a material adverse impact on revenues and cash flow. In the case of the FPL Group, its CWIP amounts to only $204 million, or just over 2 percent, of total PP&E. This low CWIP position is a very positive investment indicator.

Current and Other Assets

An electric utility has relatively insignificant accounts receivable and inventories, which, in the case of inventories, are mainly comprised of consumable materials, parts, and supplies.

Liabilities/Equity

The key consideration on this side of an electric utility's balance sheet is the composition of its capitalization. As a general rule, financial analysts prefer a split of debt and equity of roughly 55 percent and 45 percent, respectively. To be conservative, I would classify short-term borrowings, the current portion of long-term debt, long-term debt, and preferred stock with sinking fund or redemption requirements as the debt component of capitalization. Nonredeemable preferred stock and shareholders' equity qualify as the equity component. A satisfactory capitalization profile might look something like this:

Shareholders' equity	.45
Preferred stock	.10
Long-term debt	.40
Short-term debt	.05
Total capitalization	1.00

Using FPL Group numbers, its capitalization profile would calculate as follows:

Shareholders' equity	$4,845	.58
Preferred stock	$ 226	.03
Long-term debt	$2,949	.35
Short-term debt + Current maturities	$ 332	.04
Total capitalization	$8,352	1.00

Needless to say, FPL Group's capitalization position is very favorable and makes a positive contribution to the company's investment quality.

EXHIBIT 13.2 • Income Statement—FPL Group

Consolidated Statements of Income

	(In millions, except per share amounts)		
Years Ended December 31,	**1997**	1996	1995
Operating Revenues	**$6,369**	$6,037	$5,592
Operating Expenses			
Fuel, purchased power and interchange	**2,255**	2,131	1,722
Other operations and maintenance	**1,231**	1,189	1,206
Depreciation and amortization	**1,061**	960	918
Taxes other than income taxes	**594**	586	549
Total operating expenses	**5,141**	4,866	4,395
Operating Income	**1,228**	1,171	1,197
Other Income (Deductions)			
Interest charges	**(291)**	(267)	(291)
Preferred stock dividends – FPL	**(19)**	(24)	(43)
Other – net	**4**	(7)	19
Total other deductions – net	**(306)**	(298)	(315)
Income Before Income Taxes	**922**	873	882
Income Taxes	**304**	294	329
Net Income	**$ 618**	$ 579	$ 553

Current and Other Liabilities

These accounts are usually not material and usually consist of normal accounts payable, accrued expenses and taxes, and various deferred items.

THE INCOME STATEMENT

The income statement for an electric utility is a straightforward presentation. FPL Group's income statement is reproduced in Exhibit 13.2. Operating revenues are offset by a fairly standard set of operating expenses to arrive at operating income, which is then adjusted according to entries for other income (expense) and taxes to arrive at net income. There are no cost of sales or gross profit considerations as with a regular business.

Operating Revenues

Operating revenues for a utility are the equivalent of sales in a regular business. An electric utility's operating revenues are affected by the rates that can be charged, levels of consumption (which tend to be affected by weather), the size of the customer base, and the customer mix (e.g., residential versus commercial). FPL Group recorded total operating revenues of $6,369 million in 1997, up significantly for an electric utility from $5,592 million in 1995.

Operating Expenses

Basically, a utility's operating expenses involve the cost of its fuel, purchased power, and net power interchange costs. General operating expenses are included in the entry for other operations and maintenance. Depreciation, because of a utility's large fixed asset investment, represents another major charge (noncash) against income. Some taxes are considered recoverable, and these are included under operating expense. FPL Group's total operating expenses amounted to roughly $5.1 billion.

Operating Income

Operating income is a key income figure that is used in the calculation of various performance ratios that will be discussed later in this chapter's section on investment evaluators.

Other Income (Deductions)

Obviously because of the large debt positions that electric utilities must carry, interest charges are generally the principal item in this section.

Two unusual items, which do not appear in FPL Group's income statement, are peculiar to utility companies. The allowance for borrowed funds used in construction (AFUDC) and the allowance for other funds used during construction (also considered as AFUDC) are presented as separate entries for other income. These are noncash credits to income that represent the capitalized cost of debt (the former item) and equity (the latter item) used to finance construction. AFUDC is nothing more than an accounting entry. Investors need to be aware that in periods of high construction activity, AFUDC can contribute significantly to a utility's earnings but nothing to cash flow. Also, earnings that are inflated by AFUDC are not considered quality earnings (i.e., those produced from real operating revenues). Good quality electric utility profits have a low percentage of AFUDC in them. The FPL Group has no AFUDC component in its income figure.

Net Income

Taxes deducted from pretax income produce a company's net income results. As with any company, this is another key figure used to measure the profitability of an electric utility. For the FPL Group, net income was $618 million.

CASH FLOW STATEMENT

The cash flow statements of a regular business and those of electric utilities are exactly the same. Investors can apply the same analytical criteria to a utility's cash flow as those discussed in the earlier chapters on industrial, commercial, and service companies. Exhibit 13.3 illustrates FPL Group's statement of cash flows.

KEY INVESTMENT EVALUATORS

The liquidity measurements applied to a regular business are not relevant to a utility company. The conventional asset productivity ratios have some relevance but, because a utility's assets are comprised principally of property, plant and equipment, it's that asset that is measured rather than total assets. A utility's leverage ratios focus on capitalization and the funding of fixed assets. Utility profitability measurements are somewhat similar to those of regular companies, with the exception of the use of multilevel profit margin analysis. Cash flow and per share data indicators and ratios are basically the same for both regular and utility companies. The following investment evaluators, using the FPL Group's 1997 financials, are suggested for use with electric utilities:

Assets

Asset concentration ratio. This indicator measures construction work in progress as a percentage of total property, plant, and equipment. As discussed previously, because of the uncer-

EXHIBIT 13.3 • Cash Flow Statement—FPL Group

Consolidated Statements of Cash Flows

	(Millions of Dollars)		
Years Ended December 31,	**1997**	**1996**	**1995**
Cash Flows From Operating Activities			
Net income	$ 618	$ 579	$ 553
Adjustments to reconcile net income to net cash provided by operating activities:			
Depreciation and amortization	1,061	960	918
Decrease in deferred income taxes and related regulatory credit	(30)	(76)	(90)
Increase (decrease) in accrued interest and taxes	(79)	39	10
Other – net	27	90	119
Net cash provided by operating activities	1,597	1,592	1,510
Cash Flows From Investing Activities			
Capital expenditures of FPL	(551)	(474)	(661)
Independent power investments	(291)	(52)	(37)
Other – net	45	—	(4)
Net cash used in investing activities	(797)	(526)	(702)
Cash Flows From Financing Activities			
Issuance of long-term debt	42	—	178
Retirement of long-term debt and preferred stock	(717)	(338)	(574)
Increase (decrease) in short-term debt	113	(179)	(56)
Repurchase of common stock	(48)	(82)	(69)
Dividends on common stock	(332)	(320)	(309)
Other – net	—	3	(18)
Net cash used in financing activities	(942)	(916)	(848)
Net increase (decrease) in cash and cash equivalents	(142)	150	(40)
Cash and cash equivalents at beginning of year	196	46	86
Cash and cash equivalents at end of year	$ 54	$ 196	$ 46

tainties inherent with CWIP, it is preferable that this ratio be as low as possible because of rate base and cost recovery issues. FPL Group's ratio calculates as follows:

$204 ÷ $9,354 = .0218 or 2.2%

Asset turnover ratio. Operating revenues are divided by the average net amount for property, plant, and equipment, which represent a utility's operating property, not its total assets. Because utilities carry such a heavy fixed investment, most often larger than its revenue amount, this ratio is usually less than one, which is the case for the FPL Group:

Step 1:	$9,384 + $9,354 = $18,738 ÷ 2 = $9,369
Step 2:	$6,369 ÷ $9,369 = .6780 or 67.8%

Leverage

Debt/capitalization ratio. In this ratio, the debt component of capitalization is compared with the utility's total capitalization. The lower the percentage the better. Here again, FPL Group's ratio is considerably below the general utility industry range of 45 to 50 percent:

$2,949 ÷ $8,020 = .3677 or 36.8%

Long-term debt/property, plant, and equipment ratio. For the FPL Group and other electric utilities, this ratio indicates the degree of real asset collateral behind the debt contracted to support a company's capital investment. It also indicates a company's degree of dependence on debt to fund these expenditures. FPL Group's ratio reflects a relatively conservative posture:

$2,949 ÷ $9,354 = .3153 or 31.5%

Profitability

Operating expense ratio. Management's operational efficiency is indicated by this ratio, which reflects the relationship between total operating expenses and total operating revenues. Obviously, the lower the percentage the better. FPL Group's operating expense ratio is calculated as follows:

$5,141 ÷ $6,369 = .8072 or 80.1%

Net income/property, plant, and equipment ratio. This is a utility company's version of the conventional return on assets measurement, but in the case of utilities the focus is narrowed to a company's fixed assets. The return on average PP&E for the FPL Group is illustrated below:

Step 1:	$9,384 + $9,354 = $18,738 ÷ 2 = $9,369 average PP&E
Step 2:	$618 ÷ $9,369 = .0660 or 6.6%

Return-on-equity ratio. This is the conventional ROE indicator, which for the FPL Group is calculated accordingly:

Step 1: $4,592 + $4,845 = $9,437 ÷ 2 = $4,719 average equity

Step 2: $618 ÷ $4,719 = .1310 or 13.1%

Cash Flow

Because we have discussed these ratios previously in Chapter 6, I will simply calculate those cash flow ratios, using FPL Group's figures appropriately applied to electric utilities:

Capital expenditures/Operating cash flow ratio:
  $551 ÷ $1,597 = .3450 or 34.5%

Dividends paid/Operating cash flow ratio:
  $332 ÷ $1,597 = .2079 or 20.8%

Total capital expenditures + dividends/Operating cash flow ration:
  $551 + $332 = $883 ÷ $1,597 = .5529 or 55.3%

Free cash flow ratio:
  $1,597 – $883 = $764 ÷ $1,597 = .4784 or 47.8%

Dividend payout (Dividends paid/Net income) ratio:
  $332 ÷ $618 = .5372 or 53.7%

In closing our discussion of electric utilities, it is worthwhile noting that in prior years these companies customarily made large dividend payouts. In general, the industry practice was characterized by dividend payout ratios of around 80 percent. In view of the new economic environment for electric utilities, the FPL Group was one of the first companies in the industry to recognize the unsustainable nature of this level of dividend payment. While the industry's financial character will continue to vary somewhat from that of mainstream companies, the electric utilities' indicators of financial condition and performance will now become more closely matched to those of regular businesses.

What Have You Learned?

Investing wisely takes practice—lots of practice. Smart investors need to develop a variety of skills to help them make well-informed decisions. What I have tried to do in this book is to teach investors the fundamentals of one aspect of researching an investment opportunity. Being able to decipher and interpret financial statements and financial statement information is an important investment analysis skill that can contribute significantly to the process of selecting winning stocks.

What I have provided you in this book is just the beginning. If you are motivated to further develop your financial statement skills, I would highly recommend three books, which are listed in the bibliography:

1. Charles H. Gibson, *Financial Statement Analysis*
2. Leopold A. Berstein, *Analysis of Financial Statements*
3. Ferris, Tennant, and Jerris, *How to Understand Financial Statements*

Over the years, I have benefited from all three books in any number of ways. As self-education materials, these books require some "heavy lifting" by the reader. They will require an above-average investment of time (to digest) and money (to acquire), but the payoff for the serious investor will be a breadth and depth of financial statement know-how that will pay a lifetime of dividends.

However, before leaping to the next level of financial know-how, what have you learned, so far, about financial statements and the investment process from this book? Most important, you should now understand, in the words of Messrs. Ferris, Tennant, and Jerris (Prentice Hall, 1992), that "with a modicum of effort and a minimal accounting background, it is possible to make a reasonably well-informed assessment of a company's performance and its quality of reported earnings, assets, and cash flows." A company's financial statements are full of clues to its investment qualities. And now you have a basic knowledge of how to go about getting inside those financials to come up with useful information. This is what investment professions do.

If you work with a financial adviser, the next time you talk about one of his or her stock recommendations, you can talk intelligently about the strength of the company's balance sheet, earnings, and cash flow. At the very least, you will be able to ask good questions.

Let us say that the adviser's recommendation warrants a look at the company's annual report. Instead of your eyes glazing over at the thought of reading this document beyond the first couple of pages, you can look at the company's financials in the document, crunch some numbers, and track key investment evaluators over a reasonable period to pick up some trends. The financial statement worksheets in Appendix B come in handy for this purpose. Also, supplemental information like the auditors' report, the MD&A section, and the notes to the financials provide additional valuable insights about the company's financial condition and performance. The next step is to look for some validation on your findings from other sources of investment information.

Where do you get this help? A Value Line Report on the company is most likely available at your local library. Or try your brokerage firm to see if they can get you a Standard & Poor's stock report. Both of these investment information services provide a wealth of data on thousands of companies; and you can make better use of their data now that you have some financial statement know-how. Until now, all those numbers might have been a little overwhelming.

The company continues to look interesting. Either through your adviser or Internet investment information services, you obtain an investment research report. These reports can be biased and not completely objective. As long as you know that, however, often they also contain a lot of information about a company. Here again, your newly acquired financial statement skills will allow you to make independent judgments about the company's financial position. While you are on the Internet, perhaps you tap a service such as Hoover's Online, a respected provider of comprehensive background and financial data on some 5,000 companies. All of this information is predigested for you and presented in a series of reports, including a company's financials and a comprehensive presentation of financial ratios. Again, you have a basis for understanding and interpreting this material.

During the course of your research effort, you come across an article on the target company in one of the many investment periodicals currently available. The writer provides some worthwhile insights about the company, including comments about leverage, free cash flow, and margins that now make sense instead of falling into the same category as an unknown foreign language.

Whether you, as an investor, go through the investment research process on your own, work with a professional adviser, or use a combination of both approaches, the ultimate investment decision that you make will be based on fairly solid ground. You will have done your homework. An important component of that homework involves developing the ability to work with a company's numbers to see what they tell you about its investment potential.

I will end my remarks here with an appropriate quote from Martin D'Amico (*How to Predict Year-End Cash*. Englewood Cliffs: Prentice Hall, 1998): "Three thousand is just a number. By itself it has absolutely no meaning. It could be dollars, units, a sale or a cost. But when you attach a meaningful description and compare it to other numbers within a business, it becomes a powerful tool for measuring the health of a business." I hope you have learned something about how to use this powerful tool and will use it to improve your investing know-how.

"The Numbers Game"

Arthur Levitt, chairman of the Securities and Exchange Commission, spoke at the New York University Center for Law and Business, New York, NY, September 28, 1998, on the general subject of corporate financial reporting and specifically about earnings management in a speech entitled, "The Numbers Game." The following remarks have been excerpted from this speech, with permission, and focus on the issue of a company's quality of reported earnings:

ACCOUNTING HOCUS-POCUS

Our accounting principles weren't meant to be a straitjacket. Accountants are wise enough to know they cannot anticipate every business structure, or every new and innovative transaction., so they develop principles that allow for flexibility to adapt to changing circumstances. That's why the highest standards of objectivity, integrity, and judgment can't be the exception. They must be the rule.

Flexibility in accounting allows it to keep pace with business innovations. Abuses such as earnings management occur when people exploit this pliancy. Trickery is employed to obscure actual financial volatility. This, in turn, masks the true consequences of management's decisions. These practices aren't limited to smaller companies struggling to gain investor interest. It's also happening in companies whose products we know and admire.

So what are these illusions? Five of the more popular ones I want to discuss today are "big bath" restructuring charges, creative acquisition accounting, "cookie jar reserves," "immaterial" misapplications of accounting principles, and the premature recognition of revenue.

"Big Bath" Charges

Let me first deal with "big bath" restructuring charges.

Companies remain competitive by regularly assessing the efficiency and profitability of their operations. Problems arise, however, when we see large charges associated with companies' restructuring. These charges help companies "clean up" their balance sheet—giving them a so-called big bath.

Why are companies tempted to overstate these charges? When earnings take a major hit, the theory goes, Wall Street will look beyond a one-time loss and focus on future earnings.

And if these charges are conservatively estimated with a little extra cushioning, that so-called conservative estimate is miraculously reborn as income when estimates change or future earnings fall short.

When a company decides to restructure, management and employees, investors and creditors, customers and suppliers all want to understand the expected effects. We need, of course, to ensure that financial reporting provides this information. But this should not lead to flushing all the associated costs—and maybe a little extra—through the financial statements.

Creative Acquisition Accounting

Let me now turn to the second gimmick.

In recent years, whole industries have been remade through consolidations, acquisitions, and spin-offs. Some acquirers, particularly those using stock as an acquisition currency, have used this environment as an opportunity to engage in another form of "creative" accounting. I call it "merger magic."

I am not talking tonight about the pooling versus purchase problem. Some companies have no choice but to use purchase accounting—which can result in lower future earnings. But that's a result some companies are unwilling to tolerate.

So what do they do? They classify an ever-growing portion of the acquisition price as "in-process Research and Development, so—you guessed it—the amount can be written off in a one-time charge—removing any future earnings drag. Equally troubling is the creation of large liabilities for future operating expenses to protect future earnings—all under the mask of an acquisition.

Miscellaneous "Cookie Jar Reserves"

A third illusion played by some companies is using unrealistic assumptions to estimate liabilities for such items as sales returns, loan losses, or warranty costs. In doing so, they stash accruals in cookie jars during the good times and reach into them when needed in the bad times.

I'm reminded of one U.S. company who took a large one-time loss to earnings to reimburse franchisees for equipment. That equipment, however, which included literally the kitchen sink, had yet to be bought. And at the same time, they announced that future earnings would grow an impressive 15 percent per year.

"Materiality"

Let me now turn to the fourth gimmick—the abuse of materiality—a word that captures the attention of both attorneys and accountants. Materiality is another way we build flexibility into financial reporting. Using the logic of diminishing returns, some items may be so insignificant that they are not worth measuring and reporting with exact precision.

But some companies misuse the concept of materiality. They intentionally record errors within a defined percentage ceiling. Then they try to excuse that fib by arguing that the effect on the bottom line is too small to matter. If that's the case, why do they work so hard to create these errors? Maybe because the effect can matter, especially if it picks up that last penny of the consensus estimate. When either management or the outside auditors are questioned about these clear violations of GAAP, they answer sheepishly . . . "It doesn't matter. It's immaterial."

In markets where missing an earnings projection by a penny can result in a loss of millions of dollars in market capitalization, I have a hard time accepting that some of these so-called non-events simply don't matter.

Revenue Recognition

Last, companies try to boost earnings by manipulating the recognition of revenue. Think about a bottle of fine wine. You wouldn't pop the cork on that bottle before it was ready. But some companies are doing this with their revenue—recognizing it before the sale is complete, before the product is delivered to a customer, or at a time when the customer still has options to terminate, void, or delay the sale.

Financial Statement Worksheets

The material in Appendix B can be reproduced freely without requesting permission. Formula guides are provided for the first column (where a base year is needed, the formula begins in column B), which then can be replicated for the other columns. Please note that the formulas indicated relate to a manual computation of the various subtotals, totals, indicators, and ratios for each worksheet, which are organized in five designated columns, A through E. these formula guides can help computer users configure the cells as per the requirements of an EXCEL spreadsheet.

BALANCE SHEET WORKSHEET

COMPANY NAME:
AMOUNTS IN:
FISCAL YEAR-END:

CODE	BALANCE SHEET FISCAL YEAR	A	B	C	D	E
	ASSETS					
1	Cash and Equivalents					
2	Temporary Invested Funds					
3	Accounts Receivable					
4	**Total Quick Assets**					
5	Inventories					
6	Other Current Assets					
7	**Total Current Assets**					
8	Noncurrent Invested Funds					
9	Property, Plant & Equipment					
10	Other Noncurrent Assets					
11	Intangible Assets					
12	**Total Assets**					
	LIABILITIES					
13	Short-Term Borrowings					
14	Current Portion Long-Term Debt					
15	Accounts Payable					
16	Accrued Expenses					
17	Other Current Liabilities					
18	**Total Current Liabilities**					
19	Long-Term Debt					
20	Redeemable Preferred Stock					
21	Noncurrent Liabilities					
22	**Total Liabilities**					
23	Minority Interest					
	EQUITY					
24	**Total Shareholders' Equity**					
25	**Total Liabilities & Equity**					
	INVESTMENT EVALUATORS					
26	Days Sales Outstanding (days)					
27	Inventory Turnover (days)					
	Operating Cycle (days)					
	Fixed Asset Turnover (x)					
	Return on Assets (%)					
	Liability/ Asset Ratio (dcml)					
	Liability/ Equity Ratio (x)					
	Capitalization Ratio (dcml)					
	Adj. Capitalization Ratio (dcml)					
	Book Value per Share ($ amt)					
	NOTATIONAL DATA					
28	Operating Leases					
29	Number of Common Shares					
30	Net Sales					
31	Cost of Sales					
32	Net Income					

Formula Guide for the Balance Sheet Worksheet

Total Quick Assets	Code 4	A1+A2+A3
Total Current Assets	Code 7	A4+A5+A6
Total Assets	Code 12	A7+A8+A9+A10+A11
Total Current Liabilities	Code 18	A13+A14+A15+A16+A17
Total Liabilities	Code 22	A18+A19+A20+A21
Total Liabilities & Equity	Code 25	A22+A23+A24
Days Sales Outstanding (days)	Code 26	
	Column B	((A3+B3)÷2)((B30÷365)
Inventory Turnover (days)	Code 27	
	Column B	((A5+B5)÷2)÷(B31(365)
Operating Cycle (days)	Column B	B26+B27
Fixed Asset Turnover (x)	Column B	B30÷((A9+B9)÷2)
Return on Assets (%)	Column B	B32÷((A12+B12)÷2)
Liability/Asset Ratio (dcml)	Column A	A22÷A12
Liability/Equity Ratio (x)	Column A	A22÷A24
Capitalization Ratio (dcml)	Column A	(A14+A19)÷(A14+A19+A24)
Adj. Capitalization Ratio (dcml)	Column A	(A14+A19+A20+A28)÷(A14+A19 +A20+A28+A24)
Book Value per Share	Column A	A24÷A29

Notional data is obtained from the company's financial statements and the notes to the financial statements. The data obtained are entered directly into the worksheet.

INCOME STATEMENT WORKSHEET

COMPANY NAME:
AMOUNTS IN:
FISCAL YEAR-END:

CODE	INCOME STATEMENT FISCAL YEAR	A	B	C	D	E
33	Sales/Revenues					
34	Cost of Sales					
35	Gross Profit					
36	Selling Expenses					
37	General & Administrative					
38	Research & Development					
39	Total Operating Expenses					
40	Operating Profit					
41	Interest Expense					
42	Other Income					
43	Other Expense					
44	Pretax Income					
45	Provision For Taxes					
46	Minority Interest					
47	Special Items					
48	Net Income					
49	Per Share—Basic					
50	Per Share—Diluted					
51	Number of Average Shares					
	INVESTMENT EVALUATORS					
	Gross Profit Margin (%)					
	Operating Profit Margin (%)					
	Pretax Profit Margin (%)					
	Net Margin (%)					
	Return on Equity (ROE) (%)					
	Return on Capital Empl.(ROCE) (%)					
	Sales Growth (%)					
	Net Income Growth (%)					
	Sales per Share ($ amt)					
	Earnings per Share ($ amt)					

Formula Guide for the Income Statement Worksheet

Cost of Sales	Code 34	Negative number
Gross Profit	Code 35	A33 – A34
Selling Expenses		
General & Administrative		
Research & Development	Codes 36, 37, and 38	Negative numbers
Total Operating Expenses	Code 39	A35 – A36 – A37 – A38
Operating Profit	Code 40	A35 – A39
Interest Expense	Code 41	Negative number
Other Expense	Code 43	Negative number
Pretax Income	Code 44	A40 – A41+A42 – A43
Provision for Taxes	Code 45	Negative number *
Minority Interest	Code 46	Negative number *
Special Items	Code 47	Negative number *
Net Income	Code 48	A44 – A45 – A46 – A47
Net Income Per Share – Basic		
Net Income Per Share – Diluted		
Number of Average Shares	Codes 49, 50, and 51	Notional data from statement
Gross Profit Margin (%)	Column A	A35÷A33
Operating Profit Margin (%)	Column A	A40÷A33
Pretax Profit Margin (%)	Column A	A44÷A33
Net Margin (%)	Column A	A48÷A33
Return on Equity (%)	Column B	A48÷((A24+B24)÷2)
Return on Capital Empl.(%)	Column B	A48÷((A24+B24+A14+B14+A19 +B19)÷2)
Sales Growth (%)	Column B	(B33-A33)÷A33
Net Income Growth (%)	Column B	(B48-A48)÷A48
Sales per Share ($ amt)	Column A	A33÷A51
Earnings per Share ($ amt)	Column A	A48÷A51

* Generally these numbers are negative, but the reader should be aware that there are instances, albeit in frequent, where these numbers could be positive.

CASH FLOW STATEMENT WORKSHEET

COMPANY NAME:
AMOUNTS IN:
FISCAL YEAR-END:

CODE	CASH FLOW STATEMENT FISCAL YEAR	A	B	C	D	E
52	Sales					
53	Operating Cash Flow					
54	Capital Expenditures					
55	Dividends Paid					
56	Free Cash Flow					
57	Business Acquisitions					
58	Short-Term Debt					
59	Total Debt					
	INVESTMENT EVALUATORS					
	Operating Cash Flow/Sales (%)					
	Cap. Expenditures/ Op. Cash Flow (%)					
	Dividends/ Op. Cash Flow (%)					
	Cap. Expd.+ Div./ Op. Cash Flow (%)					
	Free Cash Flow/ Op. Cash Flow (%)					
	Op. Cash Flow/ Short-Term Debt (x)					
	Op. Cash Flow/ Total Debt (%)					
	Cash Flow per Share ($ amt)					
	Dividends per Share ($ amt)					

Formula Guide for the Cash Flow Statement

Capital Expenditures	Code 54	Negative number
Dividends Paid	Code 55	Negative number
Free Cash Flow	Code 56	A53 – A54 – A55
Operating Cash Flow/Sales (%)	Column A	A53÷A52
Cap. Expenditures/Op. C.F. (%)	Column A	A54÷A53
Dividends/Op. Cash Flow (%)	Column A	A55÷A53
Cap. Expd. + Div./Op. C.F. (%)	Column A	(A54+A55)÷A53
Free Cash Flow/Op. C.F. (%)	Column A	A56÷A53
Op. C.F./Short-Term Debt (x)	Column A	A53÷A58
Op. C.F./Total Debt (%)	Column A	A53÷A59
Cash Flow per Share ($ amt)	Column A	A53÷A51
Dividends per Share ($ amt)	Column A	A55÷A51

BANK WORKSHEET

COMPANY:
AMOUNTS IN:
FISCAL YEAR-END:

CODE	BALANCE SHEET	YEAR	YEAR	YEAR	YEAR	YEAR
1	Cash & Banks					
2	Invested Funds					
3	**Total Primary Assets**					
4	Gross Loans					
5	Loan Loss Reserve					
6	Net Loans					
7	Premises & Equipment					
8	Other Assets					
9	**Total Assets**					
10	Total Deposits					
11	Borrowings					
12	Accrued Expenses					
13	Other Liabilities					
14	Long-Term Debt					
15	**Total Liabilities**					
16	**Shareholders' Equity**					
17	**Total Liabilities & Equity**					
	INCOME STATEMENT					
18	Interest Income					
19	Interest Expense					
20	**Net Interest Income**					
21	Fees, Commisions & Other					
22	**Total Income**					
23	Provision for Loan Losses					
24	Employee Expense					
25	General Operating Expense					
26	**Total Operating Expense**					
27	Pretax Income					
28	Special Item					
29	Taxes					
30	**Net Income**					
	SUPPLEMENTAL DATA					
31	Dividends Paid					
32	Employees (actual year-end)					
33	Average Earning Assets					
34	Average Total Assets					
35	Average Total Equity					
36	Average Gross Loans					
37	Nonperforming Loans					
38	Loan Charge-Offs					

Formula Guide for Bank Worksheet

Total Primary Assets	Code 3	A1+A2
Total Assets	Code 9	A3+A6+A7+A8
Total Liabilities	Code 15	A10+A11+A12+A13+A14
Total Liabilities & Equity	Code17	A15+A16
Interest Expense	Code 19	Negative number
Net Interest Income	Code 20	A18–A19
Total Income	Code 22	A20+A21
Provision for Loan Losses	Code 23	Negative number
Employee Expense	Code 24	Negative number
General Operating Expense	Code 25	Negative number
Total Operating Expense	Code 26	A24+A25
Pretax Income	Code 27	A22–A23–A26
Special Item	Code 28	Negative number *
Taxes	Code 29	Negative number *
Net Income	Code 30	A27–A28–A29
Average Earning Assets (Line 33)	Column B	(A3+A4+B3+B4)÷2
Average Total Assets (Line 34)	Column B	(A9+B9)÷2
Average Total Equity (Line 35)	Column B	(A16+B16)÷2
Average Gross Loans (Line 36)	Column B	(A4+B4)÷2

* Generally these numbers are negative, but the reader should be aware that there are instances, albeit infrequent, where these numbers could be positive.

BANK INVESTMENT EVALUATORS WORKSHEET

COMPANY:
FISCAL YEAR-END:

RATIOS	YEAR	YEAR	YEAR	YEAR	YEAR
CAPITAL ADEQUACY					
Tier 1 Capital (%)					
Total Capital (%)					
Leverage (%)					
Equity/ Assets (%)					
Dividends/ Net Income (%)					
LOAN ASSET QUALITY					
Loan Loss Reserve/ Gross Loans (%)					
Nonperforming Loans/ Gross Loans (%)					
Nonperforming Loans/ Loan Loss Reserved (%)					
Loan Charge-offs/ Average Gross Loans (%)					
MANAGEMENT EFFICIENCY					
Net Margin (%)					
Efficiency (%)					
Gross Loans per Employee (amt millions)					
Total Income per Employee (amt millions)					
PROFITABILITY					
Return on Assets (%)					
Return on Equity (%)					
LIQUIDITY RATIOS:					
Gross Loans/ Total Deposit (%)					
Total Primary Assets/ Total Deposits (%)					

Formula Guide for the Bank Investment Evaluator Worksheet

Tier 1 Capital		
Total Capital		
Leverage	Data is obtained from the bank's financial statements and the notes to the financial statements.	
Equity/Assets (%)	Column A	A16÷A9
Dividends/Net income (%)	Column A	A31÷A30
Loan Loss Reserve/Gross Loans (%)	Column A	A5÷A4
Nonperforming Loans/Gross Loans (%)	Column A	A37÷A4
Nonperforming Loans/Loan Loss Res. (%)	Column A	A37÷A5
Loan Charge-Offs/Avg. Gross Loans (%)	Column B	A38÷A36
Net Margin (%)	Column B	A20÷A33
Efficiency (%)	Column A	A26÷A22
Gross Loans per Employee (amt millions)	Column A	A4÷A32
Total Income per Employee (amt millions)	Column A	A22÷A32
Return on Assets (%)	Column A	A30÷A34
Return on Equity (%)	Column A	A30÷A35
Gross Loans/Total Deposits	Column A	A4÷A10
Total Primary Assets/Total Deposits (%)	Column A	A3÷A10

Bibliography

Accounting Trends and Techniques 1997. New York: American Institute of Certified Public Accountants, 1997.

Bernstein, Leopold A. *Analysis of Financial Statements*. 3rd ed. Homewood, Ill.: Dow JonesIrwin, 1990.

Donnahoe, Alan S. *What Every Manager Should Know about Financial Analysis*. New York: Fireside/Simon & Schuster, 1990.

Downes, John, and Jordan Elliot Goodman. *Barron's Finance and Investment Handbook*. Woodbury, N.Y: Barron's Educational Series, Inc., 1986.

Drucker, Peter E. "If Earnings Aren't the Dial to Read." *The Wall Street Journal*, October 30, 1986, p. 49.

Ferris, Kenneth R., Kirk L. Tennant, and Scott I. Jerris. *How to Understand Financial Statements*. Englewood Cliffs, N.J.: Prentice Hall, 1992.

Follett, Robert. *How to Keep Score in Business*. Chicago: Follett Publishing, 1978.

Forst, Brian. *Power In Numbers*. New York: John Wiley, 1987.

Fridson, Martin S. *Financial Statement Analysis*. New York: John Wiley, 1991.

Gahlon, James M., and Robert L. Vigeland. "An Introduction to Corporate Cash Flow Statements." *AAII Journal* (January 1989): 14–18.

Gibson, Charles H. *Financial Statement Analysis*. 7th ed. Cincinnati: South-Western College Publishing, 1998.

Horngren, Charles I., and Gary L. Sundem. *Introduction to Financial Accounting*. Englewood Cliffs, N.J.: Prentice Hall, 1987.

Lipay, Raymond J. *Understand Those Financial Reports*. New York: John Wiley, 1984.

Loth, Richard B. *How to Profit from Reading Annual Reports*. Chicago: Dearborn Financial Publishing, 1993.

_____. *The Annual Report Glossary*. Edwards, Colo.: FIPS Partners, 1988.

_____. *The Shareholder's Dictionary*. Edwards, Colo.: FIPS Partners, 1990.

Lynch, Peter. *One Up on Wall Street*. New York: Simon & Schuster, 1989.

Markese, John. "Financial Statements: The Balance Sheet, The Income Statement and How to Interpret Them." Series. *AAII Journal* (July, August, and September 1986): 33–35, 34–35, and 31–34, respectively.

Myer, John N. *Understanding Financial Statements*. New York: New American Library, 1968.

O'glove, Thorton L. *Quality of Earnings*. New York: The Free Press, 1987.

Robert Morris Associates. *Credit Considerations—Volumes 1, 2 & 3*. Philadelphia: RMA, 1986.

Ruth, George E. *Analyzing Financial Statements*. 5th ed. Washington, D.C.: American Bankers Association, 1998.

Securities and Exchange Commission. *Management's Discussion and Analysis of Financial Condition and Results of Operations.* Reprint. New York: Sorg, 1989.

Server, Andrew Evan. "Cashing In on Cash Flow." *Fortune,* May 23, 1988, pp. 113–14.

Spurga, Ronald C. *Balance Sheet Basics.* New York: Franklin Watts, 1986.

Tracey, John A. *How to Read a Financial Report.* New York: John Wiley, 1980.

Understanding Audits and the Auditor's Report. New York: American Institute of Certified Public Accountants, 1989.

Glossary Of Financial Statement Terminology

accelerated depreciation A method of depreciation used mostly for tax-reporting purposes that results in lowering a company's current earnings, thus lowering its income tax payments.

accounting policies The accounting methods employed by a company under generally accepted accounting principles (GAAP) for the preparation of its financial statements. These policies are enumerated in the notes to the financial statements.

accounting principles The basic concepts and assumptions that accountants use when preparing financial statements. Examples of accounting principles include, among others, conservatism, historical cost, materiality, and revenue recognition.

accounts payable A current liability representing amounts owed by a company to suppliers for the purchase of goods and services under varying terms of payment and referred to as trade credit (aka accounts payable).

accounts receivable A current asset that represents amounts owed to a company that are to be collected within the next 12 months. Generally, trade receivables, amounts due from customers for the goods and services they have purchased, account for practically all of the receivable amount. A note receivable usually represents the sale of some other asset or the conversion of a trade receivable from open account to a note basis (aka receivables).

accrual basis The basis used by most companies for their financial reporting, whereby revenues are recognized when they are realized (goods shipped or services rendered) and expenses to produce these revenues are recognized when they are incurred.

accruals (See **accrued expenses**.)

accrued expenses A current liability in the balance sheet that records accumulated obligations as of the statement date for such items as payroll, employee benefits, insurance premiums, interest due, rent, sales commissions and, in some instances, taxes.

accrued income (See **deferred credits**.)

accumulated depreciation The cumulative amount of all depreciation, generally shown as a deduction from the historical cost of fixed assets in a balance sheet or in the notes to financial statements.

acid test ratio (See **quick assets ratio**.)

additional paid-in capital A component of shareholders' equity in a balance sheet that records the amount of equity capital paid by shareholders over the amount designated as par value for the company's common stock (aka capital in excess of par or stated value, capital surplus, paid-in capital, and additional capital).

allowance for doubtful accounts Management's estimate of the uncollectible amount it expects on its customers' trade accounts receivable. Accounts receivable in the balance sheet are always stated net of the allowance

American Institute for Certified Public Accountants (AICPA) The professional organization for certified public accountants, which has been influential in the development of the accounting profession and generally accepted accounting principles.

amortization A gradual reduction of the value of intangible assets and leasehold improvements on a systematic basis over a given period. Amortization also is used to describe the regular, periodic repayment of debt, particularly long-term obligations such as bonds and term loans.

annual report A formal, detailed record of a publicly held company's financial condition and performance. The company's financial statements, the notes to the financial statements, the management discussion and analysis, and the auditors' report are all found in this document. This report is issued yearly to shareholders but also is available to the general public three to four months after the fiscal year-end.

asset turnover A ratio that compares average total assets with net sales and is an indicator of a company's ability to generate sales from its asset base.

assets Everything of value that a company owns or is due, that can be measured objectively. Assets generally are separated into current and noncurrent components of the balance sheet.

audit The examination of a company's accounting records and supporting data under prescribed procedures by independent certified public accountants.

audited statements Financial statements that have been the subject of an audit.

auditors Outside or independent auditors; usually a firm of certified public accountants (CPAs) that examines a company's financial records according to generally accepted accounting standards.

auditors' report After auditing a company's financials, the auditors provide their findings in a brief report that accompanies the financial statements. The findings provided by the auditors, after auditing a company's financials, in a brief report that accompanies the financial statements (aka independent accountants' report or opinion, accountants' report or opinion, independent certified public accountants' report or opinion, independent auditors' report, certified public accountants' report, or auditors' opinion).

authorized shares The maximum number of shares of capital stock that a company may legally issue under the terms of its incorporation (aka authorized stock).

average cost One of the principal methods used to value the cost of a company's inventory. The average cost method, as the term literally implies, produces a gross profit somewhere between that obtained from the impact on the cost of sales under the last-in, first-out (LIFO) and first-in, first-out (FIFO) methods of valuing inventory cost (aka weighted-average method).

balance sheet A financial statement that lists, as of the date of the fiscal year-end, a company's assets (those items of value it owns), liabilities (what it owes), and shareholders' equity (the owners' interest).

bond A form of long-term borrowing by which a company issues a written promise to pay a fixed amount of money on or by a specified date at a stipulated interest rate.

book value An accounting term for the original cost of an asset, less accumulated depreciation or amortization, reflected in a company's accounting records (aka carrying value). However, the term also is used frequently to describe shareholders' equity, particularly on a per-share basis.

book value per share (See **book value.**)

bottom line Financial vernacular for net income—the "bottom" or last line in a company's income statement.

business combinations A term that refers to the acquisition of one company by another; accounting uses two methods to record the acquisition of one company by another—the purchase method or a pooling of interests. The former accounts for a business combination on the basis of the market value of assets of the acquired company; the latter is based on the book value of the acquired company's assets.

capital Money invested in a business by its owners; sometimes considered just equity, but there are really two kinds of capital—long-term debt and equity.

capital asset (See **property, plant and equipment.**)

capital employed Synonymous with capital structure, capitalization, and invested capital, it refers to the permanent funds—debt and equity capital—employed to support a company's operations.

capital expenditure The outlay of money to acquire or improve a capital asset.

capital goods Fixed assets, particularly machinery and equipment, used for the production of other goods.

capital invested in excess of par value (See **additional paid-in capital.**)

capital investment An investment in capital goods or capital assets of long-term benefit to a company.

capitalization Generally used in financial writing to refer to a company's permanent capital, long-term debt, and equity. Sometimes referred to as invested capital or capital employed. (See **market capitalization.**)

capitalization ratio A measurement that indicates the debt component of a company's capitalization, (i.e., the extent the company's debt is used in relation to the total amount of the company's permanent capital).

capitalize A term that refers to a company, under certain circumstances, being allowed to record a cost as an asset (that is, subject to amortization) on the balance sheet instead of charging it to the income statement (e.g., deferred charges).

capitalized lease (See **capital lease**.)

capital lease A lease for capital goods that essentially provides all the attributes of ownership to the lessee company. Accounting conventions, therefore, require that a capital lease be reflected as a fixed asset and a long-term liability in the lessee company's balance sheet.

capital stock The ownership shares of a company consisting of all common and preferred stock.

capital structure Synonymous with capitalization, refers to a company's relative amount of long-term debt and equity and these resources' relationships with each other and the assets they support.

capital surplus (See **additional paid-in capital**.)

cash The most liquid of assets that appears as the first line item in current assets in a company's balance sheet. It is money on hand and on deposit in banks.

cash equivalents A company's short-term, temporary investments for earning interest on cash in excess of current requirements.

cash flow Usually (the term has several definitions) the funds generated by a company to operate the business, make capital investments, amortize debt, and pay dividends. Cash flow originates from a company's operations, financing, and investment activities.

certified public accountant (CPA) (See **auditors' report**.)

charge A term regularly employed in financial reporting to indicate an expense in the income statement.

commercial paper Short-term corporate obligations or promissory notes, unsecured, interest bearing with flexible maturities. They normally are issued by top-rated companies or backed by bank lines of credit that guarantee their liquidity.

commitments Pledges, such as for the future purchase of capital goods or leasing obligations, that companies indicate in the notes to financial statements.

common stock A unit of ownership in a corporation entitling the owner to voting rights and dividends. As part of a company's capital stock, common stock is a component of shareholders' equity in the balance sheet.

compensating balances A term that refers to a certain level of deposit balances that lenders, if possible, attempt to require borrowers to maintain with them as one of the conditions of a loan or credit agreement. These funds, however, should not be thought of as restricted cash.

consolidated financial statements Financial statements in which consolidation of the financial positions of the parent and its majority-owned subsidiaries reflects the combined activities of a number of separate legal entities into one economic unit

contingent liabilities Potential liabilities not recorded on a company's balance sheet, the most common of these being obligations related to litigation and guarantees (aka contingencies).

continuing operations A term often used in a company's income statement to distinguish income of a recurring nature as opposed to that produced by extraordinary events and/or discontinued operations.

cost (See **historical cost**.)

cost and profits in excess of billings A current asset usually found in the balance sheet of a company working with a customer on a long-term contract basis. As of the statement date, the company has completed work but not yet billed the customer (aka cost and estimated earnings in excess of billings).

cost in excess of fair value of net assets acquired (See **goodwill**.)

cost in excess of net assets of acquired businesses (See **goodwill**.)

cost of sales The cost of producing a company's inventory; that is, the cost of raw materials, labor and production overhead used to produce finished products. For nonmanufacturing companies, this represents the cost of merchandise purchased for resale. Service companies do not have a cost of sales (aka cost of goods sold and cost of products sold).

covenants Conditions placed in a loan or credit agreement by a lender to protect its position as a creditor of a borrowing company (aka restrictive covenants).

creditor Anyone who lends money to a company—a financial institution, bondholder, investor who buys the issuing company's commercial paper, and a supplier of goods and services that extends trade credit.

credit ratings Formal credit risk evaluations by credit rating agencies of a company's ability to repay principal and interest on its debt obligations, principally bonds and commercial paper.

cumulative effect of change in accounting policies A special item, not part of recurring earnings, that requires specific disclosure in a company's income statement. As the term implies, a change has occasioned an earnings gain or loss outside the flow of continuing or normal operations.

current A term synonymous with short term, generally meaning less than one year.

current assets Assets in the balance sheet of a company that are cash or are reasonably expected to be converted into cash within the company's next fiscal year.

current liabilities Liabilities in the balance sheet of a company representing obligations that are due and payable within the company's next fiscal year.

current portion of long-term debt Classified as a current liability, the amount of longterm debt that is due and payable, as of a company's year-end statement date, during the next fiscal year. It is considered a fixed charge.

current ratio A popularly used test of short-term liquidity that measures the amount of current assets available to pay current liabilities.

days sales in inventory A measurement used to determine a company's inventory turnover.

days sales outstanding A measurement used to determine a company's trade receivables turnover (aka DSO and days sales in receivables).

debenture The technical term used to describe an unsecured bond.

debt Generally considered to be funds a company has borrowed from a creditor, implying the payment of principal and interest. This is a liability, current or long-term, that has a high priority ranking for payment.

debt issuance costs (See **deferred charges.**)

debt service A term that refers to a company's obligation to make payment, of interest and principal, on the current maturities of outstanding debt to keep its loans on a current status. In other usage, debt service implies just the payment of interest to keep borrowings current.

deferred charges A noncurrent asset representing a cost that has been capitalized, such as a deferred financing cost (investment banking fees) for a securities placement.

deferred credits A term generally associated with unearned, accrued, or deferred income that appears in a company's balance sheet in the liability section. Deferred items represent the collection in advance for goods delivered and/or services rendered, and rather than owing cash payments to the customer, the company has an obligation to provide the goods or services to the customer.

deferred financing costs (See **deferred charges.**)

deferred income (See **deferred credits.**)

deferred income taxes A long-term liability that is an accounting estimate of tax payments deferred because a company is permitted to use different accounting methods for taxes and financial reporting.

depletion The term applied to the use of natural resources such as oil and gas, minerals, and timberlands. As assets in a company's balance sheet, the resources eventually will be used up; therefore, as they are depleted, a loss in value is recorded much like the depreciation of fixed assets.

depreciation The accounting procedure that allocates the cost of a fixed asset (plant and equipment—land is not depreciated) over its estimated useful life.

depreciation expense The annual amount of depreciation expense generally included in the cost-of-sales component of the income statement. In the statement of cash flows, depreciation expense, as a noncash charge that adjusts net income, appears as an addition to cash from operations.

dilution A term that refers to the effect on earnings and book value per-share calculations when, over time, the number of shares issued by a company increases disproportionately to the growth in the company's earnings. Net income is reported on a per-share basis as basic and diluted.

discontinued operations Operations that have been or will be discontinued and are reported separately from continuing operations in a company's income statement. The purpose is to distinguish results from continuing operations and thus improve the comparability of earnings from year to year.

dividend A payment in the form of cash or stock by a company to its shareholders.

dividend payable A current liability on the balance sheet that reflects a declaration by the board of directors of a dividend to be paid by the company to its shareholders.

dividend payout ratio A measurement of that portion of net income that is being paid out in dividends rather than retained in the business.

dividend yield A measurement that provides the yield, as a percentage, on a company's common stock by dividing the dividends per share by the market price per share.

earned surplus (See **retained earnings**.)

earnings A term used interchangeably with income and profit.

earnings per share (EPS) A term that indicates the net income (after preferred dividends) per share of common stock.

earnings report (See **statement of income**.)

effective tax rate A term that refers to the calculation of the percentage resulting from dividing income tax expense by pretax income in a company's income statement.

employee stock ownership plan (ESOP) A tax-qualified benefit plan that provides employees with an ownership interest in their company. There are two types: nonleveraged and leveraged. A leveraged ESOP has balance sheet implications, whereby the ESOP borrows the money to buy the company's stock and the company provides or guarantees the loan.

equity The general term used to describe the investment that the shareholders have in a company. It is the difference between total assets and total liabilities, the owners' share of the business (aka shareholders' or stockholders' equity and shareholders' investment).

equity capital A term synonymous with equity that represents what the owners put into the business as opposed to debt capital that comes from creditors.

equity in earnings of affiliates The amount of earnings, as recorded in the income statement, that belongs to the investor company from the operations of unconsolidated affiliates and subsidiaries.

equity method The accounting method used for recording the value of the investments of an investor company representing 50 percent or less ownership in unconsolidated subsidiaries and affiliates.

estimated useful life For financial statement purposes, and in accordance with GAAP, the period of time that a company establishes to depreciate a fixed asset.

expenditure The term generally used to describe an outlay of funds by a company for the acquisition of an asset. The immediate effect is on the balance sheet. Later, as the asset is depreciated or amortized, the expense is passed on to the income statement.

expense The term generally used to describe an outlay or accrual of funds by a company to cover costs incurred for selling; general and administrative functions; interest; taxes; and other items affecting the income statement.

extraordinary item The type of entry in a company's income statement meant to disclose an unusual or infrequent item that is not part of recurring or continuing operations (aka special item).

fair market value of assets (See **market value**.)

FASB (See **Financial Accounting Standards Board**.)

FIFO (See **first-in, first-out method**.)

finance company subsidiary Generally, a wholly owned subsidiary that exists primarily to finance the parent company's sales to customers. Manufacturers of high-value capital goods often use this mechanism to support their distributors and largescale sales transactions.

Financial Accounting Standards Board (FASB) Beginning in 1973, the primary organization for the development of generally accepted accounting principles. Prior to 1973, the American Institute of Certified Public Accountants (AICPA) undertook this function. The FASB consists of a seven-member board of certified public accountants, academics, and representatives of industry and government. Supported by a staff of experts, the FASB conducts research, issues rulings (Statements of Financial Accounting Standards—SFAS) and, in general, is the watchdog for proper financial reporting.

financial leverage The expression that refers to a company's use of debt as opposed to equity to support its assets (aka leverage).

financial statements Generally considered a company's balance sheet, income statement, statement of cash flows, and statement of shareholders' equity/retained earnings (aka financials).

first-in, first-out method One of the commonly used methods for valuing the cost of inventory whose effect tends to maximize earnings.

fiscal year A company's business year, usually a 12-month accounting period that does not necessarily correspond to the calendar year.

fixed assets The financial professional's shorthand for property, plant, and equipment (aka fixed capital, fixed investment, or capital assets).

fixed capital or investment (See **fixed assets**.)

fixed charges Those obligations, generally interest and current maturities of longterm debt, that a company must meet to maintain a good record with creditors.

footnotes (See **notes to financial statements**.)

foreign currency translation A term that refers to translating the financials of international operations in foreign currencies to the U.S. dollar. The effects of foreign exchange fluctuations are recorded in a special equity account to avoid distortions in reported earnings (aka currency translation adjustment, translation or cumulative translation adjustment, and foreign exchange translation adjustments).

foreign exchange gains (losses) Transaction gains or losses from buying and selling foreign exchange or taking payment for a sale in foreign currency. These are not the same as translation gains or losses and are reported through the income statement as realized exchange gains or losses.

Forms 10-K and 10-Q For publicly held companies, filing requirement forms of the Securities and Exchange Commission. Form 10K is similar to an annual report but with more detail. Form 10Q contains detailed (quarterly) information on a company's operations and financial position.

free cash flow An expression that indicates the amount of cash available after capital expenditures (and sometimes cash dividends) are subtracted from net operating cash flow.

fully diluted earnings Earnings per share expressed after the assumed exercise of warrants and stock options, and the conversion of convertible securities.

funded debt Technically, that portion of a company's long-term debt composed of bonds and other similar long-term, fixed-maturity type of borrowings. Some definitions simply equate funded debt with long-term debt.

furniture and fixtures A fixed asset, subject to depreciation, that often is included as a component of the property, plant, and equipment account grouping in a company's balance sheet.

GAAP (See **generally accepted accounting principles**.)

generally accepted accounting principles (GAAP) Principles according to which financial statements are prepared. They represent a body of accounting research, precedents, and agreed-upon standards of financial reporting that have evolved over the years.

generally accepted auditing standards Standards characterized by adequate planning, an understanding of internal controls, and the gathering of sufficient evidence to prepare an audit report. Audit work is to be performed by competent professionals with an independent attitude. (See **auditors' report**.)

goodwill An intangible asset that arises from business combinations accounted for under the purchase method. It represents the cost to the acquiring company in excess of the fair value of net assets (equity) of the acquired business (aka purchased goodwill).

gross margin (See **gross profit**.)

gross profit The difference between a company's sales and its cost of sales.

historical cost The accounting principle that values assets at their purchase price; for example, fixed assets are listed in a company's balance sheet at their historical cost less accumulated depreciation (aka cost).

identifiable assets The term used in the business segment information note in an annual report to identify those assets of the company that are used by each product line or line of business and geographic area of the company's overall activities.

income A term synonymous with profit and earnings. The terms are used interchangeably to indicate gains to the company.

income before taxes The statement of income after the cost of sales, operating expenses, other income/expense and special items have all been deducted from the company's revenues. The only remaining expense is taxes (aka pretax income).

income statement (See **statement of income**.)

income tax Generally, a major expense item in the income statement. The deduction from pretax income, usually identified with the caption "provision for income taxes," results in net income. The tax entry represents levies by state, local, and foreign governments and the federal government on a company's earnings (aka federal income taxes and taxes).

income tax payable This line-item caption that identifies a company's current tax liability. It is an accrued expense, but because of its relative importance as an obligation, it usually is stated separately in current liabilities.

independent accountants' report (See **auditors' report**.)

industry practice An expression used by companies to explain their application of an accounting policy that runs counter to general practice but conforms to industry usage.

intangible assets Noncurrent assets in a balance sheet representing nonphysical items such as patents, financing costs, and purchased goodwill. The value of these intangibles is reduced by amortization over varying periods of time.

intercompany transactions Business transactions that take place within the corporate family and are eliminated in the consolidated financial statements so as not to inflate the numbers of the consolidated entity

interest expense Generally, a line item in the income statement reflecting the interest costs on a company's borrowings and considered a fixed charge.

interest income Interest earned by a company on its temporary investment of cash.

interest rate swap A financial product that companies use to protect themselves against their exposure to debt-related changes in interest rates.

inventory Generally identified in the balance sheet's current assets in its plural form as inventories. For manufacturers, inventory will consist of raw materials and supplies used in production, work in process, and finished goods. Wholesalers, distributors, and retailers basically have a finished goods inventory. Service companies have little or no inventory, with some exceptions such as transport companies that have supplies inventory used by the business.

inventory turnover The number of times inventory is replaced during a company's fiscal year.

invested capital (See **capitalization**.)

investment in unconsolidated subsidiaries (See **investment**.)

investment A noncurrent asset that represents a company's equity ownership in unconsolidated subsidiaries and affiliates.

last-in, first-out method One of the commonly used methods for valuing the cost of inventory whose effect tends to understate earnings.

lease commitments Pledges generally disclosed in a note to the financial statements in a company's annual report that (1) details the amount of assets under capital leases in property, plant, and equipment; (2) discloses the present value of minimum capital lease payments, which is the amount recorded as part of long-term debt; (3) indicates the total minimum operating lease payments; and (4) provides the annual rental expense for operating leases for the three fiscal years being reported in an annual report.

leasehold improvements A fixed asset component of the property, plant, and equipment account in the balance sheet. A leasehold represents a right to the use of a property under a lease. Leasehold improvements represent expenditures, which are capitalized, for installations, renovations, and remodeling of such property These expenditures are subject to amortization.

leverage (See **financial leverage**.)

liability A term defined as what a company owes to others—creditors, suppliers, tax authorities, and the like. As a section of the balance sheet, it is divided into current liabilities and long-term liabilities.

LIFO (See **last-in, first-out method**.)

line of credit A term related to a company's borrowing relationships, generally with commercial banks, that represents an agreement that sets the terms and conditions for borrowing up to a set amount of money.

liquid assets A term associated with the most liquid of current assets—cash, cash equivalents, marketable securities, and trade receivables—that can be quickly converted to cash.

liquidity A much-used phrase in financial reporting that refers to the ease with which a company's assets can be converted to cash. A business is said to be liquid when it holds a high proportion of largely liquid assets (cash, cash equivalents, marketable securities, and accounts receivable).

loan or credit agreement A formalized, contractual arrangement between a lender and a borrower that sets the terms and conditions for borrowing.

London interbank offered rate (LIBOR) The equivalent of the prime rate as applied to eurodollar loans.

long term A term used to indicate a period that extends for more than one year.

long-term debt As presented in a balance sheet, a long-term liability and an important component of a company's capitalization. Long-term debt represents borrowed funds, usually subject to a formal loan or credit agreement, that are due for payment after one year and usually over several years.

long-term investments (See **investments**.)

long-term liabilities Obligations that fall due after one year and follow current liabilities in a company's balance sheet presentation.

lower of cost or market An accounting term representative of the generally accepted accounting principle of conservatism. The valuation having the least favorable effect on a company's financial position is the one applied and the term is seen most often with inventory and marketable securities.

management's discussion and analysis Referred to as MD&A, a report that appears in a company's annual report or Form 10-K in which management comments on the results of operations (the income statement), liquidity, and capital resources for the years under review. The comments should include prospective information on these and other activities of the company.

marketable equity securities Securities representing ownership of common and/or preferred stock that are listed, thus providing ready marketability and conversion to cash.

marketable securities Securities representing a company's temporary investment of cash in safe, highly liquid instruments for interest or dividend yield.

market capitalization A measurement of company size—giant, large, medium, and small—used by investment professionals. It is computed by multiplying a company's stock price by the number of its outstanding shares. A company's market cap should not be confused with its capitalization, which is a financial accounting concept. (See **capitalization**.)

minority interest A balancing entry that appears below the liabilities section of the balance sheet for companies with consolidated subsidiaries that are not wholly owned.

minority interest in earnings Just as the balance sheet is affected by minority interest, so too is the income statement. For example, when the parent company consolidates 100 percent of the earnings of a subsidiary that is 80 percent owned, 20 percent of earnings is deducted from the parent's earnings.

net income Figure arrived at when expenses are deducted from total revenues (sales and other income) and is the bottom line of the income statement. A net loss is obviously the opposite of net income. Net income is a major contributor to cash flow and is used to compute a variety of profitability indicators (aka net earnings and net profit).

net sales A term that represents the value from the sale of a company's goods and services (aka sales or revenues).

net working capital A term synonymous with working capital, which is the difference between current assets and current liabilities.

net worth A term synonymous with equity, shareholders'/stockholders' equity, or investment, all of which refer to the ownership interest in a company as stated in its balance sheet. In financial parlance, tangible net worth signifies that a company's intangible assets have been deducted from its balance sheet net worth.

noncash charge An expression used to refer to those expense items in a company's income statement that, as accounting entries only, reduce earnings but do not represent an outflow of cash. These noncash items are added back to net income, which, along with some other adjustments, result in operating cash flow in the cash flow statement.

noncurrent A term synonymous with long term.

nonrecurring An expression used in reference to items in the income statement, which are supposed to be unusual, extraordinary, or one-time events.

notes payable A current liability in the balance sheet for money owed by a company as evidenced by a written promissory note; generally used to denote bank financing.

notes receivable (See **accounts receivable**.)

notes to financial statements Notes that are an integral part of a company's financial statements; they provide additional disclosure of information of critical importance to understanding a company's financials (aka footnotes).

off-balance sheet A term generally referring to debt or debtlike obligations such as operating leases that don't appear in the balance sheet. However, conservative analysis considers these items as debt in the calculation of a company's debt measurements.

operating cycle The number of days it takes to convert accounts receivable and inventory into cash and a key indicator of a company's liquidity,

operating expenses A term synonymous with a company's selling, general, and administrative expenses.

operating income The level of income in a company's income statement after operating expenses are deducted from gross profit. Some analysts use this figure instead of net income to calculate profitability ratios.

operating lease A contract by which the lessor company maintains formal ownership of the property or equipment and grants the use of the item(s) to a lessee company in return for rental payments. These payments are charged to the income statement as rental expense. Conservative analysts consider operating leases as off-balance sheet financing.

operating working capital A term that refines the conventional definition of working capital by excluding cash, short-term investments, and short-term borrowings. Changes in operating working capital items are reconciled in the operations section of the cash flow statement and affect the outcome of a company's net operating cash flow.

other assets A catchall category for miscellaneous assets that is usually used in the noncurrent section of assets in the balance sheet.

other current assets Some item(s) that management expects to convert to cash within the next fiscal year.

other current liabilities Obligations due within the next fiscal year that have not otherwise been specifically identified as accrued expenses or accruals.

other income/expense Nonoperating items that appear in the statement of income. As income, they could include interest earnings, sale of assets, royalties, dividends, equity in earnings of affiliates, and other sundry gains. As an expense, foreign exchange losses, asset write-offs, and other miscellaneous charges would be included. If not specifically stated, interest expense may become lost in an aggregate amount or net number.

other postretirement employee benefits (OPEB) A rule proposed in 1989 by the Financial Accounting Standards Board (FASB) that would require companies in 1993 to record the expense for postretirement healthcare benefits on an accrual basis, the way pension retirement benefits presently are handled (aka other postretirement benefits).

paid-in surplus (See **additional paid-in capital**.)

par value The stated value on the face of a stock certificate.

patents (See **intangible assets**.)

payables (See **accounts payable**.)

pension and retirement plans A company's pension plan status that is now the subject of a significant disclosure in the notes to financial statements in an annual report. In general, the note will provide a description of (1) the plan or plans, (2) pension expense components, (3) a reconciliation of each plan's status, and (4) the actuarial assumptions employed.

pooling of interests (See **business combinations**.)

preferred stock A form of capital stock that represents ownership in a company. Preferred stock has precedence over common stock regarding its owner's rights to the receipt of dividends and the distribution of assets in a liquidation. It generally carries no voting rights or only under certain conditions. The dividend rate usually is fixed; if the stock is designated as cumulative preferred stock, any arrears (for dividends not paid) must be paid before any dividend payment is made to common shareholders.

prepaid expense A current asset representing an advance payment, generally for services and supplies, that is classified as current in the balance sheet.

present value A concept that measures the value today of a future inflow or outflow of money

pretax income Income before taxes.

price-earnings ratio A ratio much used by the investment community that shows the relationship between a company's earnings per share and its market price per share (aka earnings multiple or just multiple).

prime rate A base rate used by lenders for establishing interest rates on a company's borrowings. Major money center banks, typically located in New York, are the most influential in establishing the prime rate, which is the rate that commercial banks charge their most creditworthy customers.

profit A term used interchangeably with earnings and income.

profitability A term used to comment on the ability of a company to produce profits. There are numerous measurements of a company's profitability; some of the more widely used indicators include comparisons of gross profit, operating income, pretax income, and net income with net sales as well as comparisons of net income with average equity, capitalization, and assets.

pro forma A manner of presentation of unaudited financial information, often employed in the note on acquisitions in an annual report, showing the combined full-year results of the parent and acquired company. It assumes that business purchases are affected at the beginning of the fiscal year.

property, plant, and equipment Commonly referred to as fixed assets, the formal term that usually appears as the account title of a noncurrent asset in the balance sheet (aka fixed capital, fixed investment, and capital assets).

provision for income taxes (See **income tax**.)

purchase method (See **business combinations**.)

purchased goodwill (See **goodwill**.)

quality of earnings A term that refers to how a company generates its earnings. High-quality earnings are characterized by a company's application of (1) conservative accounting policies, such as LIFO inventory, accelerated depreciation, and short-term amortization of deferred charges, goodwill, and so on; (2) increased sales from volume; (3) costs that are stable or, better yet, lower than previous years; and (4) the absence in the statement of income of nonrecurring, extraordinary items (gains) that artificially inflate earnings.

quick assets ratio A liquidity measure that further refines the current ratio by comparing current assets that are cash, cash equivalents, marketable securities, and trade receivables with total current liabilities (aka the acid test and quick ratio).

reclassifications A term that usually appears in the note on accounting policies and that refers to a common practice of restating certain financial statement accounts in a previous year, or years, to conform with the most recent presentation. This restatement makes the statements more comparable.

redeemable preferred stock A line item in a company's balance sheet that falls into a kind of no-man's-land between the liability and equity sections. The SEC will not allow preferred stock with mandatory redemption requirements to be shown as part of equity. Conservative analysis views redeemable preferred stock as having more of the characteristics of debt (it is included in long-term debt calculations) than of equity.

research and development (R & D) expense An investment in R&D is important for many companies, and they often prefer to highlight these expenses in their income statements as opposed to having R&D expenses buried in a summary account such as selling, general, and administrative expense.

restrictive covenant (See **covenants**.)

restructuring A practice that can cover a multitude of sins but is often related to the losses ("restructuring charges" as special items in the income statement) incurred when a company divests itself of poorly performing businesses.

retained earnings An important component of the shareholders' equity account in a company's balance sheet that represent profits kept in the business. They have not been distributed (paid out) as dividends but rather retained in the company as permanent working capital or to finance fixed investments (aka undistributed earnings or profits, earned surplus, accumulated profits, and retained income).

return on Measurements of profitability that tend to appear in corporate financial reporting with little standardization of usage. Four "return on" profit indicators reflect a company's return on assets, capital employed, equity, and sales by comparing either net income or operating income with previously mentioned financial statement elements.

revenues A term, used inconsistently in financial reporting, that is generally a caption in the income statement indicating the gross or total inflow of funds to a company. By far the most important source is net sales, to which is added such nonoperating income sources as interest income or equity in earnings of affiliates. This form of presentation is characteristic of the single-step format for the income statement. In other instances, however, and particularly with service companies, revenues are synonymous with sales.

sale-leaseback An off-balance sheet financing mechanism by which a company sells a fixed asset, generally property, to another party and then leases it back. A sale-leaseback transaction generates an immediate inflow of cash, and the lease is structured as an operating lease so that the company pays for the continued use of the asset as an expense, but no debt is shown on the balance sheet.

securities A broad term that includes both debt and equity instruments, short term and long term.

segment information The term referring to a note to the financials of a company that operates in more than one line of business and that provides a breakdown of each line according to selected income statement and balance sheet information as well as geographic scope of each of the company's major business segments.

selling, general, and administrative (SG&A) expense A company's operating expenses that appear as a major entry in a company's income statement.

shareholders' equity Synonymous with equity, a term used in the balance sheet to identify the ownership interest in the company (aka stockholders' equity and shareholders' investment).

shares A company sells (issues) shares to the public that become publicly traded, in an amount to provide it with sufficient equity capital to operate the business. It issues these shares from an authorized number of shares approved as capital stock by the company's articles of incorporation.

short term A term synonymous with current, which comprises a period of no more than 12 months.

sinking fund A regular accumulation of a fixed amount of cash or securities in a special fund specifically dedicated to pay or redeem an issue of a company's bonds or preferred shares. Such a feature prompts conservative analysts to consider the related obligation as debt.

solvency A general term used to describe a company's ability to meet its long-term debt obligations; a counterpart to considerations of liquidity, which focuses on a company's ability to meet its short-term obligations.

statement of cash flows A financial statement used by companies to measure and report on the flow of money in and out of a business.

statement of financial accounting standards (SFAS) (See **Financial Accounting Standards Board (FASB)**.)

statement of income One of the three key financial statements used in financial analysis that summarizes a company's revenues and expenses.

statement of retained earnings A statement, sometimes presented separately from the statement of shareholders' equity, that reflects the changes in a company's retained earnings, a component of shareholders' equity in the balance sheet, for the period reviewed in a corporate annual report.

statement of shareholders' equity One of the four financial statements generally presented in a corporate financial communications that provides a reconciliation of the changes in the various components of a company's shareholder equity over a three-year period. It is not used for financial analysis purposes.

stock plans Information that generally appears as a note in corporate annual reports and provides details about the incentives a company provides to its executives and employees in the form of stock plans, which could include stock options, stock appreciation rights, and stock grants.

stock repurchase plan A program by which a company undertakes a systematic approach to purchasing its own stock in the open market. Such buybacks create treasury stock, which, because it lowers the amount of stock outstanding, reduces shareholders' equity in the balance sheet.

subordinated debt A term describing a form of longterm debt that is "junior," or in a secondary position, vis-à-vis the claim on a company's assets for the payment of its other debt obligations. The other creditors therefore are in a "senior" position, that is, the repayment of their debt has priority over subordinated debt, which is generally considered quasiequity by financial professionals.

subsequent events Information that has a material effect on the financial statements for such events or transactions as debt incurred or an acquisition occurring after the fiscal year-end but prior to the issuance of the audited statements and that appears as a note to the financials.

subsidiary A corporation owned or controlled by another company and commonly referred to as the parent company. Any fraction of ownership above 50 percent constitutes control. Subsidiaries are separate legal entities but in consolidation they become part of the parent company's financial statement presentation as one economic unit.

tangible net worth A stringent measurement of a company's equity position that reduces net worth by the amount of intangible assets.

temporary differences The expression now used (*timing differences* was the previous term) to describe the origin of deferred income taxes. Companies are allowed to use different accounting methods for their tax returns and financial statements. For example, the difference between the faster-paced depreciation by the accelerated method (tax return) and the slower-paced depreciation of the straight-line method (financial statements) generates an accounting estimate of deferred tax payments—a temporary difference. Many other forms of temporary differences relate to the timing of profit recognition.

trade A general term that refers to the commercial relationships of a company. The trade prefix used with receivables and payables identifies transactions occurring within the mainstream of a company's commercial activities. Trade credit identifies the payment terms a company grants to its buying customers and receives from its suppliers. Trade discounts, usually for prompt payment, cut costs to the buyer and accelerate cash flow to the seller.

trade receivables (See **accounts receivable**.)

treasury stock A term that appears as an adjustment entry to the shareholders' equity in a balance sheet. Treasury stock represents stock that has been issued (sold publicly) and then subsequently repurchased by the company. Because the stock no longer is outstanding but has not been retired, a company's holding of treasury stock requires a reduction in the company's equity base.

turnover An expression used by financial professionals to indicate the number of times an asset moves in and out of a business; generally applied to receivables, inventory, and total assets and expressed as a times multiple or in days.

unaudited The opposite of audited, a term applied to information supplied by a company in its annual and quarterly reports that is outside the audit conducted by its independent auditors.

unconsolidated subsidiaries A company's subsidiary operations that have not been consolidated, which means that the parent company owns less than 50 percent of the subsidiary. The parent company carries these subsidiaries in its balance sheet as investments in the noncurrent assets section.

undistributed earnings (See **retained earnings**.)

unearned income Also known as deferred income, a term describing a company's liability, either current or long-term, to a customer for income received prior to the delivery of goods or the rendering of services.

unrealized gain (loss) A recognition of a change in value in a company's financial statements with respect to the current market value of an asset in comparison with its cost prior to its liquidation. For example, a company may recognize a loss in value (unrealized loss) for an investment in equity securities prior to the actual sale of the securities.

unusual charges (See **extraordinary item**.)

value In general, a term implying the worth of something as measured in monetary terms. For example, a company's machinery assets have a market value—what someone would pay for them; also referred to at times as fair value. Machinery also has a replacement value—what it would cost the company to replace the same machinery assets. In accounting terms, these two values —market and replacement—are considered too subjective to be used for preparing financial statements. Therefore, historical cost, or original cost, subject to depreciation is the basis used for determining financial reporting values (book value).

warranty obligations A term reflecting that the ultimate liability for a company's product guarantees and warranties cannot be determined precisely. Therefore, if warranty obligations are material, management estimates an amount for these obligations that is expensed through the income statement and carried as a reserve on the company's balance sheet as a longterm liability and/or accrued expense.

weighted average of outstanding shares of common stock A calculation provided for the shareholder in an annual report. It is used as the numerator in the formula for the various per-share measurements, for example, earnings and book value per share. The weighted average simply gives proportional consideration to the shares outstanding during the fiscal year (aka weighted average shares outstanding or outstanding shares).

working capital The difference between a company's current assets and current liabilities. Working capital is widely used by creditors and investors as a measure of a company's liquidity (aka net working capital and net current assets).

working capital ratio A measure of a company's funding adequacy that compares working capital with net sales to indicate the volume of business a company is conducting on a given working capital base.

write-down An accounting term used to describe the partial reduction in value of an asset from its cost to a lesser value, such as inventory write-downs caused by obsolescence.

write-off An accounting term used to describe the complete reduction in value of an asset. A write-off recognizes that the asset no longer has any value to the company.

zero-coupon bond A debt security issued at a deep discount (no interest payments are made) to its face value, thus deferring the payment of cash interest and principal for several years until its maturity.

Index